T0317928

TURTLE BUNBURY is an author, historian, public speaker and TV presenter based in Ireland. His previous book, *Ireland's Forgotten Past*, was described by Sebastian Barry, the Laureate for Irish Fiction, as 'a delicious and stirring atlas of Irishness'. His other books include *The Irish Pub* and the award-winning *Vanishing Ireland* series.

TURTLE BUNBURY

THE IRISH

TALES OF EMIGRATION, EXILE AND IMPERIALISM

WITH 29 ILLUSTRATIONS

CONTENTS

EMERALD EXODUS

Ireland's first inhabitants were born in other lands. We know not where but our current thinking is that they sailed up from more southerly latitudes in the millennia that followed the melting of the ice 12,000 years ago. Since that time, the island has been entirely surrounded by the salty seas. Until the twentieth century, the only way off was by boat. The hardy Neolithic people who lived 5,000 years ago took to the water in tree trunks that were hollowed out by human hand. The next wave of immigrants to Irish shores are thought to have arrived by boat from present-day Portugal. Archaeology provides tantalizing hints of their integration with other parts of Europe, including items of jewelry imported from eastern France in the late Bronze Age.

Profitable trade is, of course, one of the fundamental motives for travel. Among the most lucrative commodities in prehistoric times was mankind itself, the slaves who could be put to work fighting wars, rowing ships and building the cities and temples of the ancient world. It seems reasonable to suggest that some of the earliest members of the Irish diaspora were luckless souls captured and then sold to toil and die in foreign lands. Ireland's slave industry certainly boomed during the centuries when the Romans occupied neighbouring Britain.

St Patrick, the man credited with introducing Christianity to Ireland, was himself a slave. Perhaps the greatest legacy of the church that he represented was the remarkable number of missionaries, ascetics and educators who set out from Irish shores to bring Christ's revolutionary messages of love, forgiveness and humility into the perilous depths of Europe. The first of these holy men were the *peregrinatio pro Christo* ('exiles for Christ'), whose zealous wanderings would often bring them to a martyr's grave. The most famous was St Columba, one of the senior members of the Uí Néill dynasty, who is said to have gone into self-imposed exile to assuage his guilt after precipitating an internal war in Ireland that left thousands dead. In 563 he founded a monastic settlement on Iona, an island off the west coast of Scotland, which became the epicentre for an early Christian renaissance. As the Venerable Bede put it, Iona was 'a great school of Christian education…specially designed to prepare and send forth a body of clergy trained to the task of preaching the Gospel among the heathen'.

These gutsy souls travelled alone or in small groups, their scalps symbolically tonsured, or shaved from ear to ear. Some devoted their lives to proselytizing along the old trade routes and Roman roads. Others opted for seclusion and became hermits. For many more, their dream was to simply reach Rome, where the apostles Peter and Paul lay buried, or perhaps even to set foot in the Holy Land.

In the centuries after Columba, religion, trade and warfare would bring Irish people deep into Europe and, by the sixteenth century, westwards to the Americas. For many of the 40 million US citizens who claim some form of Irish ancestry today, their family story begins with the Great Hunger (p. 132), the cataclysmic period of starvation and disease that crucified Ireland between 1845 and 1850. Understandably, those who fled Ireland at this time felt deep bitterness towards the authorities that had presided over the catastrophe, a sensitivity that has intensified with the passage of time, leading to extreme accusations that the British government orchestrated a deliberate genocide.

The generation that arrived during and after the famine soon found themselves thrust into another maelstrom: the American Civil War (1861–65). At least 200,000 Irish-born soldiers served in the conflict, including the Waterford-born Young Ireland leader Thomas Francis Meagher (later the acting governor of Montana), Galway-born bandmaster Patrick Sarsfield Gilmore (author of the song 'When Johnny Comes Marching Home') and Louth-born Mary Hodgers (p. 140). Based in Chester, Pennsylvania, John Roach of Mitchelstown, County Cork, emerged as the most prominent shipbuilder in America by the end of the war.

'My forefathers were the men who followed Cromwell and who shared in the defence of Derry, and in the victories of Aughrim and

8

the Boyne,' acknowledged US president Theodore Roosevelt, the descendant of a Scots-Irish immigrant from County Antrim. When he went on to praise the Scots-Irish as 'a bold and hardy race', he encapsulated the lesser-known truth for many millions of 'Irish' settlers in the United States whose roots lay not in the misery of the Great Hunger but in the religious turmoil and oppression that ripped through Britain and Ireland in earlier centuries. During the 1700s, an estimated 200,000 Scots-Irish, or Ulster Scots as they are also known, sailed for North America, including the ancestors of at least sixteen US presidents and the grandparents of Sam Houston, the first president of Texas. Their forebears were among the thousands of families, predominantly Presbyterian, who originated in Scotland, settled in Ireland for a few generations and then crossed the Atlantic to North America. The Scots-Irish exodus coincided with the emigration of wealthier Irish Catholics such as Charles Carroll of County Laois, who moved to Maryland in 1688; his grandson and namesake was the sole Catholic signatory of the United States Declaration of Independence in 1776.

The story of the Irish abroad is a tale of empire as well as emigrants. Many of those who left Ireland for foreign shores did so under Britain's imperial flag. The empire provided its citizens with the ideal opportunity to explore and exploit. The civil service that oiled it was thick with Irish men, and occasionally Irish women, throughout its hierarchy. Hundreds of thousands of Irish fetched up in Australia, including at least 48,000 convicts. New Zealand also experienced a high influx of Irish, initially from Leinster but later predominantly from Munster and Ulster. Over 4.4 million Canadians claim Irish descent – over 12 per cent of the population. Three 'Fathers' of the Canadian Federation were Irish, including the ill-fated Thomas D'Arcy McGee (p. 144). Seven viceroys of India were born in Ireland, as were at least seven governors of Hong Kong. As Britain's first envoy to China, Antrim-born George Macartney led the initial attempt to open up trade with the Chinese Empire in 1792. Only two British prime ministers were born in Ireland, although David Cameron, Tony Blair, John Major and Jim Callaghan all have Irish ancestry.

The Irish were especially active in the British forces. In the early nineteenth century, an estimated 40 per cent of the British army were Irish, as were a third of the 140,000 sailors in the Royal Navy. Over 200 Irishmen won the Victoria Cross, the highest military honour in the empire, including Charles Davis Lucas (the earliest 'chronological' winner) and Roscommon-born Luke O'Connor (the first soldier to win). Among the many Irish-born soldiers who rose to the very top of their profession were the Duke of Wellington, Lord Kitchener and General Gough (p. 83), who won both Hong Kong and the Punjab for the empire.

On Oliver Cromwell's watch, between 6,000 and 10,000 Irish men and women were rounded up in the 1650s and sent to work as indentured servants on the Caribbean island of Barbados. Life on the island was frequently hideous for these people who were compelled to work in gruelling and sometimes fatal conditions on the sugar plantations. Every single day was spent either sowing, tending or harvesting the crop, or extracting and boiling the juice from the sugar cane in order to turn it into sugar and molasses. They worked alongside African chattel slaves, but there was a clear hierarchy: should an Irish servant catch an African slave committing theft, he could kill the slave without fear of legal consequence. Indeed, while the slaves were considered legally sub-human, and their slavery itself was perpetual and hereditary, indentured servitude for the Irish was at least temporary and non-hereditary, and they were considered legal persons.

When their indentures expired after 1660, many Irish freemen (former servants) clearly opted to remain in Barbados as, in 1667, nearly half of the colony's 4,000-strong militia were recorded as Irish. Among them was the ancestor of Robyn Fenty, better known as the singer-songwriter Rihanna. However, up to 10,000 freemen left Barbados in the 1660s, including many Irish who settled on the nearby island of Montserrat. By the late seventeenth century, almost 70 per cent of Montserrat's white population were Irish-born and the island is known today as 'The Emerald Isle of The Caribbean'.

The transatlantic slave trade is a scar upon all our pasts, a fact that was so dramatically underlined by the intensification of the

Black Lives Matter movement in 2020. During the eighteenth and early nineteenth centuries, Irish port cities such as Dublin, Cork and Waterford enjoyed an especially buoyant export of food and provisions to the plantations of the West Indies and the American South. Many of the sugar, cotton, rice and tobacco plantations in Georgia, the Carolinas, the Caribbean and elsewhere were owned or run by people from Ireland. The 1939 movie *Gone with the Wind* (based on a book by Margaret Mitchell, great-granddaughter of an Irish emigrant) centres on a Georgia plantation called Tara and prominently features families named O'Hara, Kennedy and Butler. The latter surname brings to mind Carlow-born Pierce Butler, a Founding Father of the United States who was also one of the biggest slave owners in the country. Butler was the principal promoter of the 1787 Fugitive Slave Clause in the US Constitution, which ensured that enslaved people who fled from one state to another could be returned to the state from which they escaped if captured. This vile clause was mostly obliterated, but not repealed, by the Thirteenth Amendment in 1865.

Fortunately, there is no adulatory plaque in Carlow to Pierce Butler. Nor is there any homage in Ennis to Richard Brew (p. 58), one of the earliest and most successful slave traders operating on the African coast. Dick Dowling (p. 135) was among 20,000 Irish who fought for the Confederacy in the US Civil War. His statue was removed from public view in Houston in 2020. Should his plaque be removed from Tuam Town Hall?

Or what of Hercules Mulligan (p. 70) whose espionage reports were dependent on the pluck of his slave Cato? Or the Kilkenny-born architect James Hoban (p. 76) whose construction team on the White House included at least 200 slaves? Or the saintly Margaret of New Orleans (p. 127) who bought at least six African slaves at the city market? Or should we focus instead on the goodly deeds of the Marquess of Sligo, a descendant of the Pirate Queen, Grace O'Malley, who oversaw the abolition of slavery in Jamaica during his tenure as the island's governor in the 1830s? It is all very complicated and deeply unsavoury but context, of course, is everything.

Throughout the eighteenth and nineteenth centuries, America and Ireland kept getting closer. With the invention of longitude and

Ben Franklin's breakthrough on how best to use the Gulf Stream, the journey time had been reduced to less than four weeks by the close of the eighteenth century. In 1838, the paddle steamer *Sirius* left Cork Harbour and arrived into New York after a record-breaking eighteen days. Indeed, such a relatively short trip meant that during the Great Hunger, numerous ships sailed to Ireland from the United States laden with food and provisions supplied by the Irish diaspora in America. The Irish continued to stream into the United States, which, in 1892, opened its famous immigration station at Ellis Island. The first person through it was Cork-born Annie Moore (p. 180).

Nine years after Annie Moore arrived, Guglielmo Marconi, a kinsman of the Jameson whiskey distilling family, made the first transatlantic radio communication between Ireland and America. By 1907, a regular transatlantic radio-telegraph service was in operation. 'Have I done the world good or have I added a menace?' Marconi would later wonder as radio became mainstream. The first spoken words were transmitted across the Atlantic from the seaside town of Ballybunion, County Kerry, in March 1919.

At that time, the quickest sea crossing between Ireland and the United States still took the bones of a week. Everything changed that autumn when John Alcock and Arthur Whitten Brown completed the first non-stop transatlantic flight, crash-landing in a Connemara bog after flying 3,040 km (1,890 miles) above a featureless ocean, with blizzards pelting them in their open cockpit. As the first startled witnesses to the crash ran towards the peat-drenched aircraft, Alcock stood up from his seat, removed his goggles and announced: 'We are Alcock and Brown. Yesterday we were in America.' The older generation were particularly stunned: the voyage had previously taken weeks and yet this flying contraption had done it in sixteen hours. America was suddenly less than a day away.

In the century since Alcock and Brown's historic flight, about two and a half million people have emigrated from the island of Ireland. Although many subsequently returned, especially when air travel's popularity began to boom in the 1960s, there are still upwards of a million Irish-born men and women living abroad today. 'Diaspora' – from the Greek verb *diaspeiro*, meaning 'I scatter' – is not always a word immediately understood and yet it is an apt description for the global redistribution of a community, conveying the notion of seeds that are scattered and sown on alien soil, some at random, others with a clear strategy in mind, reminiscent of the biblical Parable of the Sower. 'The Irish Diaspora' refers not only to current emigrants but also to the descendants of previous Irish emigrants, constituting perhaps 80 million people alive in 2021. The broader story of the diaspora also encompasses the untold millions of Irish people who have been and gone from this earthly existence.

In these pages, I have homed in on a few of the men and women from the island who have made their mark on the wider world over the past fourteen centuries. Every which way I look, there are more contenders for a book such as this. Should I have considered the writer James Joyce, who lived in Trieste and died in Zurich? Or Oscar Wilde and Samuel Beckett, both buried in Paris, or W. B. Yeats, who died in the south of France? Or the politicians with Irish roots who turn up in unexpected places? Chaim Herzog, the sixth president of Israel, was the son of the Chief Rabbi of Ireland. Che Guevara descended from Patrick Lynch, a Galway man. Edelmiro Farrell, president of Argentina from 1944 to 1946 and mentor of Juan Perón, was the son of an immigrant from County Longford. Or what of Dublin-born Charles Dickinson West, who became Japan's most revered naval architect during the Meiji era?

To an extent I mention these names simply to prove how the Irish made indents in latitudes all across the globe. In this book, a cast of missionaries, explorers and philanthropists share the stage with inventors, tycoons and warriors, as well as a composer, a doctor, a would-be assassin and a football manager. These disparate souls are the prisms through which I have attempted to tell some of the broader, more complex tales of the Irish abroad. The reasons why they left Ireland are many and varied. Some were emigrants seeking a better life. Others were political émigrés. Still more marched off under the flag of the British Empire. A few were simply born under a wandering star. It is my hope that collectively their stories will showcase the remarkable contribution – mostly good, occasionally bad – that people from Ireland have made upon the world's stage.

1

COLUMBANUS AND
THE MEROVINGIAN KINGS

For all we Irish, inhabitants of the world's edge,
are disciples of Saints Peter and Paul.

COLUMBANUS TO POPE BONIFACE IV, 613

Bregenz, Austria, 611. Columbanus was unimpressed. The barbarian horde had brewed up a giant barrel of beer that they were now about to present as an offering to their god Wodan. The Irishman marched up to the cask and breathed on it. 'And lo!', recounted Jonas of Bobbio, a disciple of Columbanus, 'it broke with a crash and fell in pieces so that all the beer ran out. Then it was clear that the devil had been concealed in the cask, and that through the earthly drink he had proposed to ensnare the souls of the participants.'

Establishing facts is notoriously difficult when it comes to validating the lives of pioneering holy men like St Columbanus. Much of our apparent understanding of such people is based upon semi-fictional, semi-romantic hagiographies and hyperbolic martyrologues etched with inky feathers long decades, or even centuries, after they purportedly lived. Competing agendas are concealed behind every word. Occasionally we are presented with fragments of skulls and bones, or croziers, staffs, crosses and bells, which are said to have belonged to these holy men. Much of this is connected to the emergence of numerous cults of supposedly 'Irish' saints (p. 29) that arose across Europe in the High Middle Ages (1000–1300).

Yet the life of Columbanus is more credible than most. There is at least some documentation about the twenty-five years that he spent proselytizing in Europe, not least because he was no stranger to controversy. Some of his own writings also survive, primarily monastic rules and hymns, but also some letters and, perhaps, a boating song.

He is widely assumed to have been a Leinsterman, possibly a member of the royal Uí Bairrche dynasty that dominated in present-day

County Carlow. Jonas, who knew him in later life, maintained that his first attempt to become a monk had been thwarted in his late twenties by his attraction to women generally or perhaps to one woman in particular. Either way, when he expressed his conundrum to a female hermit, she advised that his wisest course of action would be to 'take himself to a place of stronger pilgrimage' abroad.[1]

He made his way north to the monastery of Bangor on the shores of Belfast Lough, where he became a disciple of Comgall, the monastery's founder and first abbot. As a young man, Comgall is said to have accompanied St Columba on a proselytizing mission to the Picts in northern Scotland and certainly Bangor enjoyed strong links with Columba's foundations at Iona. One wonders if Columbanus adopted Columba's name in honour of a man who had likewise abandoned the land of his birth to embark upon a 'stronger pilgrimage' in faraway lands.

Columbanus was a middle-aged man by the time he crossed the seas to Brittany in about 590. Like the other *peregrinatio* who had gone before him, his pilgrimage was to be perpetual, a lifelong sentence, combining missionary zeal with private penance and stringent asceticism.

After a short period on the Morbihan peninsula of Brittany, he ventured deeper into the kingdom of the Franks, the realm that had arisen from the ashes of the fallen Roman Empire in the middle of the fifth century. Comprising much of present-day France and Germany, the kingdom was ruled by the Merovingian dynasty who had, for the most part, converted to Christianity.

For Columbanus, this was the perfect landscape to establish his monastic utopia. His strict devotion to purity and frugality found favour with Guntram, the elderly Merovingian king of Burgundy, who invited him to found a monastery amid the ruins of an abandoned Roman fortress at Annegray in the Vosges Mountains of eastern France. It proved such a popular destination for pilgrims that, with Guntram's backing, the Irishman established two more monasteries at nearby Luxeuil-les-Bains and Fontaine-lès-Luxeuil.

Columbanus had arrived in the Merovingian Empire at a time when large swathes of present-day France were already converted to Christianity. However, always the outsider, his determination to run his communities independently of any ecclesiastical authority set him at odds with the Frankish church hierarchy, with whom he hotly argued about the true date of Easter. He enjoyed a degree of protection from Theuderic II, Guntram's young heir, for whom he served as a sort of spiritual advisor for several years. However, he was unable to win over the king's grandmother, Brunhilda, the queen consort and real power behind the throne. Things reached a head in 610 when he refused to bless various illegitimate sons that Theuderic II had sired by his concubines. Brunhilda banished Columbanus from the kingdom and, for good measure, she ordered all those monks who had followed him from Ireland and Britain to leave too. Given that Theuderic II was then engaged in a brutal war with his older brother, Theudebert II, it was perhaps no bad time to move on.

Columbanus turned his evangelical eyes eastwards and set off up the Upper Rhine, reputedly composing a Latin poem while his men heaved upon the oars and brought his boat along that majestic river. If so, this surely ranks as one of the world's earliest-recorded boat songs. One stanza runs:

> En silvis caesa fluctu meat carina
> Bicornis Rheni et pelagus perlabiter iuncta.
> Heia viri! Nostrum reboans echo sonet heia!

> ['Lo, cut in forests, the driven keel, passes on the stream
> Of the twin-horned Rhine and glides as if anointed by the flood.
> Heave, my men! Let resounding echo sound our Heave!']

Christianity was still a largely unknown entity east of the Rhine when Columbanus arrived in Alamannia (present-day Switzerland and west Austria). He spent the next two years preaching to the Alemanni and founded an oratory on the shores of Lake Constance. It was during this time that he is said to have destroyed the beer vat in Bregenz, which was precisely the sort of behaviour that ultimately led him to be ousted from the region. He decided to cross the Alps into northern

Italy but, before he left, he entrusted the ongoing conversion of the Alemanni to St Gall, one of his most loyal disciples. If truth be told, St Gall, or Gallus, was also born in Ireland and lived to be ninety-five.

Meanwhile, Columbanus and his other disciples clambered through the Alps and came down into the kingdom of the Lombards, which covered much of modern-day Italy. They duly introduced themselves at the court of King Agilulf in Milan. The Lombard monarch warmed to Columbanus and offered him a sliver of land on the banks of the Trebbia River, near Piacenza, between Milan and Genoa. The place was called Bobbio and it was here that Columbanus founded his final monastery and so concluded an odyssey of more than 3,200 km (2,000 miles) since he first arrived in Brittany. In the centuries to come, Bobbio Abbey would become universally recognized for the excellence of its library. Dissolved in 1803, it also provided the inspiration for Italian novelist Umberto Eco when he sought a location to set his bestselling murder mystery, *The Name of the Rose*, in 1980.

Columbanus's surviving writings show that he remained deeply proud of his Irish origins until the day that he died at Bobbio in 615. However, he remained virtually unknown in Ireland until interest in his life was reignited by men such as Luke Wadding (p. 37) during the Counter-Reformation a thousand years later. As patron saint of the world's 200 million motorcyclists, St Columbanus now has one of the biggest flocks of all.

2

VIRGILIUS OF SALZBURG

Luminous as bishop and worthy through merit and character
Ireland brought him to the light of this world.

VIRGILIUS INSCRIPTION, ALCUIN OF YORK, C. 784[1]

Rome, 747. For the second time in two years, Pope Zachary found himself having to play the peacemaker between the Anglo-Saxon legate and the Irishman. Both men commanded his respect. On the one side there was St Boniface, né Winfrid, the Devon-born archbishop of Mainz, who had done so much to bring Christianity east of the Rhine. On the other, there was Virgilius, the Irish-born ruler of the diocese of Salzburg in present-day Austria. The last time they came before him was when Boniface complained that he had not been consulted by Virgilius when the latter assigned the conduct of his episcopal duties to a fellow Irishman, Dub dá Chrích. The archbishop had also had cause to reprimand Virgilius for allowing an 'unlearned priest' to incorrectly baptize some Bavarians.

Virgilius's latest activities had brought fresh dismay to Boniface. Not only had he wrongfully claimed that he had papal permission to occupy the Salzburg bishopric, he had also apparently made the heretical assertion that there was 'another world and other men beneath the earth', as well as perhaps a second sun and a second moon. The Pope expressed alarm at such 'perverse and abominable teachings' and ordered a synod to investigate the allegations.[2] When Virgilius himself was summoned to Rome to explain himself, his supporters must have anticipated his imminent expulsion from the Church. No record of his visit survives but he defied the odds. Indeed, he weathered the storm so well that as well as retaining his abbey, he was also formerly appointed bishop of Salzburg in 749. Perhaps tellingly, his consecration was put on hold until after the death of Boniface in 755; the archbishop had been murdered by bandits in the present-day Dutch province of Friesland.

The formative years of Virgilius are shrouded in a typically impenetrable medieval fog. The most popular and utterly unverifiable accounts state that: he was born in 700; he may have been from Trim in present-day County Meath; he was originally known as Fergil; he was schooled at the island monastery of Iona, where he learned Greek; and he fetched up as the abbot of Aghaboe Abbey in County Laois. The latter is an attractive conjecture: Aghaboe was one of Ireland's foremost educational centres in the eighth century and excelled at teaching its students the intricacies of commerce, agriculture and geography. The abbey ruins, all but destroyed in the Tudor Reformation of the sixteenth century, still stand today.

However, there is simply no evidence for any of these assertions, save for a tentative connection to Iona. What is known is that he found himself centre stage to European court politics in 743, just as the Carolingian dynasty established by Charles Martel was consolidating its power over the dying Merovingian kingdom of the Franks. Somehow, the scholarly Irishman made his way across northern France to the palace of Quierzy-sur-Oise in Picardy. This was the court of Pepin, a son of Charles Martel who was serving as *majordomo* ('master of the household') to Childeric III, the king of the Franks. Pepin, who had been educated by Benedictine monks in Paris, would become known to posterity as Pepin the Short, not for his stature but for his closely cropped hair, which contrasted with the flowing locks of his contemporaries. By the time Virgilius secured an audience with him, Pepin was *de facto* king of the Franks, although the throne itself was still occupied by the ineffectual Childeric III, who was fated to be the last of the Merovingian kings.

Virgilius belonged to a new wave of Irishmen who settled in Europe during the Carolingian age. Many were well-educated clerics who found work as teachers in the empire's schools and courts. Their impact is hinted at through various manuscripts, correspondence, administrative records, theological works, contemporary annals and other fragments of the past that are extant in libraries and museums from Stockholm and St Petersburg to Rome and Vienna. Such sources help to colour in the remarkable rise of Virgilius.

Pepin's patronage paved the way for him to advance, via short stints in Normandy and Bavaria, to Salzburg, where the Duke of Bavaria, Pepin's brother-in-law, consented to his election as the abbot of St Peter's monastery in 745. The abbey's lucrative estates included several of the salt mines from which Salzburg, meaning 'salt fortress', derives its name. St Peter's would later achieve a degree of global celebrity when it appeared in the Hollywood musical, *The Sound of Music*.

Virgilius is thought to have provided the impetus for Pepin's game-changing use of royal unction at his coronation when he formally ascended the throne as the king of the Franks in 751. This, in turn, may have derived from a description of the ordination of kings in an Irish legal text called *Collectio canonum Hibernensis* (Irish Collection of Canon Law). In any event, Pepin's anointment proved such a powerful blessing for the Carolingian takeover that this biblical rite became standard practice at coronation ceremonies for generations of European monarchs to come.

As well as his legal skills, Virgilius was an astute and broad-minded geometer, correctly predicting the existence of humanity south of the equator. This was a revolutionary thought for orthodox Christians at the time, as was his near damnable proposal that the Earth was spherical and that there might be a second sun, which prompted Boniface's accusations of heresy.

During his thirty-four-year-reign as bishop, Virgilius rebuilt his cathedral, expanded the jurisdictive borders of his see and established Salzburg as an important centre of missionary activity. He oversaw the conversion of the Alpine Slavs of Carinthia (present-day southern Austria and northeastern Slovenia) and dispatched missionaries into Hungary. Among his principal assistants was the aforementioned Dub dá Chrích, who later took charge of the island monastery of Herrenchiemsee in the Chiemsee lake of southern Bavaria.

Shortly before his death in 784, Virgilius initiated one of the earliest-known codices, the *Liber confraternitatum ecclesiae S. Petri Salisburgensis* (also known as the Salzburg Codex), an invaluable record that names a thousand deceased and living regal and ecclesiastical figures from across Europe, including the first nineteen abbots of Iona. St Boniface, his former nemesis, did not secure an entry. Virgilius was canonized in 1233 by Pope Gregory IX, a close friend of St Francis of Assisi.

3

THE CAROLINGIAN IRISH

Almost all of Ireland, despising the sea, is migrating to our shores, with a herd of philosophers.

HEIRIC OF AUXERRE, 870[1]

Tours, France, 803. Alcuin of York was nearing the end of his remarkable life. The old world was also changing rapidly. In Alcuin's native England, the kingdoms of Mercia and Northumbria were in crisis, while every spring brought news of yet more terrifying attacks by pagan marauders from the north. Since 793, the Norsemen had laid waste to numerous monastic communities along the coasts of Scotland, England and Ireland, including the abbey at Iona that St Columba had established nearly two and a half centuries earlier. Indeed, the 'terror' of such raids had triggered a fresh wave of monks from Ireland seeking a new life in Continental Europe.

Alcuin had known plenty of Irishmen since his arrival at the Palace School in Aachen (in modern-day Germany) in 1782. Among them was the 'luminous' Virgilius, for whom he penned the poetical epitaph that once adorned the church in Salzburg that the Irish bishop had founded (p. 18). Since his arrival at Aachen, Alcuin had also helped engineer the rise of Charlemagne, his Carolingian patron, who had been crowned Imperator Romanorum ('Emperor of the Romans') in 800. With the wily grace and good humour that he had shown throughout his life, Alcuin now penned a letter to his patron in which he remarked upon 'the daily increasing influence of the Irish at the School of the Palace'.

Charlemagne, the eldest son of Pepin the Short (p. 18), held the Irish in 'special esteem'. When he founded his Palace School in Aachen, one of its first teachers was a poet and grammarian known to posterity as *Hibernicus exul* (Hibernian exile), whose works included thirty-eight poems that are now held at the Vatican Library. Among its subsequent heads was Magister Clemens, another Irishman, whose surviving manuscripts include a codex containing the letters of St Paul in Latin that was profusely annotated in Old Irish, making it one of the oldest written forms of the Old Irish language in existence.

When Charlemagne expressed concern about the occurrence of two solar eclipses in 810, he was both impressed and calmed by an Irish astronomer named Dungal, who provided an intelligent explanation of an orderly planetary heaven. Fifteen years later, Louis the Pious, Charlemagne's son and heir, appointed Dungal as master of the School at Pavia (forerunner to the University of Pavia) in Lombardy. Louis was also patron of the Irish geographer Dicuil (p. 25), who belonged to a colony of Irish teachers at Liège in present-day Belgium.

Eager to run a multi-ethnic Christian empire, Charlemagne and his Carolingian successors happily encouraged the notion that Europe had been led out of the darkness by unblemished 'preachers of truth' and 'seekers of wisdom' from Ireland. Understandably, the Irish monks did nothing to distance themselves from their blooming reputation as a race of incomparable scholars. Indeed, many proudly adopted the name 'Scottus', or 'Scotus', which, rather confusingly, was the Latin word for people from Ireland. Among Dicuil's colleagues at Liège was Sedulius Scottus, a prolific Irish poet and Latin grammarian who roundly rejected austerity in favour of a merrier life. He is sometimes said to have been the author of the Carmen Paschale, a stylistically innovative Easter song. Immortalized in one of the few surviving illuminated manuscripts from the Carolingian era, the Carmen Paschale can be seen at the Plantin-Moretus Museum in Antwerp, Belgium.

Arguably the most successful Irish scholar of the Carolingian era was Johannes Scotus Eriugena (*c.* 815–*c.* 877), a philosopher, poet and theologian, whose face featured on Ireland's £5 banknotes before the conversion to the unmemorable euro notes. He also taught at the Palace School at Aachen, where he is believed to have specialized in the liberal arts, comprising the quadrivium (music, arithmetic, geometry and astronomy) and the trivium (grammar, logic and rhetoric).[2] The school was then under the patronage of Charles the Bald, a grandson of Charlemagne, who ruled over the kingdom of West Francia from 843 to 877. As one of the most prolific writers of his generation, Eriugena would become known as the last philosopher of the Greek Neoplatonist school.

Emperor Lothair (r. 840–55), another grandson of Charlemagne, was the patron of St Donat (Donagh), also known as Donatus of Fiesole, who is said to have both studied and taught at the monastic island school of Inis Cealtra in Lough Derg in Ireland. Donat and St Andrew Scotus, a fellow Irishman, were returning from a pilgrimage to the tombs of the Apostles in Rome when they called into Fiesole, a town north of Florence, where the citizens were just preparing to elect a new bishop. As Donat entered the cathedral, all the bells began ringing and the lamps and candles burst into light. The congregation, not unreasonably, deduced that the intrepid Irishman should become their bishop. Given that they had drowned their previous bishop, it is possible that demand for the job was not high.

Donat proved a sound choice and held the office for more than half a century, with Andrew Scotus as his archdeacon. The perils of the post were exposed when a Saracen army attacked the town and sacked his palace in 846. As well as advising Lothair and writing a metrical *Life of St Brigid*, Donat attended the Roman Council of 861 and the coronation of Lothair's son, Louis II. Shortly before his death in about 876, he founded a hospice at Piacenza, in Italy's present-day Emilia-Romagna region, for the use of Irish pilgrims. Dedicated to St Brigid of Kildare, this was later bequeathed to the abbey at Bobbio founded by St Columbanus (p. 14). Donatus remains one of the most popular saints in Tuscany, where his name is to be found in numerous churches and place names.

4

BRENDAN THE NAVIGATOR
AND THE MONKS OF ICELAND

Seljaland caves, Iceland, c. 815. The identity of those who carved the large Christian crosses onto the walls of the man-made caves is an unknown and probably unknowable thing. The carvings themselves lay undiscovered until about a decade ago when the first of the twenty-four crosses was found amid the caves that run near the Seljalandsfoss waterfall on the south coast of Iceland. Similar crosses have been found cut into rocks elsewhere on the island and on the Heimaklettur cliff face of the Westman Islands, 6.5 km (4 miles) southwest of Iceland.

According to the twelfth-century Íslendingabók (Book of the Icelanders), Iceland was home to a community of hermetic monks known as the *papar* ('fathers') when the first Norse settlers arrived in 874. They are said to have fled the volcanic Arctic island overnight, leaving their bells, books and croziers behind. Perhaps they also bequeathed a more aesthetic heirloom to posterity; the Seljaland crosses certainly provide a compelling case for the notion that Irish monks were living in Iceland long before the Vikings arrived.

Irish monks certainly made their mark in the numerous islands along the way to Iceland – the Hebrides, the Orkneys, the Shetlands and the Faroes, as well as the western islands of Scotland, where St Columba's monastery on Iona would become among the most proactive Christian communities on the planet. The most famous Irish monk to take to the seas was St Brendan of Clonfert, or Brendan the Navigator, whose adventures in the early sixth century are relayed in the *Navigatio Sancti Brendani Abbatis* (Voyage of Saint Brendan). Although written several hundred years after Brendan's purported lifetime, the *Navigatio* is partly steeped in Ireland's oral tradition, itself a legacy of the Druidic age, which gives it a considerable if imprecise antiquity. It includes episodes of brilliant veracity amid Brendan's more fantastical encounters with sea-monsters, psalm-singing birds and the forlorn soul of Judas Iscariot seated on a cold, wet rock in the middle of the storm-tossed seas.

Of particular note are the portrayal of an erupting, submarine volcano and of icebergs 'the colour of silver', both of which indicate an awareness in Ireland of the landscape around Iceland. The 'Paradise of Birds' that Brendan visits twice on his voyage corresponds with Mykines, the westernmost of the eighteen Faroe Islands, which remains one of the world's most important breeding sites for seabirds. Likewise, Brendan's useful stopover on the 'Island of Sheep', where his crew converted a luckless ewe into mutton, may refer to the island of Faroe itself, 'Faroe' being derived from *føroyar*, the Old Norse word for sheep.

On a nearby island, Brendan meets Paul the Hermit, a naked monk who had been fed by a kindly otter for the past forty years. Fiction crosses a path with fact when one observes that Dicuil, a distinguished Irish geographer and astronomer at the Frankish court, noted that the Faroes were home to *heremitae ex nostra Scotia* ('hermits from our land of Ireland') in *De mensura Orbis terrae*, a geographic book compiled in 825.

Dicuil also referenced a six-month scientific mission undertaken in the last years of the eighth century to an island known as Thule. The bulk of present-day Scandinavian scholarship maintains that Thule was probably Iceland and the 'clerics' who participated in the mission were Irish monks. Their astronomical quest was to examine the cause and effect of solstices and equinoxes. They evidently made such a detailed record of their findings that Dicuil was to rather bizarrely describe Thule as being so bright during the midnight sun that one could 'pluck lice from a shirt' without difficulty.

While Iceland's hermits may have vanished in tandem with the arrival of the Vikings, the Irish influence on Icelandic culture was to deepen over the next few centuries. In the holds of many of the weather-beaten longships that berthed upon Iceland's shores were hundreds, if not more, of Irish and part-Irish women and children that the Norsemen had abducted or otherwise acquired during their raids on Ireland. Although most of these appear to have at least started out as slaves, there were also many 'free' Irish, including brides, concubines, foster children and paid servants.

The *Landnámabók* (Book of Settlements), an early Icelandic manuscript, records the names of the first 435 landholders who settled in Iceland between 870 and 930, of whom at least sixty have markedly Gaelic names. The magnificent Icelandic Sagas were also undoubtedly inspired by Ireland's Gaelic literary tradition. *Njáls Saga*, for example, poetically recounts how Sitric Silkbeard, the king of Dublin, sought help from the rulers of Orkney and the Isle of Man ahead of his showdown with Brian Boru at the Battle of Clontarf in 1014.

In 1976, the explorer Tim Severin and his crew famously sailed a replica of St Brendan's currach (boat), made from timber, wattle and animal hide, across 7,200 km (4,500 miles) of ocean, via Iceland, to Newfoundland, employing neither navigational tools nor guiding maps. The expedition proved that it was not beyond the realms of possibility that hardy Irish monks managed to traverse the 1,400-km (870-mile) stretch of ice-cold North Atlantic waters that lay between Ireland and Iceland all those centuries ago.

Perhaps those who set off into the unknown before the Viking Age were simply following the skein of the pale-bellied Brent geese that honk high in the skies above as they make their annual springtime migration to Iceland and the glaciated lands to its north. In the present century, many of the first Brent geese to arrive back in Ireland land in Tralee Bay at the end of every August. It seems serendipitous that this is the same bay from which Brendan the Navigator is said to have set sail over 1,500 years ago.

5

HELIAS OF COLOGNE

Cologne, Germany, 1028. As he awaited the arrival of the king of Dublin, one wonders what was going through Abbot Helias's mind. His emissaries had surely kept him up to date about the king's pilgrimage to meet the Pope in Rome. Did the venerable Benedictine briefly ruminate upon the simplicity of his long-distant childhood amid the drumlins of County Monaghan in Ireland? Did he grow anxious about his impending union with Sitric Silkbeard, the nemesis of the late Brian Boru, who had ruled Dublin for much of the past forty years? How would the Hiberno-Norse monarch feel when he was reunited with his blind cousin Bran?

Helias of Cologne is identified by the *Annals of the Four Masters* as Ailill of Muckno, near Castleblayney, County Monaghan. It is believed he arrived in present-day Germany as a young man and that he was among the first Benedictine monks to enter the monastery of St Pantaleon. Built on the ruins of a Roman villa just outside Cologne, St Pantaleon's was founded in about 955 by Bruno, Archbishop of Cologne and Archduke of Lotharingia, a brother of Otto I, the Holy Roman Emperor.

Bruno had been an enthusiast for the Irish since his childhood, when he was taught by an Irish cleric who went by the name of Israel. His dream of turning Cologne into a new Rome would continue after his death when a second Benedictine monastery, Great Saint Martin Church, was established in the city. This quickly became a stronghold for Irish Benedictines in the Rhineland. By the time the austere Helias became its abbot in 1019, most of the monks in the Cologne community are thought to have come from the present-day counties of Monaghan, Louth and Meath.

As the principal churchman in Cologne, Helias managed to have the feast days of St Medoldus of Muckno (13 May) and St Tigernach of Clones (4 April) added to the community's martyrology. His rules were notoriously strict but he was reputedly a musical enthusiast. One of the monks who prayed under him was Aaron Scotus, a future abbot, who was credited with introducing the Gregorian *nocturns* (evening service) into Germany.

During Helias's twenty-one-year rule as abbot, the Cologne monastery became something of a retirement home for Irish royals. Among them was Donnchad, Abbot of Dunshaughlin, a son of the king of Southern Brega whose realm incorporated present-day north County Dublin, as well as the south of counties Meath and Louth. When Donnchad was buried at Cologne in 1027, he was hailed in the annals as 'the most learned of the Irish'. He certainly enjoyed a better life than the wretched ex-king Bran of Leinster, a first cousin of King Sitric. Bran had succeeded to the kingdom when his father Máel Mórda mac Murchada was slain at the great Battle of Clontarf in 1014. Subsequently deposed and blinded by his enemies, Bran had also retired to Cologne, where he died in 1052.

Sadly, there are no concise records of Sitric's visit to Cologne in 1028, so we know not if he met with Bran. The Dublin king was following in the footsteps of his friend and overlord, Cnut the Great, King of Denmark, England and Norway, who had visited Cologne just two years earlier. It seems likely that Sitric was accompanied by Flannacán Ua Cellaig, another king of Brega, who had journeyed with him to Rome.

When Sitric returned to Dublin, he immediately put in motion the necessary steps for the foundation of Holy Trinity Church, later to become Christ Church Cathedral. Although it later came under the control of Augustinians, the cathedral started its life in 1030 as something of an adopted daughter house of the Benedictine church in Cologne. The wonderful 'continental' crypt at Christ Church is unquestionably reminiscent of a style found in the Rhineland. Dúnán (Donatus) and Gilla Pátraic (Patricius), the first and second bishops of Dublin, were both almost certainly trained at Great Saint Martin. Presumably with Abbot Helias's blessing, Sitric procured at least five of Christ Church's foundation relics directly from Cologne, including parts of the staff and chains of St Peter, a sandal that had belonged to Pope Sylvester I (314–35) and 'the relics of the 11,000 virgins', handmaidens said to have been beheaded by barbaric Huns long centuries earlier. All the relics were fated to be lost or destroyed during the Tudor Reformation of the sixteenth century.

Abbot Helias, 'Superior of the Irish monks in Cologne', died in 1042 but the Irish supremacy at Great Saint Martin Church would continue for another sixty years. In 1056, for example, the Cologne community received Marianus Scotus, a monk from the Bangor monastery in County Down, who had been exiled by his abbot for what he deemed a trifling offence. Over the next thirty years, Marianus would become one of the greatest chroniclers of his age. After visits to Fulda and Würzburg, he settled at Mainz, where he completed *Cronica Clara* (Clear Chronicle), a history of mankind since the creation of the world, which is now held at the Vatican Library.

6

THE CREATION OF THE
IRISH SAINTS

Regensburg, Germany, 1127. There must have been quite a turnout
on the day the five men set out from the Bavarian capital for the
Rock of Cashel in County Tipperary. Two of them were German:
a carpenter by the name of Konrad and his friend Enul, a joiner.
Then there were the two nobles, unidentified except that they were
Irishmen who could apparently speak German. The fifth man, the
leader of the group, was Dirmicius, the abbot of the imperial city's
Schottenklöster (Irish Benedictine monastery). At least, Dirmicius
is the name that the Benedictine abbot is generally referred to in
the annals. Sometimes it is Dyonisius, occasionally Dermot. He
was probably a MacCarthy (or Mac Cárthaigh), a scion of the great
house that had been so powerful in Munster prior to the arrival of
the Cambro-Norman warlords in the previous century.

It is thought that Abbot Dirmicius's visit to Ireland was part of
an expedition to raise funds for the various Irish monasteries under
his command across central Europe. It seems reasonable to assume
that he travelled with a carpenter and a joiner because he sought
to impress his kinsman Cormac MacCarthy, the king of Munster,
who was then in the throes of completing the construction of the
magnificent building known today as Cormac's Chapel on the Rock
of Cashel. Indeed, there is a strong likelihood that the Benedictines
of Regensburg established a small priory in Cashel but, like Konrad
the Carpenter's handiwork, its exactitudes are hard to discern.

The Rock of Cashel had been the seat of the kings of Munster since
the fifth century. In 1101, it was the setting for the Synod of Cashel,
an assembly of churchmen and laymen summoned by Muirchertach
O'Brien, the king of Munster, a great-grandson of the famous Brian
Bóruma. During the synod, Muirchertach declared himself to be
high king of Ireland. Clearly understanding the wisdom of keeping
the church on side, he simultaneously gifted the 'city of Cashel' to

God and Saint Patrick. Ten years later, he hosted the Synod of Ráth Breasail, near Mountrath, County Laois, at which the Irish church effectively signed up to the new diocese and parish-based structure initiated by the Gregorian Reforms.

Nonetheless, Muirchertach would spend much of his reign at war, defending his claim to the high kingship from rivals including the MacCarthy Mór, the former vassals of the O'Briens, in southern Munster. In 1118, the MacCarthys joined forces with the Ua Conchobhairs (O'Connors) of Connacht and Muirchertach was deposed. By the time of his death in Lismore, County Waterford, the following year, Munster had been divided into three kingdoms – Thomond (ruled by the O'Brien dynasty), Desmond (ruled by the MacCarthy Mór) and the short-lived Airgíallaunder (ruled by the Kennedys).

The ascendance of the MacCarthy family would reverberate across Europe to Regensburg, where the first Irish Benedictine community was founded in the 1080s by Muiredach mac Robartaigh (also known as Marianus Scotus of Regensburg). His family were vassals of the O'Donnell family of south Donegal, where they served as hereditary keepers of the Cathach of St Columba, the oldest surviving manuscript in Ireland, and the second-oldest Latin psalter in the world. Many of Regensburg's early monks appear to have been from Ulster, but the balance of power had shifted to Munster by 1120 when all of the Irish Benedictine monasteries in southern Germany were combined as one congregation under a motherhouse at Regensburg – the recently founded, MacCarthy-sponsored Schottenklöster of St James. The MacCarthy connection to Regensburg throws light on an extraordinary aspect of the diaspora story, namely the origination of a welter of fictitious Irish saints that are still widely revered across Europe today.

When Dirmicius died in 1133, he was succeeded by Christianus McCarthy [sic] who was, unquestionably, a cousin of King Cormac. During his twenty-year run as abbot, Christianus's greatest legacy was to sponsor the construction of a hostel in Würzburg, a city 200 km (125 miles) northwest of Regensburg. The hostel was to enjoy a lucrative business accommodating pilgrims visiting the nearby shrine, which apparently comprises the skulls of St Kilian and two fellow

Irishmen. The tale runs that Kilian and eleven of his followers had been ordered by Pope Conon to convert the pagan Duke of Thuringia. Although they managed to woo the duke and various other citizens, Kilian's refusal to sanctify a marriage between the duke and his late brother's widow earned the wrath of the latter, who had Kilian beheaded alongside two of his trusty disciples.

Encased in glass, the shrine is on view at Würzburg Cathedral to this day. Visitors are chillingly informed that the building in which they stand occupied the exact spot where the three Irishmen were executed. However, suspicions of skulduggery arise when it emerges that, while there *are* some accounts of St Kilian from the late eighth century, the story of his martyrdom was invented in the Regensburg scriptorium on the watch of Abbot Christianus McCarthy.

During the course of the twelfth century, the fertile scriptorium produced numerous hagiographies, or medieval manuscripts pertaining to other Irish saints such as St Erhard, who was said to have made his way from Lismore to France, where he established seven monasteries, and then to Regensburg, where he built a monastery on which the great Niedermünster Abbey was built. This story has the MacCarthys' imprint all over it – King Cormac was Lismore's foremost patron, having retired to the town before his death in 1138. A number of the aristocratic canonesses at the Niedermünster Abbey were Irish and it is hard not to assume that they too were MacCarthys from Munster.

The MacCarthys also had an interest in claiming St Cathaldus of Taranto, the patron saint of the Norman kingdom of Sicily, who was reinvented as an eighth-century master of the monastic school in Lismore. While returning from a pilgrimage to Jerusalem, he was said to have been shipwrecked off the coast of southern Italy but survived to become the bishop of Taranto, miraculously protecting its citizens from a series of floods and plagues. This story was scripted in the twelfth century after Normans discovered a coffin in the ruins of Taranto's cathedral (which had been destroyed by Saracens in 927) that contained a pastoral staff inscribed 'Cathaldus Rachau' alongside a small golden cross of seventh- or eighth-century Irish workmanship. The subsequent legend of St Cathaldus proved so successful that his figure was carved into the Basilica of the Nativity in Bethlehem, the primary coronation church for the kings of the Norman crusader state of Jerusalem.

In the wake of Cormac MacCarthy's death, the O'Briens regained control of the kingship of Munster. They also took up the mantle as patrons of the Benedictines in Bavaria and paid for the rebuilding of the splendid church at Regensburg in 1166, cloister, viaduct and all. Such patronage was honoured by the Regensburg scriptorium, where the Benedictines produced the stories of two new County Clare saints, namely Flannán mac Toirrdelbaig of Killaloe and Mochuille of Tulla. For good measure, they had Flannán travel all the way to Rome in 640 to be consecrated as the first bishop of Killaloe by the short-lived Pope John IV.

The penchant for creating these saintly Irish cults extended east to Melk in Austria, the seat of the royal House of Babenberg. Melk was the burial place of St Colmán (or Koloman), an Irishman who was tortured and hanged as a spy at Stockerau, near Vienna, in 1012. A whirl of legends had already spread about his immense courage – the rope with which he was hanged sprouted flowers, his incorruptible corpse was replete with healing properties – by the time a Benedictine abbey was established on a rock above the Danube at Melk in 1189. Under the guidance of the Melk scriptorium, St Colmán's cult flourished, spreading to the Electorate of the Palatinate, Hungary and Bavaria. Pilgrims travelled in droves to view the relics of the Irishman and, while the Babenbergs' campaign to have him formally canonized never bore fruit, his tomb continues to be a popular destination.

By the thirteenth century, there were a dozen closely connected Irish Benedictine monasteries operating in southern Germany and present-day Austria, running from Erfurt in Thuringia, south through Bavaria to the shores of Lake Constance in present-day Switzerland and east to Vienna. They even had an outpost at Kiev in the Rus. Whether or not the Benedictines had a priory in Cashel is unknown but the priory at Rosscarbery, West Cork, was certainly governed from Regensburg until the fourteenth century, after which it was controlled by Würzburg until its closure in the Reformation.

The only Schottenklöster that survives today as a Benedictine institution is the Schottenstift in Vienna, which was established in 1155 by the Babenberg prince, Henry, Duke of Bavaria (later King Henry II of Austria). Henry, who was buried in the abbey, had it built beside his palace and ensured that it was populated with pious monks from the Irish abbey in Regensburg. These monks were again predominantly from the O'Brien- and MacCarthy-controlled parts of Munster. Remarkably, they would have a considerable say over how the duchy's chancery was run. Two centuries later, the Schottenstift was intricately involved in the foundation of the first university in Vienna. When the last Irish abbot of the Vienna abbey died in 1418, it was the end of an astonishing era of over 300 years in which the Irish Benedictines had directed, and frequently invented, the way in which European saints should be revered.

7

JACOBO OF IRELAND AND THE MONGOL EMPIRE

Khanbaliq, Mongol Empire, 1325. Two years had passed since Yesün Temür had taken control of the massive Mongol Empire. A great-grandson of Kublai Khan, he had come to power following the assassination of his cousin, the previous emperor, an act in which he appears to have played a leading role. Yesün Temür was to enjoy less than five years on the throne before his premature death at the age of thirty-four.

During those years, his court in Khanbaliq (later Peking, now Beijing) was awash with gold, silver, cash and silks, as well as his beloved cheetahs and perhaps some ghosts of the numerous courtiers and councillors he had executed along the way. It is not the sort of place you would expect to find an Irishman and yet this was the city where Jacobo of Ireland found himself for much of Yesün Temür's reign. Perhaps the plucky friar even had an audience with the emperor himself.

To understand Jacobo's story, we need to begin in 1309 when Pope Clement V, the first of the seven 'Avignon Popes', moved the papal see to Avignon, then part of the kingdom of Naples. Clement, a former bishop of Bordeaux, is best known as the man who fulfilled the deepest wish of Philip IV, the cash-strapped king of France, by acquiescing to the extermination of the Knights Templar, the king's bankers, in 1307.

A lesser-known story about Clement concerns his support of a proposed Frankish alliance with the Mongols against the forces of Islam. The Crusaders had lost their last grip on the Holy Land several years before he became pope but the renewed possibility of collaboration with the Mongols in 1307 cheered him 'like spiritual sustenance'.[1] Furthermore, the Mongol emperor permitted Clement to establish a Roman Catholic Archdiocese in Khanbaliq. The mission was entrusted to Giovanni da Montecorvino, a Franciscan from southern Italy, who had already built a rudimentary church in the Mongol capital in the 1290s. This was the decade in which Marco Polo's travels to Kublai Khan's court at Xanadu took place, although the purported exploits of the Venetian merchant would not be published for several decades.

The military alliance with the Mongols had petered out by the time of Pope Clement's death in 1314. However, the archbishop's mission in Khanbaliq continued to expand, with further missions at places such as Citong (now Quanzhou) and Amoy (now Xiamen); on one occasion, he bought forty slaves at an auction and promptly baptized them. He even established a mission in the Uyghur city of Xinjiang that lay 3,000 km (1,860 miles) west of Khanbaliq. The administration of so many fledgling dioceses required a team of zealous experts. A call went out through the Franciscans' extensive network and among those who responded to the request was a friar known to posterity as Jacobo de Ibernia, also known as James of Ireland. Alas, nothing more is known of his background except that he had somehow made it to the port city of Hormuz on the Persian Gulf by about 1321, from where he embarked on his remarkable mission to help convert the Chinese and Mongols to Catholicism.

Our knowledge of Jacobo's subsequent adventures comes from the journal of his travelling companion, Friar Odoric (1286–1331), whom he joined at Hormuz. Doric, as he called himself, was from Pordenone in northeast Italy, a town that lies between the Adriatic Sea and the Alps. The town had been taken over by the Hapsburgs eight years before his birth and created a city in 1314. As a young man, Doric had been on a series of missions across the Balkans and into the Mongol-controlled regions of southern Russia, where the ruling elite were tolerant of Christianity.

From Hormuz, Jacobo sailed across the Persian Gulf to India with his Italian comrade and a servant. In his journals, Doric recounts an old Irish fable, presumably heard from Jacobo, that barnacle geese, whose Arctic breeding grounds were then unknown, were the fruit of barnacles, a shallow-water shellfish that attaches itself to driftwood and ships at sea. They landed at Thane, near Mumbai, from where they made their way north to the tropical port of Sopara (Supara), once the largest town on India's west coast.

In Sopara they visited a church that held the remains of St Thomas of Tolentino and three other Franciscans, who had been beheaded two years earlier for declaring the prophet Muhammad to be the demonical 'son of perdition'. Friar Doric recorded how they then gathered up the relics of the four martyrs, including St Thomas's skull, before proceeding onwards in a junk to China by way of Sumatra, Java and Borneo. They reached the port of Canton (now Guangzhou) at about the time of Marco Polo's death in Venice in 1324. They then travelled overland for some 2,500 km (1,550 miles) to Khanbaliq via Hangzhou and Yangzhou, visiting other Franciscan missionaries along the way.

Having arrived in Khanbaliq, Jacobo and Doric spent nearly three years in the area, assisting Archbishop Giovanni with his missions. No records of their own mission have yet been found. Perhaps the plucky friars enjoyed an audience with Emperor Yesün Temür. However, things became precarious in 1328 with the death of both the archbishop and the emperor. The latter's demise triggered a civil war between rival members of the Yuan dynasty that brought widespread bloodshed to China. Perhaps anticipating such a grim turn of events, Jacobo and Doric hastily left the Mongol Empire. They journeyed overland, possibly via Tibet, certainly by northern Persia, and had both made it safely to Venice by 1330. Amazingly, they still had St Thomas's skull with them, or at least, a skull that they said was his. This was bequeathed to the Franciscan chapter in Thomas's Italian hometown of Tolentino where, encased in a silver bust, it is now on show in the Cathedral of San Catervo.

The following year Doric was on his way to meet with Pope John XXII in Avignon when he was taken ill. He about-turned for Udine, a city near his family home, where he died soon afterwards. He was buried in Udine, where his tomb can still be seen, and beatified as the Blessed Odoric of Pordenone in 1755. Fortunately, he had already told his adventures to a fellow friar, who wrote them down in Latin, and they were later published to considerable acclaim. Luke Wadding (p. 37) was a notable admirer, while much of the content was pillaged by the anonymous author of the enormously popular but entirely fictitious medieval memoir, *The Travels of Sir John Mandeville*.

The Christian missions in China seemed destined for long-lasting glory when Pope Benedict XII dispatched fifty ecclesiastics to Khanbaliq in 1338. However, the great project came to a swift end thirty years later when the Han Chinese drove the Mongols out of China, established the Ming dynasty and expelled all Christians from the empire.

'Brother Jacobus' appears to have been with Doric at his demise as the citizens of Udine voted him 2 marks, a considerable sum, in 1331. He was recorded in Udine's municipal records as the 'holy partner of the blessed Brother Odoric, loved of God and Odoric'. Nothing more is known of this remarkable Irishman who travelled to China in the 1320s.

8

LUKE WADDING AND
THE VATICAN ELITE

Rome, 1618. For thirty-year-old Padre Luca, that first visit to the Franciscan church of San Pietro on the Janiculum Hill must have been a moment of profound resonance. This, it was widely believed, was the very site on which St Peter had been crucified by Emperor Nero. Of rather more recent relevance were the tombs by the high altar where Hugh O'Neill, Great Earl of Tyrone, and Rory O'Donnell, Earl of Tyrconnell, lay buried.

Padre Luca, or Luke Wadding as he was christened, was living in the Portuguese city of Matosinhos when he learned that a ship laden with some of the most prominent Gaelic Irish aristocrats had arrived in the Continent from Ireland. In the summer of 1608, war-weary and landless, Tyrconnell had died in Rome shortly after his arrival, leaving a two-year-old son, Hugh O'Donnell, as his heir. Lord Tyrone, the head of the O'Neill clan, lived on until 1616, having spent his last years vainly plotting a return to Ireland. The 'Flight of the Earls', as their 1607 departure became known, marked the end of the Gaelic order in Ireland, and yet the decision by the two earls to go to Rome, the city where Luke Wadding was also to spend the rest of his life, simultaneously marked the start of a much deeper relationship between Irish Catholics and the Eternal City.

Such synergy would probably not have been possible without the genius of Padre Luca himself. This modest Franciscan friar established the Irish College in Rome, which would be preeminent among the twenty-nine Irish Colleges established in Europe at this time. A brilliant theologian and an exceptional diplomat, he also sowed the seeds for the global phenomenon of St Patrick's Day.

Luke Wadding was born in Waterford in 1588, just weeks after a third of the Spanish Armada was wrecked along the Irish coast. He was one of ten brothers and four sisters born to Walter Wadding, a well-heeled merchant, and his wife, Anastasia Lombard. He received an excellent early education in Waterford, numbering his own father and his older brother Mathew, a merchant, among his most attentive teachers. Tragedy struck in 1602 when both his parents succumbed to plague. The following year, Mathew brought him to Portugal, where he commenced his studies at the University of Coimbra. Another brother Ambrose went to the Jesuit University of Dillingen in Bavaria, where he would become a celebrated professor.

In September 1604, Luke Wadding entered the Order of Friars Minor, better known as the Franciscans, and made his profession a year later. Having spent his novitiate at Matosinhos, he went on to become a theology lecturer at the University of Salamanca in Spain. An exceptional linguist, he was by now fluent in Portuguese, Castilian and Hebrew, as well as Greek, Latin, English and Irish. Mastering Italian, when the time came, was no problem for him. Wadding's special interest in the doctrine of the immaculate conception of the Virgin Mary caught the eye of a Spanish bishop, who invited him to serve as his theologian on a delegation to the Vatican City in Rome, where the Franciscans were also headquartered.

Upon his arrival in Rome in 1618, Wadding was accommodated by Spanish Franciscans living near the church of San Pietro, where the Irish earls were buried. He was later introduced to the 2nd Lord Tyrconnell, now a teenager, who was so impressed by Wadding's 'merit and talent' that he urged the Pope to make him the bishop of Waterford. Tyrconnell's mentor, Florence Conry – the archbishop of Tuam, another Franciscan friar in exile – likewise applauded Wadding as a man of 'great intelligence and discipline'. Such endorsements were further enhanced when he united with his mother's cousin Peter Lombard, the exiled archbishop of Armagh, who had been living in Rome since 1598.

In the spring of 1619, Benigno da Genova, the minister general of the Franciscans, asked Wadding to write the definitive history of the 400-year-old order. This colossal project would occupy much of his time for the next three decades before he finally completed the eight-volume work, *Annales Minorum*, published in 1654. It also made the Waterford native one of the most influential men in the Vatican because not only was he granted unprecedented access to material about the order, he was also now meeting or corresponding with the leading figures from the miscellaneous Franciscan branches, including Urban VIII, who served as pope from 1623 to 1644, and the powerful Barberini and Ludovisi families.

Arguably the most important of these contacts was Ludovico Ludovisi, the ambitious and immensely wealthy nephew of the late Pope Gregory XV. Cardinal Ludovisi lived in a magnificent villa that he had built on Monte Pincio and filled with a fabulous collection of Roman antiquities, along with frescoes and other works by contemporary artists. The villa lay a stone's throw from the small friary of St Isidore's, which a small group of Spanish Franciscans had founded in 1621. When the Spaniards ran into difficulty and left Rome, the friary was offered to Luke Wadding as a base where missionaries could be trained for the Irish Franciscan province and he readily accepted the challenge.

Part of his *raison d'être* was to prove to the wider Catholic world that Franciscans were by no means opposed to education, as was often stated of the order. He now tapped into his network for financial support; the response was outstanding, with sizeable donations from the Pope and the king of Spain, as well as numerous cardinals, princes and ambassadors. Such benefactors enabled Wadding to buy the site, finish the building and formally open the College of St Isidore on 13 June 1625. It thus became the first effective Irish institution to be founded in Rome and Padre Luca would serve as its guardian until 1649.

Perhaps inspired by Ludovisi, Wadding commissioned works for the church from Baroque artists such as Andrea Sacchi and Carlo Maratti. He also furnished its library with a remarkable collection of 5,000 printed books and 800 manuscripts. The college's first lecturers were all Irish: Martin Breathnach from Donegal, Patrick Fleming from Louth, John Punch from Cork and Anthony O'Hicidh (Hickey), scion of a celebrated bardic family from County Clare.

The success of St Isidore's drove Wadding's ambition as he next sought to create a college where secular clergymen could be trained to keep the Catholic faith alive across Ireland – as the young Tyrconnell had written of their homeland, quoting from the Gospel of Matthew, 'the harvest is plentiful, but the labourers are few'.[1] As such, Wadding carefully nurtured his rapport with his patrons, paying particular attention to Cardinal Ludovisi, who had lately been appointed the cardinal protector of Ireland. Ludovisi was already in consultation with John Roche, another Irishman, about the notion of a college for Irish secular clergy in Rome. When Roche returned to Ireland as the new bishop of Ferns in 1627, he left the door open for Wadding to take up the collegiate reins.

With Ludovisi's support, Luke Wadding rented a small house on the present-day Via degli Ibernesi (Irishmen's Street), close to both St Isidore's and the cardinal's villa. This is where the Pontifical Irish College opened on New Year's Day, 1628, welcoming its first six students, who took their meals at St Isidore's. They were evidently an erudite group and Ludovisi was soon declaring his pleasure that 'the youth of my college attend with fervour to their studies'.

Within a decade of his arrival in Rome, Luke Wadding had managed to establish two Irish colleges in the city, one regular, one secular, that would do much to promote Irish Catholicism and preserve the Gaelic culture within the Vatican, as well as producing a steady stream of Franciscan novices. Some achieved prominence in the hierarchies of France, Portugal, Flanders, Italy and America, while others served as chaplains to the Irish regiments abroad. At least twenty returned to Ireland to preach during the seventeenth century, including St Oliver Plunkett, the archbishop of Armagh, who was burned and beheaded in London. At least four more former students of the Irish College became bishops in Ireland, while Paul Cullen, one of the college rectors, went on to become Ireland's first cardinal in 1866. Almost four centuries after its foundation, the Irish College is now the last remaining Irish college on the European continent that still functions as a diocesan seminary.

As for Padre Luca, he remained on close terms with the papal curia, the principal administrators of the Holy See, advising on the appointment of bishops and other senior church offices in Ireland. His shrewd diplomacy was remarkable because he was not only representing Irish interests in Rome, but also still pitching on behalf of his Spanish patrons who had initially sent him to the city. It was by no means easy – he was often entangled in the factionalism that was rife both in Rome and within the Franciscans themselves, while his 'Old English' ancestry caused resentment with some of the Gaelic members of the Irish clergy.

Since he had left Ireland as a teenager, Luke Wadding was aware of the deteriorating status of his homeland's Catholic population at the hands of the Protestant English administration in Dublin. During the 1640s he became deeply embroiled in the Irish Confederate Wars, in which a loose coalition of Catholic interests vainly attempted to wrestle back control of the island. When war broke out in October 1641, Padre Luca actively encouraged Owen Roe O'Neill, a nephew of the Great Earl of Tyrone, to return home to take the lead of his Ulster compatriots. The Vatican funded O'Neill's journey, providing him with a frigate, the *St Francis*, as well as a cargo of arms and munitions.

In 1645, three years after O'Neill's ship dropped anchor at Castledoe, County Donegal, Wadding persuaded Innocent X, the new pope, to send his papal nuncio Cardinal Rinuccini to drum up support for the Catholic Confederate cause in Ireland. Indeed, Rinuccini was due to land in the Wadding stronghold of Waterford until his ship blew him westwards to Kenmare Bay, on the southwest coast of Ireland. The Vatican also showed its support by dispatching 1,000 braces of pistols, 4,000 cartridge belts, 2,000 swords, 500 muskets and about 9,000 kg (20,000 lb) of gunpowder; such a large consignment of enemy arms would be echoed in the dramatic landing of German guns and arms at Howth harbour on Dublin Bay in 1914.

When O'Neill was victorious over enemy forces at Benburb, County Tyrone, in 1646, he sent the captured banners directly to Luke Wadding, who hung them triumphantly in the cupola of St Peter's Basilica in the Vatican. Wadding also persuaded the Pope to send O'Neill the sword of his uncle, Lord Tyrone, which was a tremendous morale booster. However, his spirit was profoundly crushed in the gloomy year of 1649 when O'Neill died of a mysterious disease eleven weeks after Oliver Cromwell arrived in Ireland to destroy the Confederacy. Father Richard Sinnott, a good friend of

Padre Luca, was one of twenty-nine Franciscan friars killed during Cromwell's ensuing conquest.

At the peak of its power in 1644, the Supreme Council of the Catholic Confederation had written from Kilkenny to the dying Pope Urban VIII, and then to his successor, Innocent X, advocating that Wadding be made a cardinal. It was not until long after his death that his Franciscan brethren discovered that it was Wadding himself who prevented such appeals from reaching the Pope, preferring to retain a less exalted position despite his contemporaries' wish to lift him higher. In 1644, and again in 1655, he received votes as a candidate for the papacy, making him the closest Ireland has come to having a pope. In the wake of his death in 1657, there were even whispers of imminent canonization.

Padre Luca was laid to rest in the college church at St Isidore. He would be survived by both his colleges, as well as thirty-six volumes of written work.[2] In the 1950s, his statue was erected on the Mall in Waterford; it now stands by the entrance to the town's French Church. The library at the Waterford Institute of Technology was also named after him. In 2007, the archive of the General Curia of the Franciscan Order in Rome was likewise named in his honour.

A mural of St Patrick above his modest tomb recalls what was perhaps Luke Wadding's most enduring legacy. As a member of the Vatican's Breviary reform commission of 1629, he entered St Patrick's Day into the universal calendar of the Church as the feast day of the patron saint of Ireland. His old friend John Roche, now a bishop, clearly anticipated the long-term repercussions when he elatedly wrote to him, 'God reward you for including his feast in the Roman calendar.' Arguably, 17 March is now the best-known feast day of any saint across the world.

9

DON GUILLÉN,
THE ORIGINAL ZORRO

Mexico City, 1641. Tempted as he was, the courtier known as Don Guillén Lombardo de Guzmán did not imbibe any of the peyote himself. Instead, the young Wexford man focused his attention on his Creole friend, Don Ignacio, who was now sipping on the hallucinogenic cocktail. All he needed was a hint, a glimmer of a vision, to reassure him that he had divine support. Perhaps he was surprised when Ignacio's voice from the otherworld intoned that Guillén would soon become a king. He certainly had a long period to reflect on it all before the Inquisition finally tired of him and condemned him to the flames.

William Lamport, as Guillén was christened, was born in Wexford in 1611. He claimed descent from Milo de Lamporte, one of the first Cambro-Norman knights to arrive in Ireland. Ensconced at Ballyhire Castle, just south of Rosslare, the Lamports remained influential until the late sixteenth century when their Catholic faith set them at odds with the Protestant policies imposed on Ireland by the English Crown. Guillén was six years old when his grandfather, a renowned pirate, was executed following a personal request by King James I.

The youngest of four children, he studied under the Augustinians and Franciscans in Wexford, and later with the Jesuits in Dublin. He excelled at theology and maths but his thirst for knowledge caused a falling out with his older brother Juan, a Franciscan friar. When the Jesuit college in Dublin was shut down, Guillén moved to Charles I's London, where he studied Greek and mathematics at Gresham College. Identified as an outspoken political troublemaker, he was soon facing arrest over an anti-monarchy satire he had published. He took a ship to France, only to be captured by pirates with whom, according to his own testimony, he then served for over a year.

By 1630 he had left his pirate friends and found favour with the Marquis of Mancera, a Spanish grandee based in the northwest region of Galicia. With Mancera's support, Guillén secured a place at a Jesuit college for young, well-to-do Irish exiles in Santiago de Compostela. By the time he won a scholarship to advance to the Irish College in Salamanca, he had Hispanicized his name to Guillén Lombardo and, for a touch of aristocratic credibility, added the honorific 'Don'. Among those who knew him was Diego Nugencio (also known as John Nugent), a Franciscan friar from Mullingar, County Westmeath, who recalled him as 'a very capable student and theologian' with 'a beautiful face and figure'. With his long red hair and sparkling eyes, Don Guillén was clearly a charming man.

In 1632, Mancera sent him to King Philip IV's court in Madrid to meet Don Gaspar de Guzmán, Count-Duke of Olivares, the Spanish king's favourite and chief minister. Like Mancera, Olivares was impressed and placed the Irishman at Madrid's elite College of San Lorenzo de El Escorial, where the monarchy's most loyal servants were trained. It was during this period that his portrait was sketched by one of Anthony van Dyck's apprentices.

A useful swordsman, Guillén's approval ratings rocketed in the Spanish court when he commanded a crack squad of Irishmen that helped to relieve a French siege of the beleaguered Basque town of Hondarribia in 1638.[1] He may have also participated in undercover assignments to Italy and Catalonia on Olivares's behalf. The minister certainly permitted Guillén to adopt his family name, de Guzmán, at this time, an honour that further enhanced his network.

While in Madrid, Guillén made a strong push to secure Spanish military support for a Catholic uprising in Ireland. However, this project slipped to one side in January 1640 when he abruptly boarded a ship bound for New Spain, as the Spanish Empire's colonies in present-day North and Central America were then known. One theory is that he was on the run having made an unmarried noble woman, Doña Ana Godoy Rodríguez, pregnant. Although this may be so, his flight was also connected to the appointment of the Marquis of Villena as New Spain's viceroy. Olivares distrusted Villena and had ordered Guillén to cross the Atlantic to spy on him.

Upon arrival in Mexico, Don Guillén lodged with one of Olivares's allies, teaching grammar to his son in lieu of rent. To maintain his cover, Olivares asked him to investigate stories of mounting discontent among New Spain's Creoles, the Mexican-born descendants of Spanish settlers. Given his own status as the Irish-born descendant of displaced Norman Catholic settlers, it is understandable that he quickly bonded with Mexico's Creoles, lodging with one of their elders. As he mingled with the Creole elite, he also became profoundly appalled by the enslavement of indigenous Mexicans and Africans, and the tyranny of those who ruled the kingdom.

The drama intensified in June 1642 when Juan Palafox, the Creole-backed bishop of Puebla, overthrew Villena in a peaceful coup that was readily supported by Don Guillén. However, there was disappointment in store when the Crown in Madrid failed to support Palafox and dispatched another viceroy to reassert direct royal authority in New Spain. This was too much for the now penniless Guillén who, convinced that the Spanish monarchy was about to collapse, began planning another coup.

It was at this time that he began meeting Don Ignacio, a Spanish-speaking Creole elder who lived near the silver mines of Taxco. Guillén later stated that his interest in peyote was inspired by memories of a hallucinogenic herb in Ireland that he called 'tams', presumed to be some form of magic mushroom. By imbibing mescaline from the peyote cactus, he hoped to induce a trance that would reveal his future. However, because he might not remember the vision, he instead mixed the peyote with wine, handed a glass to Don Ignacio and waited, pen in hand, to record what happened. Ignacio later told the Inquisition that 'nothing came...and I just felt pains all night in my head and body'. However, 'so that Don Guillen would leave me alone and let me sleep', he told the Irishman that the indigenous labourers of Taxco were ready for revolution and that Guillén himself would become king of a new, independent state.

Guillén was so convinced that he spent the next two months plotting his rebellion and devising a new family tree, which established him as a son of Philip III, the former king of Spain, and the Countess of Ross, a fictional Irish noblewoman. His aim was to seize control of Mexico City with an armed militia of 500 enslaved Africans, indigenous Mexicans and Creoles, hoping that the people would rise up in support and proclaim him king of New Spain. However, when Guillén informed his Spanish and Creole friends of his grand scheme, he was greeted with absolute incredulity. Inevitably, one of them denounced him as a perilous heretic to the Inquisition and he was arrested on 26 October 1642. When constables searched his apartment, they found a cache of documents – a proclamation of independence for New Spain, with a democratic parliament and Guillén as its king, as well as plans to establish free trade (notably naming China as the target market) and to abolish slavery and forced labour in the silver mines.

Ordinarily the solution would have been to dismiss Guillén as a fanatic, but the thirty-one-year-old's network of powerful contacts and his hitherto successful career compelled the Inquisition to treat this 'diabolic plot' with special severity. He was hauled before the court in 1642, where witness after witness came forward to castigate Guillén, including his own brother Juan. Accusations of blasphemy, treason and witchcraft followed, as well as the sensational claim that he was an illegitimate half-brother of the Spanish king. The Inquisitors painted him as an insane, malevolent, deceitful woman-izer and sentenced him to rot in jail.[2]

He spent most of the next two decades as a prisoner of the Holy Office of Mexico. On Christmas Eve 1650, he managed to escape, only to be captured plastering broadsides on the city walls soon afterwards; the posters denounced the Inquisition as a fraudulent entity that was targeting wealthy citizens in order to seize their wealth. Back in jail, he devoted the rest of his life to drafting endless seditious pamphlets as well as nearly 800 Latin psalms, still unpublished, which are said to be quite beautiful.

In 1659, the Inquisition decided to make an example of Guillén and condemned him to burn at the stake for his multiple heresies. Somehow, he managed to strangle himself on the pyre before the flames engulfed him. His last will and testament proclaimed his hope that Judgment Day was on its way, along with his certainty that the archbishop of Mexico City would be among the first to be engulfed by the fires of hell.

Don Guillén would become the most famous of the fifty or so people to be executed by the Mexican Inquisition. Despite the

Inquisitors' best efforts, posterity would record him as a brilliant humanist, a Renaissance man, a champion of the underprivileged and a martyr for Mexican independence and the rights of the indigenous population. His statue stands guard by the mausoleum inside the El Ángel monument in Mexico City.

Guillén's immortalization as Zorro began in 1872 when a retired Mexican general published a historical romance about 'Don Guillén de Lampart', an enlightened revolutionary who takes on the might of both the Spanish Empire and the Inquisition. In 1919, the American pulp novelist Johnston McCulley reinvented Don Guillén as Señor Zorro, a charming vigilante who protects the indigenous people of California from a ruthless and utterly crooked Spanish elite. The following year, Douglas Fairbanks donned a black cape, Cordovan hat and eye mask and translated McCulley's acrobatic hero onto the silver screen in *The Mark of Zorro*. The silent swashbuckler was one of the biggest hits of the 1920s, spawning over forty sequels and remakes, as well as numerous TV series and radio dramas.

10

LORD BELLOMONT'S PIRATICAL VENTURE

Execution Dock, Wapping, London, 23 May 1701. The crowd was in lively form as the condemned pirates were hauled out of the horse-drawn cart and marched towards the gallows. Captain Kidd played to them a little, as he would. He had somehow managed to find some drink, but surely the old seadog was entitled to a bit of light relief? Eight of the nine crewmen condemned to die alongside him had been reprieved. The sole exception was Darby Mullins, a 'hearty' Irishman from County Derry, who stood beside him now as the Captain delivered his final words to those gathered, warning all ship-masters to learn from his fate. He made no mention of his former patron Lord Bellomont, upon whose orders he was now about to die.

Born in Ireland in 1636, Richard Coote, 1st Earl of Bellomont, was a grandson of Sir Charles Coote, probably the most ruthless English army commander to serve in the country during the Cromwellian era. Little is known of his early life but he is thought to have lived between Moore Park, east of Navan, County Meath, and Piercetown, near Tyrrellstown, County Westmeath. During his twenties, Bellomont killed a man in a duel and married an heiress. When he succeeded his father as Baron Coote of Coloony in 1683, he also inherited extensive lands in Sligo and Leitrim, including those around Coloony (now Collooney) itself, which were later sold to the Coopers of Markree Castle.

As an ardent Protestant, he could not tolerate the pro-Catholic policies of James II, who became king in 1685. Instead he moved to Europe, where he served as a captain of horse in the Dutch army and befriended William of Orange and his wife Princess Mary. His support of William and Mary's seizure of the English throne in 1688 would pay handsome dividends when he was rewarded with a colossal 31,000 hectares (77,000 acres) in Ireland. The immensity of this land gift caused such an outcry in the Irish parliament that the king was obliged to rescind it. Nonetheless, Coote kept a large Irish estate and was created Earl of Bellomont, as well as becoming the governor of Leitrim. He also served as Treasurer to Queen Mary from 1689 until her death in 1694.

Handsome and stylish, Bellomont was part of a circle of exceptionally wealthy Whigs who had supported King William's coup. Among these were four men with strong Irish links who would play a key role in his future plan. The 'proud but drunken' Lord Romney had served at the Battle of the Boyne in 1690 and was King William's first viceroy of Ireland; he was also briefly owner of 20,000 hectares (50,000 acres) of confiscated land in the country. Lord Shrewsbury was the hereditary Lord High Steward of Ireland and would become the island's viceroy in 1713. Lord Somers also had considerable lands in Ireland, while Lord Orford was the admiral responsible for King William's navy during the final year of his war against James II in Ireland in 1691.

In 1695 Bellomont was appointed to a parliamentary committee assigned to examine the case of Jacob Leisler, one of New York's most influential citizens. Leisler claimed his father had been framed and 'barbarously murdered' on the orders of the sitting governor of New York. Bellomont championed Leisler's cause with such success that King William appointed him governor of not one but three royal colonies, namely Massachusetts, New Hampshire and New York. He was also by extension made captain of the militia of Rhode Island, New Jersey and Connecticut.

Bureaucratic cogs turned slowly in 1690s London and it was not until April 1698 that the increasingly gout-riddled governor finally arrived in New York to take up his post. He was instantly faced with the complexities of New York, a colony still plagued by the divisions that had erupted over the Leisler case, as well as ongoing conflict with the indigenous Iroquois and Abenaki over ancestral lands that had been stolen by the Europeans.

As governor, one of Bellomont's primary missions was to stamp out 'free-booting' in the region, much of it involving blatant, open commerce between pirates and merchants in the fledgling colonies, especially New York City and Rhode Island. However, the King's Admiralty were unable to finance a war on piracy because all of its available resources were being employed to sustain the Royal Navy's ongoing war with France.

In early 1696, long before he sailed for New York, Bellomont hit upon a solution that would not only rid the seas of dastardly pirates but also clear his own considerable personal debts. Enter William Kidd, a Scottish privateer who had spent the past five years living the life of a New York businessman. He had made his mark as a privateer in the Caribbean, pillaging French settlements on behalf of the Admiralty. His wealth was much enhanced when he married a woman of substantial property in New York. That he applied to marry her just two days after her husband's mysterious death understandably triggered much gossip.

Poachers, of course, often make the best gamekeepers. Bellomont met with Kidd in London and asked the Scot to return to sea as a pirate-hunter. He offered £60,000 to outfit the *Adventure Galley*, a new three-masted ship, complete with thirty-two cannons. The costs were to be met by Bellomont and four secret backers, later revealed to be lords Romney, Shrewsbury, Somers and Orford. Kidd's brief was to hunt down pirates in the Indian Ocean, recover their booty and then discreetly redistribute it among the five investors. King William was also entitled to a tenth of the proceeds. There was no mention of trying to return any stolen items to the original owners.

Kidd complied and was handed the all-important letters of assent and marque, as well as a special royal commission to tackle the pirates. In April 1696 he left London on *Adventure Galley* and set sail, via New York, for the piratical hotbed of East Africa. It was during his brief stop in New York that forty-year-old Darby Mullins joined his crew. Five years later, in defence of his life, Mullins would tell how he had been orphaned as a boy and raised on a farm near Magherafelt, County Derry, only to be kidnapped and transported to the West Indies as a teenager. He had subsequently worked on plantations in Jamaica where, having survived the ferocious earthquake of 1692, he established a public house in Kingston. He then moved to New York where, prior to joining Kidd's crew, he had worked on various ships, plundering from vessels that he believed to be owned by 'enemies of Christianity'.

Unfortunately for Bellomont, Kidd had lost some of his earlier knack. An entire year went by during which he found precious little cargo. He also narrowly avoided a mutiny after a third of his crew succumbed to disease. Confidence on board was not restored when the hot-tempered Scot smashed an iron bucket over the head of his ship's gunner and killed the man. In desperation, Kidd captured two merchant ships on the Malabar Coast, but his decision to keep the booty for himself was to prove fatal.

One of the merchant ships, the *Quedah*, was carrying a valuable cargo of silk, muslin, calico, sugar and opium, most of which belonged to one of the Mughal emperor's courtiers. The captain of the *Quedah* was an Englishman who managed to send word of Kidd's nefarious activities back to London. By now the poorly built *Adventure Galley* was leaking so badly that Kidd had to abandon her to a watery grave at Île Sainte-Marie (present-day Nosy Boraha), a pirate haven off the northeast coast of Madagascar.

Along with Darby Mullins and a handful of others still prepared to serve under him, Kidd sailed the *Quedah* to the West Indies where, to his dismay, he learned that the Admiralty had declared him a pirate and issued an arrest warrant. He made his way to Boston to negotiate with Governor Bellomont, who had promised him clemency if he handed himself in. Alas for Kidd, the Irish peer did not keep his word and the privateer was swiftly dispatched to London, along with nine of his crew, to stand trial for five counts of piracy, as well as the murder of his gunner. Meanwhile, Bellomont initiated a major search for Kidd's booty, some of which was recovered.

In what was widely regarded as a sham trial, 'the notorious pyratt' Kidd and his crew were found guilty as charged and sentenced to death. Darby Mullins argued that he had simply been obeying the orders of his superior officer and that he would have been punished had he refused. The prosecution took the view that such obedience was negated by the fact that the actions themselves were unlawful. Mullins gamely reasoned that 'the case of a seaman must be bad indeed if he were punished in both cases, for obeying and for not obeying his officers, and that if he were allowed to dispute his superior's orders, there would be no such thing as command on the high seas'.[1] It didn't convince the jury; the judge donned the black cap. After Mullins mounted the scaffold on 23 May 1701, the *Tyburn Chronicle* reported that he had 'begged pardon of God and man for the offences he had committed, and acknowledged his sins had deservedly brought upon him the misfortunes under which he laboured'.

Captain Kidd was hanged alongside him. The first attempt to hang him actually failed when the rope snapped and the fifty-six-year-old Scot tumbled to the ground. He was still conscious as the rope was reknotted. He was hoisted back up on the gallows; this time the rope did not snap. Kidd's sole consolation as the noose tightened may have been that he had outlived the deceitful Earl of Bellomont, who unexpectedly succumbed to his gout in Bowling Green, Manhattan, New York in March 1701.

11

GEORGE BERKELEY, THE 'IRISH PLATO' AND BERMUDA COLLEGE

Rhode Island, America, 1731. One wonders how many times George Berkeley re-read Walpole's remark. It was so typical of Britain's chief minister, frank and final and yet somehow rather charming. For eight long years, the Kilkenny man had harboured a dream of establishing a missionary training college on the Atlantic island of Bermuda. Three years earlier, Berkeley and his new bride had actually moved to Rhode Island, on the northeast coast of North America, in order to lay the groundwork for the enterprise. But now their mounting suspicions were confirmed. The funds that Westminster had promised were simply not going to materialize. The project was over. It was time for Ireland's preeminent philosopher to go home.

George Berkeley is thought to have been born at Dysart Castle, near Thomastown, County Kilkenny, on 12 March 1685. He was the eldest son of William Berkeley, a gentleman. After an early education at Kilkenny College, George was enrolled at Trinity College Dublin in the week of his fifteenth birthday. He was to enjoy a close association with the university for the next twenty-four years.

Berkeley thrived at Trinity where, in the space of four years, he produced three extremely influential and ground-breaking works on vision and metaphysics, all written while he was in his mid-twenties. His idealist philosophy held that, aside from the spiritual, everything in this world exists only as it is perceived by our senses, hence his own motto, *esse* is *percipi* ('to be is to be perceived'). Appointed junior dean of Trinity in 1710, he became a senior fellow in 1717. At that time, all fellows at Trinity had to be ordained in the Church of Ireland, an Anglican (Protestant) institution, within three years of commencing their fellowships. Religion was to be central to his philosophical musings over the decades to come.

One reason why Berkeley's work stood out was because he was such an eloquent and beautiful writer. This brought him into favour with

London's leading intellectuals when he went to the British capital in 1713 to oversee the publication of his latest work. His circle included the playwright Joseph Addison, with whom he guzzled champagne at the opening night of Addison's critically acclaimed tragedy, *Cato*, and the poet Alexander Pope, who credited Berkeley with 'ev'ry virtue under heav'n'. There were also two fellow Irishmen, namely Dublin-born Richard Steele (for whom Berkeley wrote essays in *The Guardian*) and Jonathan Swift (another Kilkenny College alumnus).

Shortly before he left for Dublin to become the dean of St Patrick's Cathedral, Swift presented Berkeley at Queen Anne's court. Swift also paved the way for Berkeley's first proper experience of travel by introducing him to the Earl of Peterborough, the queen's ambassador to the king of Sicily. Peterborough appointed Berkeley as his chaplain and secretary for a ten-month visit to Italy, much of which was spent in the Tuscan port of Livorno. His return to London in the summer of 1714 coincided with the death of Queen Anne and the ascension of the German-speaking Elector of Hanover as King George of Great Britain and Ireland.

Peterborough and Swift were among those who expressed disdain for the Hanoverian succession. Berkeley published an essay that urged his Tory friends not to support the Jacobite rebellion against the king, but nonetheless found himself *non grata* among the new Georgian elite. A helping hand came from St George Ashe, the bishop of Clogher, who asked him to return to Europe in 1716 as chaperone to his ailing teenaged son. The duo spent the next four years travelling extensively through Italy, visiting Sicily, Puglia, Calabria and other lesser-known regions and witnessing an eruption on Mount Vesuvius near Naples that Berkeley wrote about in detail. He also chronicled the innumerable fine mansions they called upon in a journal, and continued to pen essays on subjects such as motion and time.

The unfortunate Master Ashe died of his illness soon after their return in 1721. Britain was by then sinking into the economic doldrums brought about by the infamous bursting of the South Sea Bubble. Berkeley wisely continued onwards to Ireland, where he worked as a lecturer in Greek and Hebrew at Trinity College. He also served as the senior proctor, orchestrating the principal ceremonies at the university.

One of Berkeley's earliest patrons was the Cork-born politician Sir John Percival, later to become 1st Earl of Egmont and a founding father of the British colony of Georgia in North America. When the Deanery of Derry became vacant in 1724, Lady Percival put in a good word on Berkeley's behalf with her friend the Duchess of Grafton, whose husband was the viceroy of Ireland at the time. Berkeley was duly offered the living, including a hefty remuneration of £1,500 a year, for which he was compelled to resign his fellowship at Trinity.

At this juncture, an extraordinary bequest came Berkeley's way following the death of the Dutch heiress, Esther van Homrigh, a former lover of Jonathan Swift. (Swift invented the name 'Vanessa' for her by inserting the 'van' from her surname before 'Esse', a pet form of her first name.) Swift had spurned her in favour of his other lover, Hester Johnson, also known as Stella. Bishop Ashe, Berkeley's patron, is said to have presided over Swift's alleged marriage to Stella.

Just before she died, Esther van Homrigh rewrote her will and left half her fortune to Berkeley, whom she barely knew. Berkeley considered the inheritance to be providential, a gift from God to help him fulfil his wider dream. By 1723, that dream was to establish an Anglican college on Bermuda. In his opinion, Protestant Europe was in a state of inexorable spiritual decay and the only hope was to start anew in the fledgling British colonies of North America. The principal hurdle was the blatant shortage of Protestant clerics in the colonies while, conversely, the 'Church of Rome' was making extensive inroads in the French and Spanish colonies. Berkeley's solution was to found a college where the children of colonists and Native Americans alike could be trained as missionaries and dispatched into the wilds of the Americas to spread the Protestant faith.

Bermuda struck him as the perfect place for such a college. Annexed as a colony of the British Crown in 1684, a year before Berkeley's birth, the Atlantic island enjoyed a temperate climate. A prominent stop-off for transatlantic ships voyaging to North America and the Caribbean, it benefited from excellent connections with many of the developing ports and towns in the English colonies. Berkeley liked the reports he had received about the prudent, pennywise demeanour of Bermuda's colonial inhabitants. Most of the island's 8,500-strong population were indentured servants and enslaved people who worked on plantations or in maritime enterprises like salt raking.

Berkeley spent five years lobbying Westminster to back his crusade. He was evidently a persuasive man. In 1726, Sir Robert Walpole, the king's chief minister, undertook to give him an enormous government grant of £20,000. Parliament also presented him with an all-important college charter, signed by George I.

Now all he needed was a wife. He initially tried his luck with Anne Donnellan, a niece of Lord Percival, who was highly regarded for her support of music, art and literature. Donnellan, who described herself as 'an asserter of the rights and privileges of women',[1] declined his proposal, after which he went in pursuit of Anne Forster, the daughter of a former Chief Justice of Ireland. 'I chose her for her great qualities of mind, and her unaffected inclination to books,' Berkeley explained. 'She goes with great thankfulness, to live a plain farmer's life, and wear stuff of her own spinning. I have presented her with a spinning-wheel.'

George Berkeley and Anne Forster were married on 1 August 1728. Anne's £2,000 fortune provided enough money for the newlyweds to cross the ocean and purchase an old farmhouse on 39 hectares (96 acres) of land just north of the bustling port of Newport, Rhode Island. The surrounding landscape, Berkeley wrote, 'exhibited some of the softest rural and grandest ocean scenery in the world'. By 1729 the Berkeleys had converted the farmhouse into a manor house that, covered in clapboards, is regarded as one of the first adoptions of the Palladian style in America. Named Whitehall after the royal palace in London, the house and garden are now maintained by the National Society of the Colonial Dames of America.

Based at Whitehall, Berkeley spent the next three years awaiting word of the promised grant from Westminster. He did not make idle use of his time. Assisted by a workforce that included at least four slaves, he began developing the farm as a place to supply produce for the college in Bermuda, 1,200 km (740 miles) south. He also delivered fourteen sermons in Newport's Trinity Church, where his words inspired the creation of the philosophical society that built the Redwood Library, now the oldest community library in the United

States. Following the death of their baby daughter Lucia, she was laid to rest at Trinity Church; Berkeley would later commission an organ for the church, still extant, upon which the first organist was Charles Theodore Pachelbel, a son of the famous composer Johann Pachelbel.

Berkeley was also busy writing his book *Alciphron* (a vigorous defence of Christianity against free-thinkers, published in 1732) and corresponding with American intellectuals, as well as his extensive circle of friends back in London and Ireland. And, of course, he was persistently prodding Walpole's government into sending him the pledged funds. The problem was that with the accession of the new king, George II, in 1727, Walpole's political influence had, albeit briefly, waned. By late 1730, Berkeley must have had a strong suspicion that things were not going to plan. Early the following year, he received the final blow when Edmund Gibson, Bishop of London, advised him of Walpole's updated thoughts. 'If you put this question to me as a minister,' Walpole had told Gibson, 'I must and can assure you that the money shall most undoubtedly be paid – as soon as suits with public convenience; but if you ask me as a friend whether Dean Berkeley should continue in America, expecting the payment of £20,000, I advise him by all means to return home to Europe and give up his present expectations.'

Disappointed as he was, the forty-five-year-old Berkeley was sufficiently stoic to close his eyes and proceed on with life. 'Events are not in our power,' he surmised, 'but it always is, to make a good use even of the very worst.'[2] He began winding down his colonial enterprise and focusing on his return to Europe, where he might 'be useful some other way'. He presented his farm to Yale University on condition that its income be used to establish a fellowship, which is still in existence. Yale was also gifted the bulk of his library of 2,000 books, with the residue going to Harvard. Yale and Harvard were but two of the Ivy League colleges that would take a shine to Berkeley's pioneering thoughts on education. In time, the University of California would adopt the name of 'Berkeley' (pronounced 'Burklee' in this context) in honour of the 'Irish Plato'. However, in 2023 Trinity College Dublin declared that it would no longer name one of its principal libraries in honour of Berkeley due to his stance on slavery.

In the autumn of 1731, the Berkeleys and their newborn son made their way to Boston, from where they embarked on a five-week voyage back to Britain. The Dean of Derry, as he still was, busied himself writing and publishing a plethora of sermons, theories, discourses and principles on an extraordinary range of subjects: mathematics, morals, economics, motion, vision, medicine, the natural world and the scope and reasoning of the human mind. Despite his eccentricities and the failure of his Bermuda enterprise, his experiences and ambitions stood him in good stead with many contemporaries, including John Oglethorpe, whom he met to advise on the planned colony of Georgia.

In 1734, Berkeley was consecrated as the bishop of Cloyne and entrusted with 344,000 economically bereft hectares (850,000 acres) of County Cork, where the vast majority of its inhabitants were Roman Catholic. Having moved to Cloyne, Berkeley rarely left the diocese over the course of his nineteen-year term as bishop. Instead both he and Anne focused on the welfare of the people under his watch, being especially active to improve the lot of the poor, 'to feed the hungry and clothe the naked', as he put it. He founded a spinning school for children, a workhouse for 'sturdy vagrants' and cultivated both hemp and flax in the region.

In 1744 he published *Siris*, his last major work, which also transpired to be his foremost bestseller. The book set out to establish the medical 'virtues' of tar-water, a liquid concocted by stewing pine tar in water, as a cure for dysentery, consumptive coughs, asthma and numerous other ailments. He even argued that the consumption of tar-water provided a deeper contemplation of God.

Only three of his seven children survived childhood – George, Henry and Julia, a girl of 'starlight beauty'. When young George, later destined to be a vicar of Bray, County Wicklow, won a place at Oxford in 1752, the elderly bishop opted to escort the youngster to the college. He also wanted to take the opportunity to meet a publisher to discuss the reprinting of some of his old works, as well as a new collection of essays. However, he took ill and died in Oxford, apparently drifting off while his wife read him a sermon. In his will he directed that his body be 'kept five days above ground...even till it grow offensive by the cadaverous smell'. He was then laid to rest at Christ Church Cathedral, Oxford, where nearly 260 years later he is still celebrated as one of the preeminent philosophers of the Age of Enlightenment.

12

RICHARD BREW, SLAVE TRADER

Anomabu, West Africa, 1767. In many ways Castle Brew was a typical Irish gentleman's residence – extensive bedrooms and halls furnished with mahogany, an organ and a glass chandelier in the front hall, silverware and china at every turn, a well-stocked library, a wardrobe of exquisitely tailored waistcoats, shirts, breeches and cravats. What made it different to other Irish mansions is that it was not in Ireland; it was in Anomabu, a West African town on the coast of present-day Ghana. The castle was built for Richard Brew, an Irishman widely regarded as the most notorious slave trader in West Africa during the 1760s and 1770s.

Richard Brew's ancestors are thought to have been the Cambro-Norman family of 'de Bruwa' or 'de Bruth'. By the early eighteenth century, a branch had settled in Ennis, County Clare, where they traded in hides, tallow and butter on the banks of the River Fergus. Among them was Richard Brew, a Protestant gentleman, who ran a malt-house and brewery in Ennis in partnership with Nicholas Bindon, High Sheriff of County Clare. However, the brewery failed in 1743 and the Brew family fortunes declined.

Richard Brew, the slave trader, is believed to have been the first-born son of Richard the brewer and his wife, Ellinor O'Brien. Born in about 1725, he made his first appearance in West Africa in 1745, not long after his father's business woes. He initially served with the Royal African Company (RAC), a mercantile company established by Charles II in 1660, which focused on the exploitation of African gold, ivory and enslaved people.

By the 1740s, Africa's Gold Coast was booming, with nearly thirty European forts constructed along the seaboard from which the British, Portuguese, Dutch, French, Danish and Swedes vied for control of the coastal trade. The forts were primarily built to protect merchants from pirates and enemy ships whose covetous eyes had lit upon their cargoes of cotton cloth, wax, hides, wood, gum, pepper, ivory and, most alluringly, gold. However, the transatlantic slave trade had by now emerged as the biggest commercial enterprise on the coast. Every year, thousands of captive Africans were brought out from the interior of the continent by chieftains and sold to either European traders or African caboceers (middlemen) in exchange for gunpowder, textiles, tobacco and other goods. Most of those enslaved on the Gold Coast were prisoners of war, taken in combat by the Fante and Ashanti (or Asante) people and treated as plunder.

Prior to being sold, each person was stripped and thoroughly examined by a surgeon, who had to decide if they were strong enough to survive the Middle Passage, the horrific journey that would bring them from Africa to the New World. On being declared fit enough, these luckless souls were brutally branded with the company name using a hot iron to prevent the caboceers from secretly swapping them with unfit captives. Those deemed 'invalid' were either held captive in the European forts as 'castle slaves' or simply abandoned to wander and die in the coastal towns. Meanwhile, those selected for slavery were locked in a series of cells or compounds at slave outposts, or 'factories' as they were then known. Still naked, they were given nothing but food and water until a slave ship arrived to take them across the Atlantic.

Richard Brew was one of the traders who bought slaves and then transported them to the plantations of the West Indies and America to work as enslaved labourers. Although he principally operated on the Gold Coast, he was also involved with the slave factories at Lagos and Cape Lopez, just south of the equator. By 1751 he was commander of Dixcove, a small fortress 80 km (50 miles) southwest of the British headquarters at Cape Coast Castle. He appears to have worked closely with Acca, a prosperous Dixcove caboceer, who sent his youngest son Quomino (or Quamina) to live in Dublin at about this time. The boy was to spend seven years in Ireland living under the care of Thomas Allan, who had him baptized and educated alongside his own son.[1]

The RAC had by now been replaced by the African Company of Merchants, known as the Company. Brew served as its registrar at Cape Coast Castle and from 1751 to 1754 as chief factor of its fort at Tantumkweri. As such, he should have been one of its more diligent employees. However, his ambition was to make enough money to retire early and live the life of a gentleman; if achieving that goal meant hoodwinking his employers, so be it.

Brew's disregard for the Company's regulations ensured that, by offering higher prices, his private enterprises as a slave trader were soon eclipsing those of the Liverpool and Bristol merchants he was supposed to be protecting. The Company launched an investigation, but Brew resigned his office and set up as a private trader in the coastal town of Mumford. It quickly became apparent that the Company was impotent without his expertise and network. In July 1756 he was appointed governor of Anomabu, where a new fort was nearing completion. Over the next twenty years, Anomabu Fort (later renamed Fort William) was to become the chief slave-trading centre on the Gold Coast.

Brew's appointment coincided with the outbreak of the Seven Years' War, in which the British and French battled for global dominance. On the Gold Coast, the French endeavoured to woo Besi Kurentsi (sometimes recorded as John Currantee), a shrewd Fante chieftain who had become the region's principal caboceer. However, with Brew at the helm, it was Britain that emerged as the predominant commercial power in West Africa. His intricate understanding of the Fante mindset, combined with the 'extraordinary expenses' he used to line Kurentsi's pockets, ensured that the powerful chieftain opted to trade with the British rather than the French. To consolidate the deal, Kurentsi's daughter Effuah Ansah became Brew's 'country wife'; mixed marriages were common at the time. Effuah Ansah was the mother of his two daughters, Eleanor and Amba. Brew also had two sons, Richard Junior and Harry, with an unidentified African woman, or women. When the mother of one of these mistresses died, he paid for her funeral.[2]

Brew's first period of governorship between 1756 and 1760 was characterized by a boom in private trade at Anomabu, albeit with frequent complaints about his high-handedness and lack of respect for certain traders, many of whom were former Company employees. He was certainly the region's most dominant trader, bringing in cargo from London, Rotterdam and Liverpool on a fleet of his own ships, such as the *Albany* and the *Brew*. On Brew's ships, the enslaved men, women and children were almost certainly packed into dark, stuffy holds and 'pressed together like "herrings in a barrel"', as the Quaker abolitionist John Woolman put it in 1774.[3] Tightly shackled to one another and forced to lie in holds with a complete lack of sanitation for a voyage that lasted 6–11 weeks, such appalling conditions meant an estimated 15 per cent of captives died en route. Brew's own writings from this period suggest he looked at the enslaved Africans as nothing more than a commodity to be sold and transported, just like textiles or tobacco.[4]

Aside from the French, Brew's principal rivals were the Dutch. They were headquartered at Elmina Castle, a medieval-style fortress near Cape Coast that they had captured from the Portuguese in 1737. Records of the Dutch West Indies Company describe Brew as 'Irish by birth', 'notorious' and 'unscrupulous and hard-headed'. He was evidently a man that it was impossible not to notice, even if the impression he left was rarely favourable. His extraordinary competitive streak earned him few friends. That said, he was not averse to buying and selling Dutch merchandise when it suited, a practice greatly frowned upon by the British government. Indeed, he would later claim that nearly every governor and chief agent of Cape Coast Castle between 1763 and 1771 had either embezzled funds or sold slaves for private profit to buyers that included the hated Dutch.

In 1760, Brew announced that he was leaving the coast after thirteen years. His departure occasioned military parades and marching bands at the Anomabu waterfront, while the fort itself was plunged into crisis when the inhabitants demanded the sacking of the Company's new chief officer. Meanwhile, Brew sailed for London, where he formed a partnership with Samuel Smith, an influential merchant closely linked to the Irish linen industry. Smith also had useful connections in Waterford, as well as Britain's main slaving ports of Bristol and Liverpool.

Brew then made his way to Dublin, where he visited the merchants George Carleton and Thomas Jevers, members of the Ouzel Galley Society, who operated from Eustace Street in Temple Bar. He also spent time in London arranging for a ship to go to the Netherlands to collect a consignment of Dutch brandy and jenever.

Although Anomabu did not actually collapse in Brew's absence, its commerce dwindled to such an extent that the Company felt compelled to invite him back. Armed with a gold-fringed blue velvet umbrella for Besi Kurentsi, he returned to the fort to commence his second term as governor in October 1761. He was swiftly embroiled in fresh controversy when he was accused of dipping into the Company's coffers to fund a private shipment of 512 slaves to the colonies, and profited handsomely thereafter. He was also alleged to have traded again with the Dutch, as well as the French, another sworn British enemy. While the Company bemoaned its dependence on a man who was 'determined to be under no authority', it also glumly acknowledged that without Brew, its future security and prosperity at Anomabu could not be guaranteed.

In 1764, Brew permanently quit the Company and formally re-established himself as a private trader. He moved to Castle Brew, an impressive two-storey Palladian residence completed that same year and funded, in part, by his friend Samuel Smith. The castle, which boasted its own warehouses and defensive guns, was built directly across from Anomabu Fort and was reputedly its equal in size, capable of accommodating 300 men within its high brick walls. Parts of Brew's castle still survive today.

The middle years of the 1760s were complicated by rising tensions between the Fante and the Ashanti. Brew emerged as an unlikely peacemaker when, having plied the Fante with cloth, silk, liquor and other gifts, he persuaded them to give him custody of several well-to-do Ashanti hostages. The governor of Cape Coast Castle was unimpressed, denouncing Brew as 'shamefully abusive in his language, domineering in his behaviour and the object of everyone's hostility'. Such strong words may have been connected to Brew's attempt to extract payment from the Ashanti for their maintenance.[5] On the other hand, the easing of relations between the Fante and the Ashanti during the early 1770s prompted a renewed boom in the slave trade. As Brew observed, 'except at the time of the Ashantyn warr [sic] in the year 1765 I never knew slaves so plenty in my life.'[6]

By now he had established a string of outposts along the Slave Coast, including the factories at Lagos, Benin and Cape Lopez, while he also operated a small fleet that travelled back and forth along the coast and across the seas to the Americas and the Caribbean Islands. His ships carried enslaved Africans, as well as gold, beeswax and Ijebu clothing. Given Samuel Smith's links to Irish linen, it seems likely that Irish linen was also on offer to the African caboceers. However, Smith's unexpected spiral into bankruptcy from 1768 threw Brew's operations off-kilter. New partners came and went, but Brew only managed to continue his business by borrowing heavily from creditors both on the African coast and in England. In 1770 and 1771 he wrote lengthy epistles to the merchants of Liverpool, castigating the Company for failing to protect private traders like himself. Ironically, he had faced the very same charges during his time as governor of Anomabu.

Among his biggest clients were the New England merchants from North America with whom he regularly exchanged enslaved Africans for rum and tobacco. In 1776 he devised a plan for his schooner *Jenny* to sail directly from Cape Lopez to the Caribbean with 120 slaves. Another schooner was dispatched to Rhode Island to purchase a cargo of rum. Soon afterwards, he wrote to friends in England, announcing his plan 'shortly to return with a genteel fortune'.

However, in truth, his business had been in gradual decline for many years and was now on the cusp of collapse. He blamed it on the excess of merchant competition in Anomabu where, according to Brew, half the population were now 'gold-takers', as brokers were known. His own life was also nearing its end. Although he was only about fifty years old, his longevity was still, in many ways, remarkable. He was clearly stronger, or luckier, than the vast majority of Europeans who came to Africa only to succumb to tropical diseases. In the end it may have been the pressures of his failing business that brought on a serious illness at the end of July 1776. He drifted into unconsciousness and died on 4 August. He was buried in Anomabu later that day.

As the governor of Cape Coast Castle noted, Brew's death 'occasioned no small Revolution' at Anomabu. The revelation that he was bankrupt came as a shock and caused considerable confusion. Two officers from the Company were assigned to clear up his affairs, which were in utter disarray. They discovered that although the quantities of money he owed were small, the number of creditors were 'amazingly numerous'. 'Never did two persons take charge of an Estate with greater reluctance,' they later opined to their superiors in London. The settlement took two years to unravel, during which time ships were sent to collect Brew's property at Lagos and Cape Lopez. Castle Brew was sold to Horatio Smith, a cousin of Samuel. Further trouble for his executors ensued when some of Brew's vessels were seized during the American Revolution.

In his will, drawn up on 3 August 1776, Brew left twelve house slaves to Effuah Ansah and their two daughters, whom he named as his heirs. His Irish relatives were also keen to cash in until they learned that his inheritance was an empty purse. Brew's descendants by Effuah Ansah and his mistress or mistresses would prevail in the nineteenth and twentieth centuries. Some – including members of the Casely-Hayford family, as well as the Brews – continue to play a prominent role in Ghana and Britain to the present day.

13

THE ABBÉ DE FIRMONT

Paris, 1793. King Louis XVI of France did not say a word as the carriage set off towards his place of execution. Nor did the Abbé de Firmont, the Irish padre who sat opposite him. Instead, they sat in 'a profound silence' while they listened to the growing clamour outside. Every street, alleyway and rooftop were crammed with babbling, chanting, hissing soldiers and citizens, many armed with pikes and bayonets, others with lances, scythes and muskets. Added to the racket was the beat of the sixty drummers who marched ahead of the carriage, fulfilling the wishes of the revolutionary government to drown out any voices that might be raised in support of the condemned monarch. The king began to mumble some psalms aloud as the nightmarish journey wore on.

At length the carriage reached the Place de Louis XV (today known as the Place de la Concorde), the fabulous public square that the king's grandfather had commissioned less than four decades earlier. When the crowds parted to reveal a large elevated scaffold surrounded by cannons, King Louis turned to his clergyman and whispered, 'We are arrived, if I mistake not.'

Watching him untie his neckcloth and advance towards the scaffold, Abbé de Firmont was understandably overwhelmed with emotion. As well as everything else, he was assuredly wondering if he was likely to be hauled into the guillotine the moment His Majesty was no more.

It was all a far cry from the rectory in County Longford where the Abbé was born in 1745. Christened Henry Essex Edgeworth, he descended from an Englishman who had settled in Ireland during the reign of Queen Elizabeth I, ultimately taking ownership of a large chunk of Longford. The family estate was centred around Mostrim, where the Abbé's inventive cousin Richard Lovell Edgeworth did so much to improve the area that the Town Tenants' Association insisted the town be renamed Edgeworthstown in his honour in 1935. Richard was also an inventor of no mean skill, creating the prototype of the caterpillar track system used by present-day bulldozers, tanks and tractors. He also produced an early form of telegraph, a velocipede cycle, a 'perambulator' to measure land, a turnip cutter and various sailing carriages. Richard's daughter Maria Edgeworth would become one of the most successful novelists in the world in the early 1800s.

Henry Edgeworth's branch of the family were also unconventional. Robert Edgeworth, his father, had taken up residence in the rectory at Mostrim when appointed to look after the local Protestant community. However, following a meeting with a French bishop, Rev. Edgeworth became unexpectedly enamoured of the Roman

Catholic cause and converted. Given that it was not all that long since the government in Dublin had been considering a bill that advocated the castration of all Popish priests in Ireland, Robert was clearly aware that his conversion would not go down well with the Protestant establishment.

And so it was that the family relocated to France when Henry Edgeworth was just four years old. They settled among a community of Irish exiles in Toulouse, where he was educated at the Jesuit College. He later studied in Paris at the Séminaire des Trente-Trois and, after further studies at both the Collège de Navarre and the Sorbonne, he was ordained a priest. At this juncture, he dropped the name 'Edgeworth' in favour of 'de Firmont', a nod to a beloved hill called 'Fairymount' near his childhood home in Longford.

The Abbé de Firmont resided in Paris at the Les Missions Etrangères at 483 rue du Bac, from where he initially made his mark among the 'the lower orders' and the 'poor Savoyards', an immigrant community from the impoverished Alpine territory of Savoy. Plagued by poor health since childhood, he was eventually compelled to accept his doctor's advice to restrict his ministering to the more upmarket homes of Irish and English exiles in Paris. Nonetheless, the diligence of this humble, modest man caught the attention of the Roman Catholic hierarchy in Ireland.

In May 1789, the Right Reverend Dr Francis Moylan, Bishop of Cork, invited him to return home and take up an unspecified Irish bishopric. Declining the offer, the priest explained, 'Thirty-eight years absence have broke the very ties of blood with some of my relations and weakened them with all. The [English] language itself sounds odd in my ears for want of use.' The ink was barely dry on his reply when almost a thousand disgruntled Parisians famously stormed the Bastille on 14 July 1789, setting in motion the epochal events of the French Revolution.

While the Republicans readied the guillotine for aristocratic heads, the Abbé de Firmont held tight in Paris. In 1791 he was appointed confessor to Princess Élisabeth, the king's youngest sister. A staunch and deeply religious conservative, Élisabeth was effectively under house arrest at the Tuileries Palace in Paris at this time, along with

Louis XVI, Marie Antoinette and other royals. 'Though a foreigner, and very little worthy to be distinguished by the princess, I soon became her friend,' wrote the Abbé. The Longford-born priest rapidly formed a bond with the incarcerated members of the House of Bourbon, who evidently valued his serene but spirited countenance.

On 17 January 1793, the National Convention – the French government of the time – condemned Louis XVI to death. The king immediately requested the Abbé de Firmont be by his side when the end came, as the priest explained in a letter to a friend in London:

Almighty God has baffled my measures, and ties me to this land of horrors by chains I have not the liberty to shake off. The case is this: the wretched master [the King] charges me not to quit this country, as I am the priest whom he intends to prepare him for death. And should the iniquity of the nation commit this last act of cruelty, I must also prepare myself for death, as I am convinced the popular rage will not allow me to survive an hour after the tragic scene; but I am resigned. Could my life save him I would willingly lay it down, and I should not die in vain.[1]

Three days later, he was summoned to the Temple prison to attend to the king on the eve of his execution. He stayed with him throughout the night and they said Mass together at the break of dawn with the sounds of Paris echoing around them – 'the beating of the *générale*, the rattle of arms, the tramp of horses, the movement of cannon'.

At 9 a.m. they embarked on the hour-long carriage journey to the place of execution. As he very slowly approached the scaffold, Louis lent on the priest's arm for support. Addressing the enormous crowd, he declared his innocence, and urged forgiveness for those who had sentenced him to die, but the noise was such that few could have heard him. The Abbé de Firmont had an unenviably close view as the guillotine came down and sliced through the back of the king's skull into his jaw. A witness heard the Abbé roar out, 'Son of St Louis, ascend to heaven.' He then melted into the crowd.

Being privy to the last words of a despised monarch was a perilous position to find oneself in, not least in revolutionary France. As he later recalled, 'All eyes were fixed on me, as you may suppose; but as soon as I reached the first line, to my surprise, no resistance was made.' His escape was made easier by the fact that priest's robes had been prohibited by law so he was dressed as an ordinary citizen. 'I was absolutely lost in the crowd, and no more noticed than if I had been a simple spectator of a scene which forever will dishonour France.'[2]

Despite the imminent dangers, he refused to leave Paris, reasoning that there were others who depended on him, not least his mother and sister. He had also vowed never to desert Princess Élisabeth, who was still bring held prisoner in the Temple Tower. However, Élisabeth was also guillotined during the Reign of Terror and, shortly after his mother's death in August 1796, the Abbé de Firmont reluctantly boarded a ship for England. He spent three months in London, during which time he was widely feted for his courage and close proximity to such monumental events.

Prime Minister Pitt offered him a pension, which he proudly refused. He was also invited to take up the presidency of the Royal College of St Patrick in Maynooth, County Kildare. The college had been officially established by an Act of the Parliament of Ireland in 1795 as a seminary 'for the better education of persons professing the popish or Roman Catholic religion'.

He was actively considering a return to Ireland to take up the Maynooth presidency when he received a letter from the Count of Provence, Louis XVI's younger brother, inviting him to become his chaplain. Calling himself Louis XVIII, the count was now head of the French royalists and had established his exiled court at Blankenburg in the Duchy of Brunswick (now in Germany). The Abbé de Firmont immediately sailed back to Europe and reunited with the royal family.

In his absence, the Maynooth presidency passed to Father Peter Flood, a fellow Longford native. Prior to the Revolution, Father Flood had been superior of the Irish Collège des Lombards in Paris, an imposing four-storey building in the 5th arrondissement that has served as the Centre Culturel Irlandais (Irish Cultural Centre) since 2002. He narrowly avoided being murdered during the 'September massacres' of 1792, after which all six of the Irish colleges in France were closed by the revolutionary government. Indeed, the ecclesiastical college in Maynooth was established in direct response to such closures. Father Flood returned to Ireland, where he was appointed parish priest of the Abbé de Firmont's home town, Edgeworthstown. He would hold the Maynooth presidency from 1798 until his death in 1803.[3]

Meanwhile, Henry found himself on the move once more in 1797, when Louis XVIII was obliged to relocate his court to the Russian town of Mittau (now Jelgava in Latvia). Three years later, he was sent to St Petersburg, where he so impressed Tsar Paul that he 'bowed himself to the humblest posture at the Abbé's feet' and then awarded him an annual pension of 500 ducats. However, the Tsar was unable to resist the rapidly accelerating power of Napoleon Bonaparte and shortly before his assassination in 1801, he acceded to pressure from Napoleon and withdrew his support for Louis XVIII. The impoverished Bourbon king was compelled to move his court south to a palace near Warsaw, where it remained for the next four years before returning north to Mittau.

Despite the blessing of the new tsar, Alexander I, the French royals were in desperate financial straits, having sold most of their jewelry and furniture. The king himself was riddled with gout, his queen clad in rags. The Abbé de Firmont, who remained by their side throughout, was so destitute that he reluctantly accepted Pitt's earlier offer of a pension.

In February 1807, Napoleon's army invaded Russia and the jail in Mittau began to fill with French prisoners of war. That spring, the sixty-two-year-old Abbé was summoned to the jail to attend to some French soldiers who had taken ill. It transpired they had typhus, which the Irishman contracted. When word of his illness reached Princess Marie-Thérèse, Louis XVI's only surviving child, she raced to his bedside to be with a man she described as her 'beloved and revered invalid, her more than friend, who had left kindred and country for her family.... Nothing can prevent me from nursing the Abbé Edgeworth myself.'[4]

Henry Edgeworth, the Abbé de Firmont, died on 22 May 1807 and was buried at the sepulchral chapel in Mittau. Sometime later, his brother Ussher Edgeworth received a missive in Longford that contained a copy of the epitaph written in Latin by Louis XVIII, hailing the priest as 'an Eye to the Blind, a Staff to the Lame, a Father to the Poor, and a Consoler of the Afflicted...an example of Virtue and an Assuager of misfortune.' The king, who later that same year moved to Aylesbury in Buckinghamshire, England, would go on to reign as the king of France from Napoleon's fall in 1814 until his death in 1824.

14

HERCULES MULLIGAN, WASHINGTON'S SPY

Manhattan, New York, 26 November 1783. It was surely the most exceptional breakfast that the Mulligan family ever hosted. Seated at the table were two of the principal architects of the Patriot victory over the British redcoats, namely George Washington, commander-in-chief of the Continental Army, and Alexander Hamilton, his chief of staff. The previous afternoon, Washington had marched his forces into New York just hours after the final British troops were evacuated from the streets. And yet, even at this most momentous of times in American history, the future president did not forget to pay his respects to Hercules Mulligan, the Irish tailor who had not only risked everything as a secret agent for seven long years but whose information had also saved Washington's life on two occasions.

For all the Patriots in New York who had doubted Mulligan's loyalty, Washington's decision to breakfast at his family home was the ultimate wake-up call. As for Mulligan, when breakfast was complete, his day became even better when Washington ordered a complete wardrobe of civilian clothes before exiting the premises. It all marked a long overdue upturn for the man who had once been regarded as New York's most fashionable merchant tailor.

Hercules Mulligan was born in Coleraine on the coast of County Derry in 1740, the son of Hugh Mulligan, a devout Episcopalian, and his wife, Sarah Cooke. He was six years old when the family crossed the Atlantic and settled in New York where, after a stint as a wigmaker, his father set up practice as an accountant and became a freeman of the city.

Educated at King's College (renamed Columbia University in 1784), Hercules Mulligan grew into a tall, personable and flamboyant man; he was a gifted, silver-tongued storyteller who, perhaps deliberately, never lost his Irish accent. He had little time for the British authorities that then controlled the Thirteen Colonies, including New York. At the age of twenty-five, he joined the Sons of Liberty, a secret society that was determined to end the excessive taxes imposed on American colonists by the bankrupt British Crown. Five years later, Mulligan was present at the Battle of Golden Hill when some of the 'Liberty Boys' took on the British redcoats in New York, leaving several people from both sides wounded.

By this stage, Hercules had opened a haberdashery business in Lower Manhattan, with several skilled tailors working under him. His impressive offering of fabrics, laces, trims, loops, epaulettes, Irish linens and other ornamentations rapidly propelled him to the top of his profession. Much of the business involved making new uniforms or adjusting existing ones for British officers stationed in the city. Formal evening wear for the colonial aristocracy was another speciality. Both colonists and officers were enchanted by Mulligan's gregarious bonhomie and quick wit, and they were by no means impartial to his drinks cabinet, which he always made available to his customers. Mulligan's ties with the British elite deepened in 1773 when he married Elizabeth Sanders, a niece of Admiral Sir Charles Saunders, a former First Lord of the British Admiralty.

In 1772, Hercules Mulligan's brother Hugh, a trader, introduced him to ambitious teenager Alexander Hamilton, who had just arrived in New York from the Caribbean island of Nevis. Hugh Mulligan had helped Hamilton to sell a cargo of West Indian goods in order to pay for his further education. By 1774, Hamilton was studying at King's College and lodging with the Mulligans at Water Street, Brooklyn. As Hercules Mulligan later recalled, Hamilton 'used in the evening to sit with my family and my brother's family and write dogrel rhymes for their amusement; he was always [sic] amiable and cheerful and extremely attentive to his books'. Hamilton, who went on to become one of the Founding Fathers of the United States, would retain a robust attachment to the Mulligans until his death in a duel in 1804.

Life in the Thirteen Colonies was becoming increasingly complicated for colonists like Mulligan who, ostensibly loyal to the Crown, rejected many of the laws imposed by Parliament in London because they had no representation in that faraway assembly. Despite the fact that he was largely dependent on British officers for his business, Mulligan was closely involved with New York's Committee of Correspondence, seeking to simultaneously promote the cause of the Patriots and reduce the influence of the British. Much impressed by the way the Boston Sons of Liberty so successfully orchestrated the famous Boston Tea Party in 1773, he played a key role in securing a Patriot majority in the New York assembly elections of 1774.

The first shots of the American Revolution were fired in the Battles of Lexington and Concord in April 1775. When he learned of the encounters, Mulligan led a large group of Liberty Boys, who seized the keys to the custom house from the Crown Collector of the Port of New York. Having effectively closed the port to British vessels, they chose a group of people to run the city – known as the Committee of One Hundred – until a proper government could be elected, and Hercules Mulligan was a member of that committee. Indeed, his name was to be found on every committee that the Patriots founded over the course of that summer. He was also clocked as one of the most consistent attendees at all their meetings.

Meanwhile, twenty-one-year-old Alexander Hamilton was in command of the Corsicans, one of four companies of militia volunteers in New York. In May, Mulligan and Hamilton were involved in an incident when students from King's College attempted to tar and feather the college president for being an outspoken British Loyalist. Two months later, Mulligan led a raid on a City Corporation armoury, making off with a quantity of muskets and ammunition. In August, he was with Hamilton's Corsicans when they managed to seize a cannon from the British-controlled battery in Manhattan. When Hamilton was commissioned to form the New York Provincial Company of Artillery, Mulligan was given the contract to manufacture its splendid blue uniforms. He also played a key role in recruiting men for Hamilton's new unit, many of whom were Irish, and helped train them to be among the best in the service.

Despite all this blatant patriotism, Mulligan was still winning fresh work from British Loyalists, not least David Mathews, the mayor of New York, who was especially fond of the libations on offer at the tailor's shop. In June 1776, Mathews became so inebriated that he revealed that some of George Washington's disgruntled bodyguards were plotting to assassinate the Patriot leader. Mulligan was able to dispatch a warning down the line to Hamilton in good time for Washington to be spirited away to safety. Thomas Hickey, an Irish private in Washington's Life Guards, was subsequently arrested, court-martialled and hanged for mutiny and sedition.

On 9 July 1776, having ejected the British from New York, George Washington had the Declaration of Independence read out to his triumphant troops. Mulligan was once again to the fore when the Sons of Liberty promptly made their way to Manhattan's Bowling Green and toppled the 1,800-kg (4,000-lb) gilded lead equestrian statue of George III. By his side was William Mooney, a furniture dealer and fellow Irishman who would go on to found the infamous Democratic Party organization of Tammany Hall.[1] The lead from the statue was melted down and recast as bullets for the Patriot volunteers.

The British regained control of New York in September 1776. Given that Mulligan's name was affiliated with every Patriot committee, his arrest was hotly anticipated. He was captured on a day when much of the city was engulfed in flames and sent to the Provost Prison for about two months. Somehow, he managed to turn the situation to his advantage by charming his jailers with stories of his pre-war contacts among the British establishment, name-dropping all of the Loyalists whom he had made clothes for. Such talk is assumed to have paved the way for his early release, although he was ordered to remain within the confines of New York, which he did for the next seven years of British occupation.

Alexander Hamilton was by now a rising star in Washington's army. When the commander-in-chief sought Hamilton's advice on potential spies in New York, he proposed Hercules Mulligan. He was not an obvious candidate, given that he had been one of the loudest, most visible Patriots in the city. Nonetheless, Hamilton was on to something because, incredibly, New York's Loyalist elite were still frequenting Mulligan's haberdashery.

And so it was that, unbeknown to many Patriot sympathizers in the city, Mulligan began working as an undercover spy, gathering whatever information he could to help the Continental Army. Much of this fact-finding was in collaboration with the financier Haym Salomon, a Sephardic Jew from Poland who had been in the Provost Prison with Mulligan. Salomon had since been recruited by the British as an interpreter for the German-speaking Hessian troops who had helped the Crown forces recapture New York. As such, he was privy to all manner of information about Britain's upcoming military deployment plans.

Key to the success of his communications with Salomon was Cato, Mulligan's African American slave. The innocuous-looking Cato was ostensibly sent to Salomon to have advertisements translated into German for any Hessian officers seeking details of Mulligan's tailoring service. Salomon would then supply Cato with invaluable data about British activities, which he was instructed to bring directly to Hamilton.

Hercules Mulligan also gathered material from his brother Hugh, who had a supply contract with the British commissariat in New York, which provided an excellent insight into the Royal Navy's shipping schedule, as well as the army's provisioning and outfitting requirements. In the spring of 1777, for example, the British placed a large order for light uniforms, which the Mulligans correctly interpreted as a sign that the redcoats were planning to advance on the Patriot stronghold of Philadelphia. Cato was armed with a series of packages marked 'H. Mulligan, clothier' and dispatched by ferry across the Hudson River to meet up with Hamilton's men. One of the packages carried details about the likely British attack. Although Washington was unable to prevent the British from capturing Philadelphia, Mulligan and Cato had once again shown their prowess at espionage.

Mulligan was also now sharing information with the Culper Ring, a more formal group of spies gathering intelligence about British activities – for instance, he alerted them to a planned British attack on the Patriots' French allies at Newport, Rhode Island. Not entirely trusting the ring, however, he sent Cato direct to George Washington with the same news. Mulligan's intelligence enabled Washington to arrange a defence that caused the British to call off the attack. The Irish tailor sent another advance warning to Washington about an imminent attack on Charleston in early 1780 but, as with Philadelphia, the Patriot commander was unable to repel the British.

Meanwhile, Mulligan's cover was finally exposed when Benedict Arnold, a senior Patriot officer, defected and named him as a likely spy. He was court-martialled and sentenced to imprisonment, and appears to have been held for about five months. Cato was also taken in and badly beaten by his interrogators, but refused to betray the Patriots. Released in February 1781, Mulligan returned to his tailoring business. The fact that he seemed to maintain cordial relations with the redcoat officers made him a figure of suspicion to his Patriot neighbours. Many still did not realize that he was a spy, while some of those who did know began to wonder if he might be a double agent. With such an uncertain cloud over his name, his tailoring business went into sharp decline. Deeply in debt, he went to work for his brother but he, too, was soon struggling, especially after the exodus of so many British troops following the Patriots' victory at Yorktown in October 1781.

Mulligan's ability to loosen tongues had always been one of his most remarkable traits, not least when armed with a bottle of whiskey. Shortly after his release from jail in 1781, a British officer visited the tailor for a watch-coat and, having enjoyed a dram or two, told him of a plan to abduct George Washington in Lebanon, Connecticut, the following day. Mulligan poured the man a fresh drink, then successfully managed to relay the information to the Culper Ring, thus earning his moniker as the spy who saved Washington's life, twice.

The dark times for Mulligan finally came to an end on 25 November 1783 when Washington's forces reoccupied New York. Anyone who still doubted his loyalty had their minds put at ease when Washington and Hamilton called in to Mulligan's haberdashery on 23 Queen Street (now 218 Pearl Street) to enjoy breakfast with a man that George Washington now loudly proclaimed 'a true friend of liberty'. It is thought that the Mulligan's three sons and five daughters were also present. The chair on which Washington sat, and the plate he ate off, have been treasured Mulligan family heirlooms ever since.

Cato's fate has sadly faded into the archives. It seems relevant that in 1785 Mulligan was one of the nineteen men, with Hamilton, who co-founded the New York Manumission Society, an organization that sought to abolish slavery.

Marketing himself as 'Clothier to General Washington', Hercules Mulligan continued to work until he retired at the age of eighty in 1820. He died five years later and was laid to rest at Trinity Church, New York, where his old friend Alexander Hamilton was also buried. His fabulous name may have vanished from the annals were it not for his emergence as a character in Lin-Manuel Miranda's 2015 hip-hop Broadway smash, *Hamilton – An American Musical*.

15

JAMES HOBAN, ARCHITECT OF THE WHITE HOUSE

Washington, DC, 21 July 1792. The thirty-seven-year-old architect sat by the Potomac once more, listening to the river as it washed through the fields towards the village of Georgetown. One of the farms had been owned by a fellow Irishman, Dominic Lynch of Galway. All of these lands had been surveyed by George Washington shortly before he bought out all the owners, divided the land into lots and put them up for sale – this was the landscape on which he planned to build the new capital of the United States of America. From the architect's perspective, the farm of most significance was Pearce's Farm, distinguished by a farmhouse, an orchard and a small graveyard. This was where Washington had asked him to build a new presidential palace.

James Hoban had pitched a number of suggestions to the president. The design he finally worked to was not dissimilar to

Leinster House, the home of the dukes of Leinster in Dublin (now the seat of the Irish government). Indeed, if one was to insert an additional first floor into the present-day White House, it would look incredibly similar to Leinster House, specifically the triangular pediments, the four columns, the eleven bays, the chimneys, the windows and the mouldings. It was a design Hoban knew well. After all, he had often walked by the building in Dublin as a student, at which time Leinster House was one of the wonders of the city's flourishing architectural scene and faced out onto open countryside.

James Hoban grew up in the County Kilkenny townland of Riesk, midway between Callan and Cuffesgrange. Born in April 1755, he was the son of Edward and Martha Hoban, Catholic tenant farmers on the estate of the Cuffes of Desart Court. The Cuffe family descended from an English adventurer who had prospered in Ireland in the reign of Queen Elizabeth I. Desart Court, regarded as one of Ireland's most outstanding architectural triumphs, is thought to have been designed by Sir Edward Lovett Pearce, who also designed Parliament House in Dublin. The mansion was destroyed during the Irish Civil War in 1923.

As a boy, Hoban worked as an apprentice wheelwright in the Cuffes' carriage house but his great skill at drawing and mechanical work while studying at the estate school caught the eye of his landlords. Of particular importance was the enlightened Lord Otway Cuffe, later created Earl of Desart, who succeeded to the estate when Hoban was twelve and became the boy's patron. Hoban was transferred to the celebrated Drawing School of the Dublin Society (now the Royal Dublin Society), where he studied under the Cork-born architect Thomas Ivory. In 1780, the twenty-five-year-old won a prize from the Dublin Society that further underlined his promise as an architectural technician. As well as Ivory, he also appears to have worked under Thomas Cooley, an English architect who designed some of Dublin's foremost buildings including the Royal Exchange (now City Hall), and James Gandon, architect of Dublin's famous Custom House and the King's Inns.

The declining health of both Cooley (who died in March 1784) and Ivory (who died in December 1786) may have inspired Hoban to look elsewhere for his fortune. Alternatively, perhaps the ambitious redhead was simply motivated by the possibilities of the new United States after the British conceded defeat and withdrew its forces from its former American colonies in 1783. It was certainly a land of promise for architects.

By 1785 Hoban was in Philadelphia, the then capital of the Federal Republic, where he offered his services as an architect and master craftsman to the growing number of politicians and administrators of the new government. Among them was Pierce Butler, a young, Irish-born former British army officer from County Carlow who was a delegate to the Constitutional Convention. A future US senator, Butler's wife Polly Middleton hailed from an exceptionally wealthy family of plantation owners from South Carolina. At Butler's recommendation, Hoban moved south to Charleston in 1787 and set up his home, architectural practice, workshop and drawing school at 42–3 Trott Street (now Wentworth Street). Several other members of the Hoban family lived in the house, including his brother Joseph, as well as Hoban's business partner, Pierce Purcell, an Irish-born carpenter.

Hoban's Charleston designs included a vast theatre at the junction of Broad and New Streets, and several private residences, while he is also believed to have re-ordered the South Carolina State House, built by another Irishman, Samuel Cardy, in 1753. Having attained an excellent insight into how to teach during his time in Dublin, he also set up a drawing school in Charleston. Attendees at his evening classes included an adolescent Robert Mills, later the architect of the Washington Monument.

In 1791, George Washington went on a tour of the southern states during which, as he later wrote, Hoban was 'strongly recommended... as a person who had made architecture his study and was well qualified not only for planning or designing buildings but to superintend the execution of them'. Such endorsements came from people like Henry Laurens, a past president of the Continental Congress, and O'Brien Smith, another Irish plantation owner and congressman living in South Carolina. Washington would later concur that Hoban was 'a very judicious man'.

The following year, the president began planning the construction of a new 'Federal City', appointing three commissioners to oversee the project. One of the commissioners was Daniel Carroll, a scion of the Ely O'Carroll family of County Offaly. The commissioners rejected the original design plan, not least because it required the demolition of a house that Carroll was building at the time. Thomas Jefferson, the Secretary of State, then initiated a competition with a $500 prize for whoever could design a suitable presidential mansion and a Capitol for the Senate and House of Representatives. Such was the scepticism over George Washington's proposed city that when the competition was announced, many reputable architects declined to enter; Washington alerted Hoban and suggested that the Kilkenny man enter the contest. Hoban duly won the prize and the 300-guinea-a-year contract to supervise the project. It later emerged that Jefferson himself had been an anonymous entrant.

On 18 June 1792, Washington observed that Hoban was working on plans for both the President's House, or Executive Mansion, and the Capitol, and that he 'is now on his way to view the ground on which they are to stand'. By the autumn of 1792, Hoban had set up a massive construction site in the marshlands that surrounded the proposed location of the president's Greco-Roman mansion. The White House, as the building would become known, was Hoban's prime focus for the next eight years, although he was also periodically called in to help out at the Capitol.

Assisted by ten overseers, Hoban was in charge of a workforce of perhaps 400 labourers. At least 200 were enslaved, hired out from neighbouring farmers who received the slaves' wages in lieu of the slaves themselves. At least three of the seven enslaved carpenters were owned by Hoban and came with him from Charleston. Working and living in huts alongside the slaves were the white labourers, many of whom were Irish. They included up to sixty stoneworkers who quarried, cut and hauled the stone, and more than two dozen sawyers, entrusted with clearing the trees, as well as more than 100 carpenters and perhaps as many as fifty bricklayers. When not required at the site of the President's House, they often worked at the Capitol instead.

Seven Scottish stonemasons were brought over from Edinburgh to attend to the more sophisticated work. Among the innumerable skilled labourers recruited from Ireland to attend to the finer brick and stonework were Cornelius MacDermot Roe (who later became a land steward at George Washington's Mount Vernon estate), Patrick Roe and John Delahunty, while another Irishman, John Kearney, was employed as a plasterer.[1]

Month after month, year after year, Hoban orchestrated this massive labour force and, slowly but surely, the stoneworkers faded out as the plasterers, glazers and painters arrived to tackle the interiors. Notably, Hoban's records refer to the 'cleaning down and painting' of the sandstone exterior in 1798, and it is quite possible that the President's House was whitewashed at this time, thus giving rise to the informal name of the White House.

The building was not complete by the time sixty-seven-year-old George Washington died in December 1799. The house was briefly occupied by John and Abigail Adams during the final months of Adams's presidency in 1800, but it was still a warren of cold, damp, unplastered walls, unfinished windows, wobbly staircases and untested fireplaces. They crammed themselves into a few completed rooms on the second floor but there is a sense that when Adams lost the election in 1801, the one consolation was that they would no longer have to live in the President's House.

Nonetheless, few could deny Hoban's ability and craftsmanship. When finished, the house was a perfect replication of President Washington's vision. It would find its feet under Adams's successor, the widowed Thomas Jefferson, who was the first president to properly occupy the mansion from 1801 to 1809, where he lived, alone and informally, during his eight-year term. The final touches to the building were overseen by Benjamin Henry Latrobe, Jefferson's chief architectural advisor, who was the son of a Moravian missionary from Dublin.

Meanwhile, Hoban also spent three years supervising the building of the United States Capitol, a project hampered by impractical designs and a lack of resources. Again, he impressed with his diligence, even though the Capitol was still incomplete when the first representatives, senators and administrators assembled there in 1800.

In 1799, the forty-four-year-old architect married twenty-seven-year-old Susana Sewall in a Catholic ceremony at Holy Trinity Church in Washington, DC. The church had been established twelve years earlier by John Carroll, the founder of Georgetown College, who went on to become the first Catholic bishop in America. Two years before she married James Hoban, Susana had attended the same church as a witness at the wedding of Bett, her father's slave, to Edward Butler, a free man.[2] Like the Carrolls, the Sewalls were a prominent Maryland family. Clement Sewall, Susana's father, was a hero of the American Revolution who had recently established the City Tavern in Georgetown, today the home of the City Tavern Club. Her mother was a member of the Carberrys, a prominent Irish family that had been in Maryland for over a century.

Following their marriage, Susana Hoban insisted that the townhouse her husband had been awarded as supervisor of the Federal building projects be upgraded with the addition of a sizeable kitchen and areas suitable for entertaining. James Hoban had also acquired other property in the Washington area by now, including a farm on the outskirts of the city. They would have nine children – five sons and four daughters – before Susana's death at the age of fifty in 1822.

Hoban continued to exert his influence on many of the capital's public buildings during the early 1800s, as well as working on upmarket hotels and private residences for the Washington elite. In the coming decades, Hoban also either designed or oversaw the construction of the city's treasury, state, war and navy buildings.

In 1814, the White House was burned and ransacked by British forces commanded by Major General Robert Ross from Rostrevor, County Down. President James Madison subsequently based himself at the Octagon House, a nearby building that Hoban had worked on as a surveyor. As the British had also badly damaged the wings of the Capitol building, Hoban was commissioned to construct temporary quarters for the nation's legislators. In 1815, his second round at the White House began when Madison asked him to aid Latrobe with the restoration of the desecrated mansion. He worked closely with Madison's successor, James Monroe, having previously supervised the construction of Monroe's family mansion at Oak Hill in Aldie, Virginia. Hoban also designed the White House's south and north porticoes, which were added in 1824 and 1829 respectively.

During the formative years of Washington, DC, James Hoban played a significant role in its civic and social life. He was both founder and captain of the Washington Artillery, a militia largely made up of workers from the White House site. In 1793 he became co-founder and first Worshipful Master of what is today known as Federal Lodge No. 1 of the Freemasons. He maintained his Catholic faith, providing a building for his workers to use as a church (on the site of the present St Patrick's Church in downtown Washington), appointing a Dominican priest from Dublin as its pastor. He also supported other religious foundations in Georgetown, such as the Jesuit community, where his son Henry became a student and later a priest, and the Monastery of the Visitation Order, founded by another County Kilkenny native, Alice Lalor of Ballyragget. In 1802 he was appointed to the city council, after which he occupied various positions of responsibility during several mayoralties, including that of his wife's cousin, Thomas Carberry.

Hoban outlived Jefferson, Adams and most of the other great heroes of the American Revolution, passing away at the age of seventy-six in December 1831. In his will, he left over $60,000 (approximately $1.7 million at the time of writing), with property in the city and farms in Maryland, which was shared among his children. He was buried beside his wife in the old graveyard at St Patrick's Church. In 1863, their graves were moved to their present location at Washington, DC's Mount Olivet Cemetery. Although Hoban's personal archive was destroyed in a fire, some artefacts relating to his work survive, including his writing desk, which is now part of the White House Collection.

16

HUGH GOUGH, CONQUEROR
OF THE PUNJAB

Plymouth, England, March 1807. Frances Stephens blinked several times. It was the officer in the green uniform that she had dreamt about the night before. Tall, straight-backed, eminently handsome. Wide-open blue eyes, light curling hair, an aquiline nose. Yes, it was assuredly him. Turning to her father, General Edward Stephens, as the young officer entered the ballroom, she said, 'That is the man I saw in my dream.' She then waited patiently, her curly black hair rolling down her neck, wearing a short-waisted, skimpy muslin frock that had become the vogue across French society under Napoleon Bonaparte. At length, the man was presented to her: Major Hugh Gough of the 87th (Prince of Wales Irish) Regiment of Foot. He danced with her twice that night, then set off with his battalion to Guernsey. He was back in Plymouth at first opportunity; they were married on 3 June.

Hugh Gough would go on to command in more battles than any other nineteenth-century British soldier except his fellow Irishman, the Duke of Wellington. Although he was of Protestant and later Unionist stock, Gough always considered himself to be Irish. His family had been in Ireland since the early seventeenth century when Rev. Hugh Gough became the archdeacon of Ardfert and bishop of Limerick. His earlier ancestors included Iolo Goch, a court poet to the last native Prince of Wales, and Matthew Gough, governor of the Tower of London, who was killed during Jack Cade's Rebellion of 1450.

Bishop Gough's son or grandson built a house at Woodstown near the present-day Limerick suburb of Annacotty, where Hugh Gough was born in 1779. As his obituary in the *Irish Times* would later record, Gough was 'nurtured amid the clash of arms'. Colonel George Gough, his father, commanded the City of Limerick Militia during the 1798 Rebellion, when the United Irishmen, a republican organization, launched an abortive insurrection against the government.

The militia routed a force of 4,000 rebels at Johnstown, County Kildare, with a flying column of 500 horse, foot and guns. Hugh Gough's mother Letitia was a sister of William Bunbury, Member of Parliament for Carlow.

Commissioned into the Limerick Militia at the age of thirteen, Gough had transferred to the 76th Highlanders by 1795 when, aged fifteen, he was in the thick of the action as Britain captured the Cape of Good Hope. In 1796 he transferred to the 87th Foot, later the Royal Irish Fusiliers, the regiment that he would hold most dear. Made up of recruits from counties Tipperary, Galway and Clare, the 87th became known as the 'Faugh a Ballaghs', after its ancient Gaelic battle cry, meaning 'clear the way'. Promoted to major in 1805, Gough was back in action shortly after his marriage to Frances Stephens and advanced to Spain, where the Peninsular War was underway.

In 1809 he led the 2nd Battalion of the 87th to victory at the Battle of Talavera, despite being severely wounded when his horse was shot from under him. Two years later, he commanded the 87th at the Battle of Barossa where, outnumbered by the French two to one, the Irishmen managed to overwhelm the enemy with a series of grim but effective bayonet charges. The victory would implant an unshakeable faith in the power of a 'cold steel' charge in Gough's mind. For the next fifty years, he subscribed to the view that the artillery's role was merely to soften up the enemy before the men charged in with bayonet, sabre and lance. His triumph at Barossa was completed when Sergeant Masterton of the 87th captured the Eagle of the 8th French Regiment – the first Napoleonic eagle standard to fall – with the immortal words, 'Bejaybers boys! I have the cuckoo!' Barossa was a huge morale booster for Britain and its allies, paving the way for Waterloo and the final defeat of Napoleon's forces.

Gough led his men to several more victories in the Peninsular War campaign, including the Battle of Vitoria in 1813, where his men captured Marshal Jourdan's baton. His younger brother William was severely wounded at Vitoria but survived only to drown off Kinsale in County Cork in 1822. At the ensuing Battle of Nivelle, Gough was wounded again but won a Peninsular Gold Cross – the gateway to a knighthood – for his efforts. He also commanded the defence of

Cadiz and Tarifa, during which he received a head wound. When the battle-scarred warrior finally returned to London, he was given a hero's welcome. In 1815 he was knighted by the Prince Regent at Whitehall. He and his descendants were also given the right to use 'Faugh-a-Ballagh' as an additional motto to their arms.

Back in Ireland, he spent the next dozen years on half-pay, living the life of a country squire in County Limerick with Frances and their young family. In the early 1820s, he commanded a unit of troops that sought to suppress the 'Rockite' uprising in which at least 130 people across Munster were systematically murdered and at least sixty houses and churches burned. The anonymity of the killers, and their mythical leader Captain Rock, was to be a source of considerable frustration to Gough.

In 1837, Major General Gough and his wife moved to Bangalore in British India when he was appointed commander of the Mysore Division of the Madras Army. Four years later, he commanded 4,000 troops from India that confronted the Chinese in the First Opium War (1839–42). The conflict had been triggered after the Chinese government destroyed some 20,000 chests of 'British' opium at Canton (present-day Guangzhou) in a bid to stamp out the ruinous trade. Captain Charles Elliot, Britain's plenipotentiary in China, had advocated a diplomatic solution but, having arrived with his army, Gough overrode Elliot (whom he dismissed as 'whimsical as a shuttlecock') and captured the forts defending Canton before turning his sights on Nanking (now Nanjing), the second city of the Chinese Empire.

'Britain has gained as much by her mercy and forbearance, as by the gallantry of her troops,' Gough once wrote. 'An enemy in arms is always a legitimate foe, but the unarmed, or the suppliant for mercy, of whatever country or whatever colour, a true British soldier will always spare.' Unfortunately, the troops under his command did not heed such words, running riot in Amoy (now Xiamen) and other Chinese towns before they reached Nanking. After witnessing the aftermath of a mass suicide involving women and children, Gough wrote home, 'I am sick at heart of war and its fearful consequences.' Nonetheless, he pressed onwards, obliging the Chinese to concede defeat in the summer of 1842. The Daoguang Emperor signed the Treaty of Nanking, by which five port cities and the island of Hong Kong were ceded to Britain, thus confirming its status as the predominant European power in the region. Having already been made colonel of his beloved 87th Foot, Gough was created a baronet and received the thanks of both Parliament and the East India Company.

He was also now commander-in-chief of all British forces in India. In 1843, he led his army to victory over the Marathas of central India in the Gwalior Campaign. Two years later, he confronted the Sikhs in the Punjab (a region roughly synonymous with the present-day Punjab state in India and Punjab province in Pakistan). The Sikhs were probably the most formidable foes that Gough faced during his long military career. Their natural fighting ability had been honed by a group of mostly ex-French army officers who had taught them the Napoleonic drill and kitted them out in uniforms that replicated those worn by the East India Company army. As well as mastering European tactics, the Sikhs had British-style muskets and rifles that were every bit as good as the British weapons. Their artillery was superior to that of Gough's army in terms of numbers, calibre, weight and bore, while their gunners were often as accurate as, if not better than, their British counterparts.

Having hastily marched his army to the volatile frontier, Gough first met the Sikhs in battle during the dark of night at Mudki (now Moodkee), near Ferozepore (now Firozpur). By dint of a courageous cavalry charge and a 'cold steel' infantry advance, he defeated the Sikhs in a messy battle, losing 215 of his officers and men killed but gaining 17 of the Sikhs' 22 guns. He subsequently overwhelmed the Sikhs at the battles of Ferozeshah and Sobraon. Once again, the loss of life on both sides was high but his victory brought the First Anglo-Sikh War to an end. Under the terms of the Treaty of Lahore, signed in 1846, the Sikhs ceded all the territory between the Sutlej and the Beas rivers to Britain, while Kashmir became an independent province.

In 1848, the murder of two British officers ignited the Second Anglo-Sikh War as Gough's army sallied out once more to smother the flames of Sikh independence. He ran into trouble at the Battle of Chillianwalla in January 1849 when the Sikhs proved much stronger than anticipated and his army suffered heavily. The 24th and 29th Regiments lost all of their officers in a few minutes, while a total of 757 men were killed (mostly Englishmen) and another 1,700 left wounded or missing in the jungle scrub. Hollow as it may have been, Gough claimed victory and, after the battle, he received an ovation from his troops.

Sergeant Keay of the Bengal Artillery wrote:

> I can never forget the reception Lord Gough got from the troops as he rode along our line on the evening of the battle.... I happened to be at the General Hospital where the wounded and dying were lying in hundreds, and as soon as they caught sight of his venerable white head, there was such a cheer burst forth that it said, as plainly as could say, 'You will never find us wanting when you require us.'

Keay explained:

> It was not as a commander alone that he was respected, but as a kind-feeling and good-hearted man, who took a lively interest in the welfare of all those who were under him, and who took a pleasure in seeing everyone as comfortable as circumstance would permit. As for cavalry, infantry and artillery, I don't think that men ever could have been more attached to any commander than to old Gough. I used to see him in hospital daily, kindly asking after those who were recovering, and cheering up and consoling those who were bad.

However, even Gough's greatest admirers knew that Chillianwalla had been a close-run thing. His time-honoured strategy of softening the enemy with artillery fire before unleashing the bayonets had failed because he had been too low on heavy ammunition. The result was a disproportionate loss of men from his own rank and file, a figure that was undoubtedly increased by the excellent combat skills of the Sikhs. And while the undefeated Limerick man may have technically prevailed once again, the news of so many deaths was greeted with horror by both the British public and the directors of the East

India Company. With mounting criticism in Westminster of Gough's 'Tipperary Tactics', letters were issued ordering the commander-in-chief to stand down in place of Sir Charles Napier.

Timing is everything. Had the message reached Gough swiftly, the future may have been quite different, but as it was, he continued unaware of any impending recall. Prompted by the arrival of long-sought-for reinforcements, complete with long-range artillery, he sent his army in for one final battle against the Sikhs. As the British prepared to advance on Goojerat (present-day Gujrat in Pakistan) on 21 February 1849, Sergeant Keay recalled the 'unrestrained' enthusiasm of Gough's men as he rode down the lines in his long white 'fighting coat', sun hat in hand. Another officer recalled: 'While we were waiting, our attention was drawn to a curious sound in the far distance on the right. The noise grew louder and nearer, and we saw the regiments, one after another, cheering like mad. It was Lord Gough, at the head of his Staff, riding along the front. He soon passed out of sight, but we heard the cheering till it died away in the distance.'

The Battle of Goojerat transpired to be an overwhelming victory for Gough. The Sikhs surrendered unconditionally, the Sikh Empire collapsed and the Punjab was annexed to British India – 161,000 km (100,000 miles) of fertile soil, destined to become the breadbasket of the British Empire. Westminster hurriedly dispatched word that Gough was no longer to be sacked. Such news was particularly welcomed by Napier, who was a great supporter of 'that noble old fellow Gough...he is so good, so honest, so noble-minded'.

In June 1849, Queen Victoria elevated Gough in the peerage as Viscount Gough of Goojerat, in the Punjab, and of the city of Limerick. Parliament granted him a pension of £2,000 a year for himself and his next two successors in the viscountcy. He was also given four Sikh cannons. Like the Duke of Marlborough with Blenheim, or the Duke of Wellington with Stratfield Saye, Viscount Gough used some of the money to purchase Lough Cutra, a fine estate in County Galway. He also bought a Georgian villa in the south Dublin suburb of Booterstown called St Helen's, which is now the Radisson Blu St Helen's Hotel.

Promoted to field marshal in 1862, Gough's numerous honours included Knight of the Order of St Patrick and an equestrian statue by the eminent sculptor John Henry Foley, which hailed him as an 'illustrious Irishman'. The statue stood in Phoenix Park until it was blown up by the IRA in 1957. One suspects it may well have been toppled in more recent times in consideration of Gough's role in the Opium Wars and the conquest of the Punjab. The restored statue now resides at Chillingham Castle in Northumberland in England.

Frances, Viscountess Gough, died in 1863. Their marriage had lasted fifty-six years and produced five children. She was buried in a vault at St Brigid's Church, Stillorgan, County Dublin. When Field Marshal Gough died at St Helen's on 2 March 1869, he was buried alongside the woman who had dreamt about him on the eve of that Plymouth ball many long decades earlier.

17

PAT WATKINS, CRUSOE OF THE GALÁPAGOS

Galápagos Islands, 1812. Nobody ever identified where in Ireland Pat Watkins came from, just that he was an Irishman. Children for generations to come would shiver at the very mention of his name. 'His appearance was the most dreadful that can be imagined,' opined David Porter, captain of the United States frigate *Essex*, who entered Pat's story into his journal: 'Ragged clothes, scarcely sufficient to cover his nakedness, and infested with vermin; his red hair and beard nutted; his skin much burnt from constant exposure to the sun, and so wild and savage in his manner and appearance that he struck every one with horror.'[1]

The story runs that he had been on an English ship, a whaler perhaps, sailing around the coast of Ecuador in 1807 when, for reasons unclear, he opted to settle on Floreana, one of the Galápagos Islands, then known as Charles Island. Some say he was shipwrecked and marooned on the volcanic archipelago, others that he argued with his captain and was cast out of his ship. He would enter the history books as 'the first resident' of the Galápagos, his name immortalized in Pat's Landing on the east side of the island. He lived in a 'miserable hut' nearby, Captain Porter writes, where he cultivated a couple of acres of a valley that was 'perhaps the only spot on the island which affords sufficient moisture for the purpose'. On this small strip, he grew potatoes and pumpkins in 'considerable quantities', which he generally 'exchanged for rum or sold for cash' to the crews of the various whalers and other vessels that called into the island.

Porter's journal continues:

> For several years this wretched being lived by himself on this desolate spot, without any other apparent desire than that of procuring rum in sufficient quantities to keep himself intoxicated; and at such time, after an absence from his hut of several days, he would be found in a state of perfect insensibility, rolling among the rocks of the mountains. He appeared to be reduced to the lowest state of which human nature is capable, and seemed to have no desire beyond the tortoises and other animals of the island, except that of getting drunk.

Pat Watkins's hermetical life changed course when an American ship docked on the island and he took it upon himself to abduct one of its black crew members with the aid of an old musket. It appears his plan was to put the man to work as his slave but his strategy backfired when he dropped his guard for a moment, enabling his captive to hurl him to the ground, bind his hands behind his back and drag him back to the ship as *his* prisoner. Watkins was 'severely whipped' twice and placed in handcuffs. An English smuggler who happened to be in the same harbour then dragged the Irishman back onto the island in a bid to find his stash of cash. While the smuggler's men were smashing up Watkins's house and garden, he managed to escape. Concealed in the rocks, he used an old file to rid himself of the handcuffs and lay low until the smuggler's ship vanished over the horizon.

He got his garden back together again and recommenced selling potatoes and pumpkins to incoming ships. However, he also coaxed at least five crew members from these ships into joining him on the island, an inducement that was generally achieved, Captain Porter stated, 'by administering potent draughts of his darling liquor…and making them so drunk that they were insensible' to the departure of their vessels. The five men 'became his slaves, and he the most absolute of tyrants'.

In due course, Watkins invited the captains of two ships, one American, one English, to send some smaller boats around to Pat's Landing so that he could load them up with nutritious vegetables. However, by dint of trickery, he and his men then stole one of the small boats and took to the seas. It is not clear what their goal was, but it was evidently not achieved because the next time Pat Watkins was seen was when his open boat arrived into the port of Guayaquil, Ecuador. He was alone, the five men who sailed with him 'having perished for want of water', although Captain Porter was of the view that Watkins had killed them all when his own water supply became scarce.

From Guayaquil, Pat Watkins made his way to the Peruvian whaling port of Paita, where he teamed up with 'a tawny damsel' who agreed to accompany him back to his island paradise in the Galápagos. Unfortunately, the sight of this wild-eyed redhead had already aroused the suspicions of the Peruvian police. Suspecting him of 'improper intentions', he was arrested and locked away in Paita's jail. And that is the last record either Captain Porter or anyone else has ever made of this luckless soul.

18

CHILE'S IRISH PATRIOTS

El Roble, Chile, October 1813. As dawn broke across the mist-shrouded riverbanks, the Royalist forces launched their surprise attack. Nearly twenty Patriot soldiers were killed in the opening salvos. Hundreds more, including their commander José Miguel Carrera, took to their horses and fled, abandoning the artillery to the enemy. For the Royalists, the morning was looking like a resounding victory on the road to reasserting Spanish control over the troublesome Latin American colony of Chile.

And yet, even as the Spanish commanders congratulated themselves, a division of 200 Patriots had regrouped further up the river. At their head was thirty-five-year-old Bernardo O'Higgins, the son of an Irishman who had once been the most influential man in Chile. Riding at O'Higgins flank was his Monaghan-born comrade, John McKenna, known as Don Juan. Holding his gun high in the sky, O'Higgins dramatically rode along the lines of the Patriot army, roaring 'Lads! To me! Live with honour, or die with glory! The one who is brave is the one who follows me!'

And with those stirring words, the Patriots charged, recaptured their artillery, trounced the Royalists and won the battle. When the Chilean Republican government learned what had happened at El Roble, it issued orders for the immediate dismissal of Carrera as commander-in-chief of the Republican army in favour of O'Higgins. Juan McKenna (or MacKenna, as his name is spelled in Chile) was appointed his second-in-command.

John McKenna was born in 1771 at Willville House, a handsome dwelling that still stands on the outskirts of Monaghan town, close to St Macartan's Cathedral. His father Billy McKenna was a direct descendant of the McKenna chieftains who ruled over the barony of Errigal Truagh. This land, in the very north of County Monaghan, was known as McKenna Country for over 500 years before the Tudor armies arrived in the sixteenth century.

In 1782, just months after the American colonists defeated Britain in their war for independence, eleven-year-old Mckenna was dispatched to Madrid in Spain to stay with Count Alejandro O'Reilly, his mother's cousin. The count was one of the most successful of Ireland's 'Wild Geese' and, having left Ireland for Europe in his youth, had become Inspector General of Infantry for the Spanish Empire. In Spain, John became Juan and, under Count O'Reilly's patronage, he began his studies at Barcelona's Royal School of Mathematics. From 1785 to 1791 he studied military engineering at the city's Royal Military Academy. During this time, the young Monaghan man was appointed a cadet in the 'Regiment Irlanda' of the Irish Brigade in the Spanish army. His first action was on the north coast of Africa, where he helped defend the ancient Mediterranean city of Ceuta from a siege attack by the Sultan of Morocco.

In 1794, Lieutenant Juan McKenna advanced into the Pyrenees with the Royal Corps of Engineers. The Spanish engineers were part of a massive army dispatched by the Bourbon king under the seventy-two-year-old Count O'Reilly, now a field marshal, to defend Spain's border against a French attack. Although the count died en route, his young cousin showed his mettle on the Catalonian battlefields and was promoted to captain. He also befriended José de San Martín, the future liberator of Argentina, with whom he would later serve. In October 1796, McKenna set sail from Spain for Latin America, nearly all of which belonged to the Spanish Empire at that time. He made his way from Buenos Aires across the Andes to the Peruvian capital of Lima, where he was introduced to the septuagenarian viceroy of Peru, a fellow Irishman called Ambrosio O'Higgins.

O'Higgins is believed to have been born in Ballynary on the eastern shores of Lough Arrow, County Sligo, in 1720. His great-grandfather Sean Duff O'Higgins was Tierna (Lord) of Ballinary [sic] and married into the royal house of O'Conor. However, the O'Higgins were among the innumerable Catholic families whose power collapsed in the wake of William III's defeat of James II, the last Catholic king of Great Britain and Ireland, in the early 1690s. Reduced to being mere tenant farmers, Ambrosio O'Higgins's parents relocated to the Langford Rowley estate at Summerhill, County Meath, when he was a boy.

During his twenties, Ambrosio O'Higgins enlisted in the English army and served during the War of the Austrian Succession (1740–48). However, his Catholic Irish background put paid to his ambition for promotion and he deserted. By 1751 he had reached Cadiz, where he spent four years working in a trading house established by fellow Irishman William Butler, the ancestor of many of the present-day Butlers in Spain.

In 1756 he brought a consignment of goods across the Atlantic to the Spanish stronghold of Buenos Aires. He then managed to cross the Andes to Lima, where he operated a small general stall near the cathedral. Over the next few years, he lived the life of an itinerant trader, which gave him an immense understanding of the South American landscape and its people. By 1760 he had ceased his wanderings and settled in Santiago in Chile, where he studied engineering and, aged forty, obtained a commission to join the same Royal Corps of Engineers that Juan McKenna would join long decades later.

Ambrosio O'Higgins's knowledge of the Andes made him an invaluable addition to the Spanish army. He made his commercial breakthrough when he used this intelligence to oversee the establishment of a reliable postal service across the mountain range, complete with brickwork shelters, linking Buenos Aires to the remote backwaters of eighteenth-century Chile. He soon became one of the vital cogs in Spain's Latin American administration, simultaneously winning the respect of the Araucanian indigenous peoples by treating them with a humanity that was rare among colonial officers at this time.

Having risen through the ranks of the army, he was appointed the governor and captain-general of Chile in 1787. Dramatic improvements to the Chilean infrastructure followed as roads, bridges, docks, dykes and new towns mushroomed across the colony. In 1796, O'Higgins – now 1st Marquis of Osorno – was promoted to viceroy of Peru, overseeing the second richest colony in the Spanish Empire. 'Never was there a ruler more devoted to the Spanish interest, more zealous for the development of Chile, more remarkable for magnanimity and forgetfulness of self, than this man of Irish birth,' opined Claude Gay, the French historian.[1]

Shortly before he took office as viceroy, Ambrosio O'Higgins appointed twenty-five-year-old Juan McKenna as governor of Osorno. This sixteenth-century colonial town in the extreme south of Chile had been in ruins ever since it was destroyed by the indigenous Huilliche people nearly 200 years earlier. The young engineer from Monaghan was instructed to rebuild Osorno, which he did with considerable flair, constructing storehouses, mills and a grand new road through dense forests to the port of Puerto Montt, 108 km (67 miles) south. The Marquis of Avilés, who had succeeded O'Higgins as governor of Chile, greeted McKenna's improvements with less enthusiasm, fearing that O'Higgins and McKenna were attempting to establish a breakaway Irish colony. Such fears were unfounded; both McKenna and O'Higgins remained loyal to the Spanish crown. However, Avilés was also increasingly anxious, and rightly so, about O'Higgins's illegitimate son, Bernardo.

Bernardo O'Higgins never met his father. He grew up with his mothers' family, the Riquelmes, one of the most powerful dynasties in Chile. Isabel Riquelme was only sixteen when she became pregnant by fifty-seven-year-old Don Ambrosio O'Higgins. The Irishman swore to marry her but never did, perhaps because he was not considered of suitably high class by her family. Nonetheless, O'Higgins exerted sufficient influence to have his son sent to school in London, where he studied history, the arts and, most importantly, gained an understanding into what drove the American colonists to fight for independence. By the time Bernardo returned to South America, he had become a passionate liberal, dedicated to the concept of a Latin America freed from the shackles of European imperialism.

Ambrosio O'Higgins died at the age of eighty in 1801, leaving his son a large hacienda and estate in Chile. The young man took on his father's name (for the first time) and became a gentleman farmer, representing his locality on the Chilean council. He also became close friends with McKenna, learning much about engineering from his late father's friend. In 1809, the thirty-eight-year-old Juan McKenna moved to Santiago and married eighteen-year-old Josefina Vicuña y Larraín, from a family of Basque descent, and together they had five children.

By now the repercussions of Napoleon's conquest of Spain in 1808 were becoming apparent as France sought to claim ownership of the Spanish Empire. In 1810, the Chilean elite formed a government, or junta, which declared it would self-govern the colony, albeit in the name of the imprisoned Spanish king. McKenna joined the defence committee of the new government and was appointed governor of Valparaíso in 1811.

Deep divisions arose between Chile's Royalists and those who felt the Spanish monarchy was now superfluous. A further schism evolved between those seeking independence, with Bernardo O'Higgins emerging as the leader of a Republican faction that was eager to carry the torch of freedom to all of Spain's colonies. However, José Miguel Carrera, the most powerful man in Santiago, believed independence should be of a more localized and specifically Chilean nature. Tempers reached boiling point in 1812 when McKenna, who remained loyal to O'Higgins, was banished from Santiago having fallen foul of Carrera.

In 1813, the viceroy of Peru sent a Spanish army north to Chile to reassert Madrid's authority. The Chilean Republicans, or Patriots, quickly formed an army under Carrera as commander-in-chief. McKenna was recalled from exile, appointed General of Artillery and placed in charge of military engineering. Bernardo O'Higgins, who had retired to his hacienda in poor health some months earlier, rallied a local militia and also advanced to the front line. The Patriots had considerable success in the first part of the war: O'Higgins's finest hour probably came when he delivered his 'Braveheart'-like speech at El Roble in October 1813; McKenna's greatest triumph took place six months later when he commanded a Republican division in a successful defence against a far superior Spanish Royalist army at Membrillar.

As commander of the now exhausted Patriots, O'Higgins negotiated a compromising truce with the Royalist commander. Under the terms of the Treaty of Lircay (1814), the Patriots reaffirmed their loyalty to the Spanish king and accepted that Chile was an integral part of the Spanish monarchy. In return, the Royalists acknowledged the existence of a Chilean provisional government. However, the

1 The Irish poet Sedulius Scottus – one of Dicuil's colleagues in Liège – is said to have composed the ninth-century poem Carmen Paschale ('Easter Song'), pictured above.

2 A depiction of St Brendan on the whale from a German chapbook edition of *Navigatio sancti Brendani abbatis*, 'The Voyage of St Brendan', published on vellum in about 1475.

3 An 1838 etching of the 'Scots' Monastery founded by Irish Benedictine monks at Regensburg, Germany, in the eleventh century.

ABOVE **4** Jacobo de Ibernia, or James of Ireland, with Odoric of Pordenone in Sumatra. Illustration from a fifteenth-century edition of Marco Polo's 'Book of the Marvels of the World' (*Livre des merveilles*).

RIGHT **5** Portrait of Luke Wadding, founder of the Irish College of St Isidore in Rome, painted by Carlo Maratti in the 1650s.

ABOVE **6** Don Guillén Lamport, the Wexford man who inspired the legend of Zorro, is said to have been the sitter in *Portrait of a Young Captain* from the studio of Peter Paul Rubens.

LEFT **7** George Berkeley, the Bishop of Cloyne, was painted in 1727 by the Scottish artist John Smibert. Berkeley subsequently offered Smibert the post of professor of fine arts at the college he hoped to found in Bermuda.

TOP **8** Painted by Charles Benazech, this shows King Louis XVI of France standing at the foot of the scaffold, receiving the last rites from his Longford-born confessor, the Abbé Edgeworth.

ABOVE **9** George Washington's triumphal entry into New York City on 25 November 1783, now known as 'Evacuation Day', would prove to be a cathartic moment for the Derry-born tailor-spy Hercules Mulligan.

ABOVE **10** James Hoban's 1792 design proposal for The White House in Washington, DC appears to have been inspired by Leinster House in Dublin.

RIGHT **11** This oil portrait of Viscount Hugh Gough was painted by the Scottish artist Sir Francis Grant in 1853. It shows the Limerick-born general, holding his trademark pith helmet, in command during the Anglo-Sikh War.

ABOVE **12** General Frederick Young (1786–1874), the Donegal man who raised the Sirmoor Battalion of Gurkhas, as painted by James Prinsep Beadle in 1928.

RIGHT **13** James Barry, the Cork-born doctor, in Kingston, Jamaica, c. 1862. Also pictured is Dr Barry's servant John, a former soldier with the West India Regiment, and the doctor's trusty dog Psyche.

disgraced Carrera now staged a coup, seized control of the junta and repudiated the treaty.

McKenna was among several of Carrera's adversaries who were subsequently exiled to the Argentine province of Mendoza. Bernardo O'Higgins remained in command of the fallen government's forces and attempted to reverse events by engaging Carrera at the Battle of Les Tres Acequias in August 1814. This transpired to be a humiliating defeat for O'Higgins, who was lucky to escape without injury when his wounded horse crumpled on the battlefield; he managed to escape on a borrowed steed.

While the Republicans were so badly split, the Royalist forces had been much boosted by the arrival of the Queen's Talavera Regiment from Spain under the command of Mariano de Osorio, the newly appointed governor of Chile. Now faced with a common enemy, O'Higgins and the Carreras settled their differences and prepared to defend Chile against the Spaniards. However, de Osorio proved a superior commander, leading the Royalists to a crushing victory over the Patriots at Rancagua in October 1814, thus completing the Reconquista, as the Spanish reconquest of Chile was known.

Both Carrera and O'Higgins fled to Argentina, where they remained for three years. Their enmity was considerably increased when Carrera's youngest brother Luis gunned down forty-three-year-old Brigadier Juan McKenna in a duel in Buenos Aires on 21 November 1814. Luis Carrera was arrested and tried but escaped sentence.

In 1817, Bernardo O'Higgins, accompanied by General José de San Martín (an old school friend) and John Thomond O'Brien of Baltinglass, County Wicklow (San Martín's aide-de-camp), mounted a victorious campaign against the Royalists. O'Higgins duly became first president of the Republic of Chile – his term was essentially successful, with the opening of new markets, courts, colleges, libraries and hospitals across the land. As well as marked improvements in both farming and the military, he founded the Chilean navy and the Chilean Marine Corps.

However, his rule was overshadowed by his failure to intervene when Luis Carrera and his brother Juan José Carrera were arrested and executed under deeply suspicious circumstances. He was also implicated in the arrest and execution of José Miguel Carrera by Argentine forces in Mendoza in 1821. For many Chileans today, O'Higgins culpability in the killing of the Carreras remains as contentious as Éamon de Valera's supposed role in the assassination of Michael Collins is in Ireland.

By 1822, O'Higgins's radical policies had antagonized both the Church and the nobility, as well as much of the Creole populace. Faced with imminent bankruptcy, he borrowed a million pounds from Britain. This coincided with an earthquake that left the port city of Valparaíso in ruins. Chile's conservatives ousted him in a coup in early 1823. Summoned before the junta, O'Higgins rather spiritedly bared his chest and offered his life but the junta simply saluted him and sent him into exile.

O'Higgins was considering a return to his father's ancestral home in Ireland when he was introduced to Simón Bolívar, the Venezuelan revolutionary. Bolívar's government granted him two haciendas near Lima, where he and his family then settled. In 1842, the National Congress of Chile voted to allow him to return home. However, he had a heart attack during the journey and died in Lima that October, aged sixty-four. His remains are now to be found in the Crypt of the Liberator in Santiago.

Both Juan McKenna and Bernardo O'Higgins continue to be revered in Chile. Santiago's main thoroughfare is the Avenida Libertador General Bernardo O'Higgins, while its finest boulevard is the Avenida Vicuña Mackenna. The O'Higgins name is also recalled by a national park, a village, several Chilean navy battleships, the main research station in Antarctica and the late, lamented Banco O'Higgins. There is also a monument to Bernardo O'Higgins in Dublin's Merrion Square.

19

JOHN FIELD: A MUSCOVY NOCTURNE

Vvedenskoye Cemetery, Moscow, 1837. The Russians called it the German Cemetery, a nod to all the Germans, Catholic and Lutheran alike, who had been laid to rest here in the decades since its establishment by Catherine the Great. Lately, it had become the cemetery of choice for many of the English, Polish and Italian émigrés that died in the city. Amid the multitude of monuments and mausoleums that now rose up from the earth was a modest headstone, placed over a fresh grave that autumn day. It was simply inscribed:

> *John Field*
> *Born in Ireland in 1782*
> *Dead in Moscow in 1837*

It is a curious error: 'Dead', not 'Died'. An indication of the man's career emerges with an additional dedication on the reverse of the headstone: 'Erected to His Memory by His Grateful Friends and Scholars.' Almost nobody wandering through the Russian capital today would know of John Field but approximately 200 years ago, this Dubliner was arguably the best-known musician in Moscow.

John Field was born in 1782 in Golden Lane in the shadow of St Patrick's Cathedral. It was a musical household. His father, Robert Field, earned a decent living playing the violin in churches and theatres during those glory days when Dublin was considered the second city of the British Empire. As a toddler, John was taught the piano by his grandfather, also John Field, a professional organist who had attended Handel's famous premiere of the *Messiah* in Dublin forty years earlier. The elder John quickly identified his grandson's extraordinary ear and the boy was sent to study under Tommaso Giordani, a Neapolitan composer who dominated Dublin's opera scene at the time. The Irish capital was enjoying a commercial and cultural boom under Grattan's Parliament, attributed to a degree of parliamentary independence that Ireland secured from Britain between 1782 and 1800.

In March 1792, nine-year-old John Field made his debut, performing a pedal harp concerto on a fortepiano at one of Signor Giordani's 'spiritual concerts' at the Rotunda. A correspondent for the *Dublin Evening Post* described it as 'really an astonishing performance by such a child' with 'a precision and execution far beyond what could have been expected'.[1] Such glowing reviews led Giordani to recommend the boy as an apprentice to his Italian friend Muzio Clementi, a celebrated piano-teacher who sold pianos and other musical instruments. The conundrum was that Signor Clementi lived in London. Undeterred, the Field family moved to the cosmopolitan British capital in 1793, settling in Haymarket. As Clementi's apprentice, John Field's role was to help manufacture and sell instruments. However, Clementi noticed the boy at work, listened to the melodies that he conjured on his piano, saw how quickly he figured out the violin and deduced that he had a prodigy on his hands.

Under Clementi's agile guidance, young Field mastered the smooth legato technique and evolved into one of the greatest pianists of his generation. By the age of thirteen, his performances were drawing rapturous applause across London. Clementi was quick to spot an opportunity and, from 1795, he began publishing Field's compositions. This included his highly regarded Piano Concerto No. 1, H 7 (which he premiered in London in 1799, aged sixteen) and his first opus, a set of three intimate piano sonatas. Field's decision to dedicate his opus to Clementi underpinned a friendship that master and pupil would share for life.

Clementi was convinced that the future for his Irish protégé lay in continental Europe. In 1802 he brought him, via Paris, to Vienna, where the twenty-year-old performed a concerto in front of a much-impressed Beethoven. The youngster also received a quick lesson in counterpoint from Beethoven's elderly Austrian mentor, Johann Georg Albrechtsberger.

By the end of the year, Field and Clementi were in St Petersburg. Over the next six months, Field came to adore the Russian city with its artistic ambience and well-heeled citizens. When Clementi returned home, Field opted to stay. Always thrifty, Clementi managed to find Field a well-paid position as a teacher in Narva, 150 km (93 miles) west of St Petersburg, a city that today stands just across the Russian border in Estonia. With Clementi gone, Field launched himself into a plethora of concerts and made his debut at the St Petersburg Philharmonia. By the spring of 1805, he had gained enough momentum to set off on a fruitful tour of the Baltic states. He returned to St Petersburg for the summer, taking an apartment opposite the Winter Palace at Vasilievsky Island.

In 1806 he presented his first concert in Moscow, where his sweet tones were met with such enthusiasm that he moved there in April 1807 and became the city's most exclusive piano teacher. However, there are question marks over his teaching prowess. His sardonic, morose, pipe-smoking personality did not appeal to everyone. Moreover, he drank copious quantities of expensive champagne during classes and seduced an unspecified number of his female students. Nonetheless, his genius was such that the Fieldian school of piano-playing continues to be revered in Russia. Mikhail Glinka and Alexandre Dubuque, regarded as two of Russia's most eminent early composers, both studied under Field, as did Arkady Alexandrovich, the maternal grandfather of Rachmaninoff.

By 1810 the Russians were so keen on Field's work that Clementi shrewdly reissued some of his older compositions to raise extra funds. Field also began publishing a steady stream of new compositions, based on Russian folk songs, which sold extremely well. It was at this time that he composed the first of at least eighteen 'Romantic' nocturnes, for which he would be hailed as the Father of the Nocturne by the generations to come.

One of his most ardent fans was Frédéric Chopin who, inspired by Field's atmospheric compositions, went on to create twenty-one beautiful nocturnes of his own. To Chopin's dismay, Field would later become visibly irritated by the manner in which the Polish composer had so successfully adopted what Field felt to be *his* music. Franz Liszt was another admirer, describing the nocturnes as 'vague eolian harmonies…half-formed sighs floating through the air, softly lamenting and dissolved in delicious melancholy'. As Lizst observed,

John Field was the first person to even attempt 'this peculiar style'. The concept simply did not exist until he began to 'dream his music in moments when he entirely abandoned himself to his inspiration'.[2]

Among Field's students in Moscow was a petite French lady called Adelaide Percheron, the daughter of a war commissioner of the French fleet. Born in Pondicherry, India, she was regarded as something of a flirt by her contemporaries. The pair became an item in 1808 and married in 1810. Having moved to St Petersburg in 1811, they were spared the sight of Moscow burning on the eve of Napoleon's arrival in the city in the autumn of 1812.

Field's return to St Petersburg marked the start of the most productive decade of his life. He was prodigiously publishing ever more compositions, or reworking and improving existing ones, such as Go to the Devil and Shake Yourself, an Irish dance that he arranged as a rondo for the piano forte. He signed rewarding deals with both H. J. Dalmas and Breitkopf & Härtel, the leading music publishers in Russia and Europe respectively. Combined with his handsome income as a teacher, he was therefore perfectly placed to decline an offer to become court pianist to Tsar Alexander in 1819.

However, behind the scenes his private life was crumbling. In 1815, Field's mistress, Mademoiselle Charpentier, gave birth to a son, Leonov. Adelaide reluctantly stayed with her husband, having their only child, a son named Adrien, in 1819, but she had grown weary of his boozy hedonism and serial adultery. Together they performed a series of concerts in Moscow in 1821, at the end of which she left him, taking young Adrien with her to start a new life in Smolensk.

John Field continued to perform as a solo artist, and published more music, but much of the magic was gone. There were still moments of genius, such as an 1822 sonata he performed in collaboration with the fun-loving Austrian virtuoso, Johann Nepomuk Hummel. The two men had enjoyed an amusing first encounter when Hummel convinced Field that he was an innocuous travelling salesman and persuaded him to play a piece. When Field then asked Hummel if he had any tunes up his sleeve, the Austrian bashfully insisted that he was merely a salesman and could not possibly sully the ambience with his poor playing. Field persisted, so Hummel rolled up his sleeves and began playing such incredibly powerful music that Field's pipe literally fell out of his mouth. The two men became instant friends thereafter.[3]

However, John Field's incessant champagne-and-cognac-swilling lifestyle was catching up on him. Increasingly cantankerous, portly and dishevelled, he began cancelling concerts and was writing virtually no new works. Diagnosed with what appears to have been rectal cancer, he returned to London for treatment in 1831, giving some concerts in the British capital as well as Manchester. The critical response to his performances was fair to middling. His music seemed behind the times and it was now being whispered that he was something of a has-been, his star eclipsed by a new generation of ivory-tinkling geniuses such as Chopin, Liszt and Felix Mendelssohn, whom Field met in London. The *Belfast Commercial Chronicle* may have been close to the mark when it postulated that his Irish background served against him and suggested he might have more success if he added a 'nini' to the end of his name and pretended to be Italian.[4]

Field was still in London in 1832 when he learned of the death of Clementi, his old friend and mentor. The eighty-one-year-old maestro was honoured with a public funeral at Westminster Abbey; John Field helped to carry his coffin to the tomb in the south cloisters.

Discomfited by his lukewarm reception in England, Field was back in Paris by Christmas 1832. He embarked upon another tour, accompanied by young Leonov, but his piano-playing skills were undoubtedly in decline. Following a series of poorly received concerts in France, Germany and Italy, 'Drunken John', as he was now known, checked himself into a hospital in Naples in 1834. Nine months later, he was plucked out by Russian friends who took him to Vienna, where he stayed with the composer Carl Czerny, a past pupil of Beethoven, and gave three recitals. In 1835 he returned to Moscow with his younger son Adrien, now sixteen years old. He performed his final concert in the city in March 1836.

Later that year, stricken with pneumonia, he was confined to bed in his Moscow home. As he lay dying, he was asked to state his religion. 'I am not a Calvinist,' he wryly replied, 'but a *Claveciniste* [harpsichord player].' The fifty-four-year-old Dubliner died on 23 January 1837.

He had brought the gift of music to innumerable people across Europe and, in many ways, he continues to do so – without his influence, for example, it is arguable whether Chopin or Liszt could have had such a massive impact. His legacy would also be taken up by his two sons, who both pursued musical careers in Russia, Leonov as a tenor and Adrien as a pianist.

20

FREDERICK YOUNG, FATHER OF THE GURKHAS

Jaitak Fort, India, 1815. Lieutenant Frederick Young raised himself off the wet green grass, drew his sword and prepared to die. The leather-clad herdsmen slowly closed in, their curved kukri knives raised high. Behind them, the Donegal man could still make out the silhouettes of the Irregulars, Indian soldiers who – like him – were employed to fight for the British East India Company. The difference was that the Irregulars had fled when the Nepalese attacked. As Young awaited the flashing steel, one of the Nepalese soldiers stopped abruptly and spoke in English. 'Why did you not run away too?' he asked. 'I have not come so far in order to run away,' replied Young.

Lieutenant Young was not killed. Instead, greatly impressed by his fighting zeal, the hillmen took him prisoner. During his captivity, he learned much about Nepalese society, and the Gorkhas* in particular, mastering their language, their customs and their military techniques. Upon his release, the indomitable Irishman would use this knowledge to become the founding father of the Gurkha Brigade.

---

* The name 'Gurkha' comes from the hill town of Gorkha, from which the Nepalese kingdom expanded. In this chapter, 'Gorkha' is used to refer to the area and people from the area, while 'Gurkha' signifies the British regiment and its soldiers. In 1949, the spelling of 'Gurkha' in the Indian Army was changed to the traditional 'Gorkha'.

At least, that's how the story goes. Indeed, the tale of Frederick Young's capture by the Gorkhas is a deeply entrenched part of British military folklore. In another version, a Gorkha tells Young that the British are 'almost as brave as the Gorkhas themselves'. And in yet another, 'the merry men of the Nepalese hills' remark, 'Ah you are a brave man. We could serve under a brave man like you.' All these tales establish a scenario where the fearsome Nepalese soldiers are greatly flattered when Young duly suggests that they form a regiment and join the British East India Company (EIC).

The truth about Frederick Young's Nepalese encounter is a little harder to pin down. Most of what is known of his experience comes from a biography written by his daughter, Louisa Hadow Jenkins, published more than a century after his capture. She recounts how her father was born on the Inishowen Peninsula in the far north of County Donegal in 1786. His Presbyterian ancestors arrived from Devonshire in the 1630s as tenants of the Marquess of Donegal and settled at Culdaff, near Malin Head, where members of the Young family still live today. Rev. Gardiner Young, Frederick's father, was variously rector of Moville, Ballynascreen and Coleraine.

Young was just fourteen when he went to India to join the EIC's military service in Bengal. His first years were spent serving under General Lake, the man who destroyed the Franco-Irish forces at Ballinamuck at the close of the 1798 Rebellion. Commissioned an ensign in 1802, he was promoted to lieutenant after his service in the Second Anglo-Maratha War of 1803–5. Six years later, he was appointed aide-de-camp (ADC) to a colourful Ulsterman, Major General Sir Rollo Gillespie.

Born in Comber, County Down, Gillespie had survived shipwrecks, yellow fever, frauds, court martials, murder trials, mutinies, allegations of bigamy and a raid on his home in which he killed six of his eight assailants with a sword. Nicknamed 'The Strongest Man in Comber', he won widespread praise across the British Empire in 1806 when he quickly and brutally snuffed out a mutiny by Indian sepoys within the East India Company at Vellore.

During the first three years that Frederick Young spent as his ADC, Sir Rollo Gillespie conquered the Dutch Javanese city of Batavia (now Jakarta, Indonesia), deposed the sultan of Sumatra and killed a tiger in the open on Bangalore racecourse. In 1814, Gillespie and Young were ordered to advance into the fledgling kingdom of Nepal to confront the Gorkhas, who were challenging the might of the EIC. Young would later hail 'the superiority of the Gorkha army over any other with which the British power has come into contact'.

Twenty-two thousand troops were dispatched to bring a quick and decisive end to the Gorkhas insolence. Gillespie was assigned the task of dislodging the enemy from a strategic fort at Khalanga. This was to be his last hurrah. As he led his men in a head-on charge at the fort, a Gorkha sniper shot him through the heart and he died in Young's arms just 27 m (89 ft) from the palisade. Over the next six weeks, Young watched with mounting admiration as the 600 Gorkhas at Khalanga refused to submit. The British gradually cut off their freshwater supply and killed 520 of the defenders, but the Nepalese held steady until, at last, they slipped out of the fort under the cover of darkness.

In February 1815, the British laid siege to another prominent Nepalese fort at Jaitak. When they learned that a force of Gorkha soldiers was on its way to relieve the besieged fort, Lieutenant Young was dispatched at the head of a column of 2,000 native Indian troops to intercept. However, this was the moment when Young's Irregulars faced a surprise attack by a band of 300 Gorkhas in the Sirmur Hills, and as one contemporary put it, the British column 'incontinently fled', leaving the twenty-nine-year-old Young to face the music.

Taking a prisoner like Young was something of a novelty for the Nepalese. In their recent wars against the Chinese in Tibet and the Sikhs in the Punjab, the military protocol allowed no quarter for prisoners. Anyone left on the field of battle was simply massacred. For all their sins, the British not only accepted prisoners but also looked after their wounded enemies. This, according to contemporary accounts, greatly impressed the Gorkhas. Louisa Jenkins states that when her father was released, he was summoned to explain his experiences to his superior officers. He applauded the Gorkhas' immense soldiering qualities and vouched for the hillmen as a hardy, brave, humorous and likeable people. His opinion, she said, proved instrumental in persuading the British to enlist the demobilized Gorkhas to serve under the Crown.

However, while early histories of the Anglo-Nepalese War refer to the defeat of Young's Irregulars at Jaitak, there is no mention of his capture in any of the key sources. Such a dramatic story would surely have been recorded in official dispatches or in letters written by his friends. Nor is there any mention of the event in his obituaries. Perhaps Louisa Jenkins heard the story directly from her father when he was a whiskery old general living back in Donegal. Like any good soldier, he might have been inclined to embellish the tale, or perhaps it was purely based on his daughter's imagination.

The credit for conceiving a Gurkha regiment is generally given to Young's Scottish friend William Fraser, a cavalry officer and political agent. In April 1815, Fraser persuaded the British general Sir David Ochterlony that he should assemble all the Nepalese prisoners and deserters at Malaun into a paid, Irregular outfit under the East India Company. The hierarchy was assumed from the outset – with the British to lead and the Gurkhas to be led. Ochterlony agreed and the first Gurkha regiment was born when the Nasiri (or Nusseree, meaning 'friendly') Pulteen was raised under the British flag.

The concept was so successful that Frederick Young was then sent to raise a Gurkha battalion at Sirmoor in northern India, some 240 km (150 miles) beyond Nepal's western border. 'I came there one man', he later said, 'and I came back three thousand.' These were the men that the clergyman's son had fought at Jaitak and Khalanga but were now willing to accept his leadership. Promoted to captain, Young became the first British officer to command the Gurkhas. To his considerable pride, his 3,000-strong Sirmoor Battalion was battle-ready within six months and he would command it for the next twenty-eight years. It was the first Gurkha unit to see action against the Maratha Empire of India in 1817.

Five years later, Young was appointed political agent for Dehradun, a city in the Garwahl region of the Himalayan foothills. This was to be his base for the next twenty-four years. He had his first call to action in 1824 when 800 Gujars occupied the nearby fort of Koonja Bahadurpur, from which they launched a series of bloody attacks on the British and their allies. Young led 200 of his tough, wiry Gurkhas to the fort where, instead of besieging it, they fashioned a battering ram from a large tree, lopping its branches off with their kukri knives. They gradually smashed their way into Koonja and won the day with a brutal hand-to-hand battle that left 37 Gurkhas and 150 Gujars dead, Young narrowly avoiding being slain. In honour of the triumph, the Sirmoor Battalion wore a stylized Rams Head as its insignia. Young may also have been instrumental in choosing its famous credo, *Kafar hunu bhanda marnu niko* ('It is better to die than to live as a coward').

Young's obituaries would recall this 'genial-hearted young soldier' as 'the life and soul of the party'. As a passionate sportsman, the Dehradun Valley was something of a paradise. The forested shores of the Ganges were replete with black bears, elephants, tigers, leopards and striped hyenas. Young promptly became one of the first people to introduce hunting to India when he imported a pack of hounds. He built a shooting lodge called Mullingar, presumably named after the town in his Irish homeland, which would become the nucleus of the famous hill station of Mussoorie. He also apparently planted the first tea and potatoes ever grown in the valley. In 1825 he married Jeanette Bird, the daughter of a fellow army man, with whom he had eight children.

In 1846, Lieutenant Colonel Young left Dehradun to take command of the Ferozepore Brigade on the Anglo-Sikh frontier. Given the mounting tensions between the British and the Sikhs, he was constantly on guard for a surprise attack. After three years at Ferozepore (present-day Firozpur), he was promoted to brigadier general and transferred to Dinapore (now Danapur), the largest military cantonment in Bengal, where he served for a further five years.

The Donegal man concluded fifty-two years of military service in India following his wife's death in 1852, retiring to his Irish homeland at Fairy Hill, Bray, County Wicklow, only to lose all his money when his bank failed. Shortly afterwards he relocated to near his birthplace in County Donegal, where he received word in 1856 that he had been promoted to lieutenant general. He was promoted to full general in 1865. General Young died aged eighty-seven at

Albany, his home in the south Dublin suburb of Ballybrack, in 1874, and was buried at Dean's Grange Cemetery.

Thirty-two years after his death, the Sirmoor Battalion evolved into the 2nd King Edward VII's Own Gurkha Rifles. Along with the other 'Gurkha' battalions, it formed the backbone of the British Indian forces during the First World War. The extraordinary heroics of the 100,000 Gurkhas who fought in that war certainly elevated these courageous men to the status of mystical super-warriors – about 20,000 died, while approximately 2,000 received awards for courage, including three Victoria Crosses. Nearly 30,000 Gurkhas were killed or wounded in the Second World War.

At the partition of British India into Pakistan and India in 1947, the Gurkha battalions were divided between the British and Indian armies. Young's regiment was among those retained by the British and, in 1994, it became part of the Royal Gurkha Rifles. In 2009, following a high-profile campaign fronted by actress Joanna Lumley, 36,000 Gurkha veterans and their families were permitted to settle in the United Kingdom.

21

DR JAMES BARRY, CAESAREAN PIONEER

Cape Town, 26 July 1826. It is not known whether Mrs Munnik was still conscious when Dr Barry cut a midline incision from her umbilicus to her symphysis. Whatever the powers of sedation, she must have felt tremendous pain as the blade cut through the thick abdominal wall and the anterior surface of her uterus. Somehow, the doctor managed to reach inside, extract the baby, cut the umbilical cord and remove the blood clots and the placenta before stitching it all up again. Nobody can have expected the mother to survive, least of all Dr Barry. After all, James Hamilton, the doctor's former teacher and one of the most celebrated obstetricians in the world, had lost the mothers in both of the caesarean operations that he had performed.

And yet Mrs Munnik lived on and so did her baby boy. Thomas Munnik, the boy's father, was a wealthy Cape Town snuff merchant. He would name his son James Barry Munnik as a show of his immense gratitude to the Irish doctor who had, on that momentous day, performed the first successful caesarean section in African history on the Munniks' kitchen table. Indeed, it was the first recorded caesarean section undertaken in the British Empire by a Western surgeon in which both mother and child survived.

Dr Barry was also appointed the boy's godfather, and in turn the boy would become godfather to General James Barry Munnik Hertzog, better known as Barry Hertzog, who commanded Boer forces during the Second Anglo-Boer War (1899–1902) and served as prime minister of the Union of South Africa from 1924 to 1939.

This remarkable accomplishment by Dr Barry should in itself be sufficient to seal the surgeon's eminence as an obstetrics pioneer. Indeed, the doctor, who went on to become Inspector General of Military Hospitals, was something of a household name in the British Empire during the 1850s and 1860s. However, that reputation was entirely overshadowed in the wake of the doctor's death in 1866, when it was revealed that Dr James Barry was a woman who had lived as a man for over fifty years.

The story of Dr James Barry is one of the most extraordinary in the annals of the nineteenth century. His given name as a child was Margaret Ann Bulkeley (or Bulkley).** Born in Cork City in 1789, he was the progeny of a mixed marriage between Jeremiah Bulkeley, a Dublin-born Catholic, and his wife, Mary Anne Barry, a Cork-born Protestant. Mary Anne's parents were landlords of the Neptune, 'a genteel public house', that stood on the city's Merchant's Quay, or Cold Harbour as it was then known. At this time Cork was enjoying considerable prosperity by dint of its proximity to Cork Harbour, the British Empire's main base for provisioning the transatlantic troopships and supply ships sailing to its distant

---

** As James Barry (Margaret Bulkeley) identified as a man, male pronouns have been used throughout this account.

colonies in the Caribbean and the Americas, as well as Africa, India and, at length, Australasia.

By the time of Margaret Bulkeley's birth, his father had a shop on Merchant's Quay that appears to have combined a chandlery with a grocery. He had also secured a lucrative position at Cork's Weigh House, a rare office for a Catholic, whereby he spent much of his week weighing firkins of butter that came into the city from the surrounding farms of Cork, Kerry, Tipperary, Limerick and Waterford.

Jeremiah Bulkeley's world was turned upside down by the United Irishmen's rebellion of 1798. Although he played no known part in the insurrection, his Catholicism placed his loyalty in doubt and he was dismissed from the service in 1802. It is possible that another complication arose at about this time when Jeremiah and Mary Anne appeared with a new daughter, Juliana, who was considerably younger than their other children. There is a theory that the baby girl was in fact born to Margaret Bulkeley, then a young teenager, who may have been raped, with the perpetrator perhaps an uncle.

Further economic turmoil was in store for the family when creditors began hammering on Jeremiah Bulkeley's door. He had borrowed a small fortune in order to buy an expensive legal apprenticeship for Margaret's wayward older brother John. If John became a barrister, then he would surely attract a well-to-do bride who would resolve all the monies owed. The gamble misfired and, when Margaret Bulkeley was fifteen, his father was locked up in the Marshalsea debtor's prison by the Four Courts in Dublin, which left him and his mother in Cork 'in very indigent circumstances' – but then their luck changed.

The sign outside the Barry family pub in Cork depicted the god Neptune on one side, tridents and all, and a British warship called HMS *Neptune* on the other.[1] It had been painted by Mary Anne Bulkeley's mercurial and considerably older brother James Barry. He had long since moved to London and become a renowned Romantic artist, being admitted and then expelled from the prestigious Royal Academy in London. In 1806, the sixty-five-year-old artist succumbed to pituitary apoplexy in a London coffee house. In his will, he bequeathed some valuable assets to his sister, which she sold in order to pay for Margaret's education.

The late James Barry's legacy was also to ensure that the young Bulkeley, not yet eighteen years old, met some of his inner circle, most notably General Francisco de Miranda, the Venezuelan revolutionary. The general was a committed feminist and advocate of women's education. He invited Margaret Bulkeley to his London home, where he was encouraged to peruse the rare medical books in his library. Miranda was so impressed by the adolescent's appetite for the subject that he apparently suggested he study medicine formally and offered to give him work in Venezuela if he did.

In 1809 nineteen-year-old Bulkeley enrolled as one of over 900 students at the Edinburgh School of Medicine, regarded as one of the finest medical schools in Europe. However, women were not permitted at such institutions and so, with the knowledge of his mother as well as General Miranda and some of his late uncle's friends, he assumed the identity of a man and began calling himself James Miranda Stuart Barry.

For the next three years, he buried his head in the study of thirteen different subjects including anatomy, surgery and, significantly, midwifery. Army records would later show that only two other doctors in the entire British service mastered such a high number of disciplines. It was also during this time that the 11th Earl of Buchan, another friend of his artistic uncle, gave the industrious student use of the extensive library at his home in the Scottish Borders. College life was less successful. James Barry became a laughing stock among the boys, not least due to his penchant for wearing an unfashionable overcoat with long skirts, presumably to cover his legs. A fellow student tried to teach him how to box but gave up when the young 'Irishman' refused to strike out and kept protectively crossing his arms over his chest.

He graduated with aplomb in July 1812 and so became the first person born as a woman to qualify in medicine in the United Kingdom. Not until 1876 would Britain pass an act permitting women to enter the medical profession. However, even as the young doctor donned his gown, there was bad news from Venezuela: General Miranda had been arrested and thrown into prison, and he was to remain behind bars until his death four years later. Meanwhile, Dr Barry proceeded from the Royal College of Surgeons in London to the British Army

Medical Service where, continuing to present as a man, he served with distinction as a military surgeon in eleven different parts of the British Empire over the next forty-seven years.

His profession began with a posting to the Cape of Good Hope in South Africa where, as physician to the governor, Lord Charles Somerset, he was to dedicate long hours to improving the general sanitary conditions, starting with the colony's water system. When a friend's wife was taken ill, Somerset heartily recommended her to Dr Barry, 'whose skill has attested wonders since he has been here'. Mark Twain would later write, 'There were plenty of pretty girls, but none of them caught him, none of them could get hold of his heart; evidently he was not a marrying man.' However, the 1.5-m (5-ft)-tall Dr Barry became so friendly with Governor Somerset, a widower, that contemporaries became convinced the two were having a 'homosexual affair'. The gossips had a field day in 1824 when a lewd and sexually embarrassing placard appeared on Cape Town bridge, obliging the governor to sue for libel.

Two years later, Dr Barry performed the ground-breaking caesarean section on Mrs Munnik. Although he had studied midwifery under Professor James Hamilton at Edinburgh, the closest he had come to actually performing such an operation was experimenting on a cadaver. His success was thus a phenomenon, as indeed was Mrs Munnik's resilience. It would be more than twenty years before the arrival of anaesthesia for such procedures.

From the Cape of Good Hope, he made his way to Mauritius in 1828, before taking up his post as staff surgeon to the Jamaica garrison in 1831. His first Christmas on the Caribbean island coincided with the outbreak of the Great Slave Revolt, in which nearly a fifth of Jamaica's 300,000 enslaved population rose up against their British overlords. The rebellion was snuffed out after eleven days but Dr Barry's open opposition to slavery would earn him the hostility of the island's plantocracy. Slavery was abolished across the British Empire within two years of the revolt. Its abolition within Jamaica was overseen by the island's governor, Howe Browne, the Marquess of Sligo, an Irish peer who would become known as the 'Emancipator of the Slaves'.

Dr Barry continued to serve in multiple spheres around the empire over the next three decades. Many of the stories told about his time in colonies such as the Leeward Islands, Malta and Corfu would transpire to be hearsay, although it is true that he was briefly buried alive during a yellow fever epidemic in Trinidad. On the south Atlantic isle of St Helena, he established a new hospital for women and introduced daily surgeries for the poor.

Wherever he was stationed, he campaigned for the rights of patients – particularly those who were marginalized and oppressed – and highlighted the importance of both diet and sanitation to public health. While on an inspection tour of field hospitals during the Crimean War, he came up against Florence Nightingale, who later branded the Irish doctor as a 'blackguard' and 'the most hardened creature I ever met throughout the army'.

Presumably to embellish his identity as a man, Dr Barry dressed with marked eccentricity, often wearing a red wig and three-inch heels to boost his height. A vegetarian and a teetotaller with a famously short fuse, his most trusted companions in later life were a Jamaican manservant called John and a poodle named Psyche. Rumours would also circulate that he had enjoyed some dalliances with society women in his younger years.

His career culminated in Canada when he became Inspector General of Hospitals in 1857, the second-highest position in his chosen vocation. In this role, he made a considerable impact by proposing reforms including healthier food for soldiers, cleaner kitchens and separate quarters for married soldiers. He also stirred things up by championing the plight of otherwise ostracized leper communities.

When his posting ended in 1859, Dr Barry effectively retired on half-pay and returned to London, where he died following a case of dysentery on 25 July 1865, almost thirty-nine years to the day since he performed his operation in the Munniks' kitchen. Although the seventy-six-year-old left no will, he had asked John to ensure that his body be spared a post-mortem and that he be buried in the clothes and bedsheets he died in. It was clearly his hope that, even after death, he would maintain the gender that he had adopted fifty-five years earlier.

However, John was away at the time of his death and the woman who laid him out for burial had other ideas. Having made the startling discovery that Dr Barry was 'a perfect female', this woman – an as-yet-anonymous mother of nine – attempted to bribe the army. She was to be the only person who came forward to say she had seen the doctor's naked body, and it was also her description of stretch marks on the doctor that inspired the conceit that Dr Barry may have given birth to a baby in his teens.

The news was subsequently broken by Sophia Bishop, a young maidservant in the doctor's household, who cashed in with a series of articles published in the popular press within weeks of Barry's burial at St Mary's Roman Catholic Cemetery in Kensal Green. Major D. R. McKinnon, his doctor, opined that it was 'none of my business whether Dr Barry was a male or a female'. He said he had wondered if 'he might be neither, viz. an imperfectly developed man…but whether Dr Barry was a male, female, or hermaphrodite I do not know.'

22

THE TEXAS REVOLUTION

San Jacinto, Texas, 21 April 1836. The ambush was brilliantly executed and devastatingly quick. Within just eighteen minutes of the first boom of the Texian cannon, the 1,400-strong Mexican army broke and ran. They did not get far. Most of the 650 Mexicans who died that day were gunned down by Sam Houston's blood-crazed riflemen as they desperately tried to cross the marsh to safety. 'Remember the Alamo,' roared the riflemen, over and over again, as they pulled their triggers. 'Me no Alamo,' the Mexicans pleaded, but to no avail. A further 350 Mexicans were captured, including – a day later – the generalissimo himself, Antonio López de Santa Anna, president of the Republic of Mexico, who narrowly escaped an on-the-spot execution. The Battle of San Jacinto marked the end of Mexican control of the old Spanish province and the birth of the Republic of Texas.

The Texas Revolution – including the legendary last stand at the Alamo – has always been an inherently American story. However, it is also an Irish one because Irish-born and Irish-descent soldiers had a greater impact on the success of the revolution than any other ethnic group. At least 100 of the 910 men who served under General Sam Houston at San Jacinto were born in Ireland, as were fifteen of the soldiers who died at the Alamo.

At the start of 1836, Texas was the northernmost province of the Mexican Republic, which had won independence from Spain in 1821. In order to combat the terrifying menace of Comanche raids in the region, Mexico had invited emigrants from the United States and Europe to settle the land. By 1834 there were almost 38,000 people in Texas, of whom less than 8,000 were of Mexican descent. The vast majority of these Texians, as they were originally known, were described as 'Anglo-Celtic', being of Irish or Scots-Irish origin. They sought to escape the oppression and drudgery of the Old World, and to take advantage of the fertile lands beyond the Appalachians.

Of these, Catholic Irish immigrants comprised the largest white ethnic group, including some of the original 'Old Three Hundred' who settled on Texas soil in the early 1820s, such as John Kelly and David Fitzgerald. One of the earliest Irish towns was Corrigan, established by Jeremiah O'Toole and James O'Reilly in 1835. Many more Texians were of Scots-Irish or Protestant Irish descent, such as Sam Houston, whose grandfather was born in Ballybracken, near Ballymena, in east County Antrim. Andrew Jackson, the president of the United States from 1829 to 1837, was himself the son of Presbyterian emigrants from County Antrim (p. 234). In July 1835, the first call to establish Texas as an independent state from Mexico was issued by Patrick Usher, an emigrant from County Cork. His appeal found favour among the Scots-Irish community, who refused to accept the governance of Santa Anna's Catholic-backed military dictatorship. The Protestants were also deeply hostile to the policies of Father Miguel Muldoon, a Cavan-born priest who had been appointed vicar general of all the foreign Catholic colonies in Texas in the early 1830s. In the words of Noah Smithwick, a Protestant blacksmith from North Carolina,

'Padre Muldoon' was 'a bigoted old Irishman with an unlimited capacity for drink'.

Some Irish Catholics agreed with Usher, comparing Santa Anna's Texan policy to Britain's subjugation of Ireland. However, others felt a kinship with the Mexicans, not least because of their shared faith.

Several of the most thriving colonies that had sprung up across Texas were established specifically for and by the Irish, such as San Patricio de Hibernia and Refugio. Founded by James McGloin, a Sligo man, and John McMullen, another Irishman, San Patricio benefited from the spiritual guidance of Galway-born Father John Thomas Molloy. North of San Patricio, Refugio almost exclusively comprised Catholics from southeast Ireland, including the colony's co-founders James Hewetson from Thomastown, County Kilkenny, and James Power of Ballygarrett, County Wexford. Emphasizing the link between the Irish and Texian fights for independence, James Power's older brother Pat was apparently killed fighting alongside Father John Murphy at the Battle Vinegar Hill in the 1798 Rebellion (p. 83). Another refugee from that rebellion was John Joseph Linn, the son of a college professor from Antrim who had fled to New York when the British declared him a traitor. The younger Linn, a prosperous merchant, was among the foremost Scots-Irish leaders of the Texas colony founded by the Mexican empresario (land agent) Martin de León.

Relations between the Mexican government and the Texian new-comers rapidly deteriorated, not least when the latter flouted the Mexican law against slavery. Hostilities flared up when the Texians pushed east and a war – the Texas Revolution – erupted. The first shot was fired on 2 October 1835 by Lieutenant Colonel James Clinton Neill, a seasoned Texian fighter of Scots-Irish ancestry, who sent an artillery shell made of nails and cut-up horseshoes hurtling into a unit of 100 uniformed Mexican dragoons near Gonzales, Texas, killing two. By Christmas, the Texians had driven the Mexicans out of the region.

On 20 December 1835, ninety-one men signed what became known as the Goliad Declaration of Independence at Presidio la Bahía, Goliad. At least forty-two of the signatories were Irish Catholics, primarily from Refugio, including Thomas O'Connor, a young Wexford immigrant who signed despite having been granted 1,792 hectares (4,428 acres) of prime land by the Mexican government. Nicholas Fagan, an Irish-born rancher who had previously lived in New York's notorious Five Points, then hoisted the flag of Texas Independence, which was modelled on the coat of arms of the O'Neills of Ulster.

Goliad was a lone outpost of independence at this time. Many of the Old Texians decried the radical undertones of the declaration and, having seemingly ousted the Mexicans, they now returned to their neglected farmsteads in east Texas to get on with the spring planting. In New York, investors on Wall Street began speculating on whether the corn could be harvested before Santa Anna's army marched north again.

Meanwhile, a series of outposts along the borders were assigned to the new Texian regular army, including the Alamo, which was placed under Neill's command. The Alamo was a sprawling, 1.2-hectare (3-acre) Franciscan mission, constructed of limestone and adobe. It had been converted into a military fort more than seventy years earlier on the orders of Dublin-born Hugh O'Conor, governor of the then Spanish province. Aptly described by one defender as 'old and grey and tumbling', it had little military or strategic value. As Neill drily observed, 'If there has ever been a dollar here I have no knowledge of it.'

Neill did what he could to shore up the Alamo's defences but his appeals to the dysfunctional Texian government for more supplies, clothing and, most pertinently, weaponry and munitions fell on deaf ears. On 14 January 1836, he warned Houston that his ever-weakening men were 'almost naked' and longing to abandon the fort. Moreover, several thousand Mexican soldiers were now gathering on the near horizons. Following the humiliating defeats of 1835, the Mexicans had united under Santa Anna, the self-styled 'Napoleon of the West', who vowed to reclaim Texas or lose Mexico. As his Secretary of War declared: 'Our soldiers ever aspire to shed the blood of foreigners who seek to take away from us our rights and menace our independence. This war is righteous and should be without remorse.'

Neill advised Houston that an attack was imminent but 'we know not what day, or hour'. The best Houston could do was to send in

Colonel Jim Bowie, the iconic knife-fighter, with twenty-five men as a back-up. Bowie was ordered to 'blow up the Alamo' if he felt it necessary, but he formed a strong bond with Neill and the duo pledged to 'die in these ditches' rather than surrender the post. Neill mounted an 18-pounder, his solitary cannon of merit, on the mission roof facing the direction of Santa Anna's men and waited.

The original Alamo garrison contained eighty men and boys, mostly young volunteers who had arrived into Texas at the tail end of the revolution, eager to fight for a share of lush, bountiful Texan soil. At least fifteen were Irishmen, such as Derry-born Robert Evans, the Alamo's thirty-six-year-old Master of the Ordnance, and Stephen Dennison, a landless twenty-four-year-old from Galway. The latter had come directly from New Orleans, the closest major city, into which an estimated 20,000 Irish emigrants had poured in 1836 alone. Other Irishmen included Samuel E. Burns, James McGee, Jackson J. Rusk and Burke Trammel. Many others were the sons of Irish immigrants or of Scots-Irish or Anglo-Irish descent, with names such as O'Neill, Nowlan, Navan, Carey, Jameson and Ryan.

In mid-February, Neill was obliged to leave the Alamo to attend to a family emergency. Command was assigned to William Barret 'Buck' Travis, a charming, heavy-drinking, womanizing Alabaman attorney in his mid-twenties. The garrison was further reinforced by the arrival of Davy Crockett, the revered Tennessee frontiersman, with ten more men. Crockett's father John was born either in Ireland or on board the ship that carried his mother to the United States. Their ancestor Antoine de Crocketagne was a French Huguenot who emigrated to Bantry, County Cork, shortened his name to Crockett and operated as a commercial agent for French mercantile firms. Davy Crockett's first wife Polly was likewise the daughter of 'an old Irish woman' by the name of Jean Kennedy Finley. On 22 February 1836, Crockett played the fiddle as the garrison enjoyed a raucous celebration of George Washington's birthday with hard liquor, song and senoritas from nearby San Antonio.

The following morning Santa Anna's army advanced towards 'that mob of ungrateful adventurers' and the siege began. Twelve long days would pass, during which Mexican cannons relentlessly pounded the Alamo. Travis penned a defiant letter addressed 'To the People of Texas and All Americans in the World' vowing, 'I shall never surrender or retreat.' However, his appeal for reinforcements met with silence. Unbeknown to the Alamo defenders, the delegates of the people of Texas had made their official Declaration of Independence during a convention at Washington-on-the-Brazos on 2 March 1836. Four of the signatories were Irish-born, including James Power of Refugio. The news of this declaration would do nothing to diminish Santa Anna's retribution on the defenders of the Alamo.

Within the mission, Robert Evans did what he could to keep morale steady with his indefatigable humour, but the only real cause for cheer came during the dark night of 1 March when thirty-two mounted volunteers from the Gonzales Ranging Company slipped into the fort, including Jesse McCoy, the sheriff of Gonzales, and Andrew Duvalt, a thirty-two-year-old plasterer from Ireland.

As darkness fell on the evening of 5 March, the Mexican cannons stopped and an eerie silence prevailed along the rolling grasslands of the San Antonio Valley. Santa Anna's cannons rolled into closer proximity as he relocated his troops and moved in for the kill. Just before the break of dawn on that ice-cold Sunday morning, the 5,000-strong Mexican army – including the elite Zapadores Battalion – attacked the Alamo simultaneously from all four sides. The entire garrison was wiped out, including Travis, Bowie and Crockett. Sergeant William B. Ward, the heavy-drinking Irishman who manned the artillery at the main gate, fell to the slashing bayonets, while Robert Evans, the blue-eyed Derryman, was shot down as he vainly tried to blow up the remaining gunpowder supplies in the Alamo's chapel.

Santa Anna's army then turned its sights on Goliad, obliging its garrison to abandon the town to rejoin Houston's army at Victoria. They had reached a place called Coleto Creek when the Mexicans caught up with them and, after heavy losses, the garrison surrendered on 20 March. On Palm Sunday, three weeks after the Alamo fell, over 400 of these 'Texan' prisoners were systematically executed by musket-fire on Santa Anna's orders. Many were Irishmen from the Catholic colonies of San Patricio de Hibernia and Refugio.

The massacre at Goliad was subsequently overshadowed by the dramatic showdown at the Alamo, possibly because those who died at Goliad were already somewhat ostracized from the Texians when they were massacred. Nonetheless, the two events galvanized the Texians to act and down their farming tools, take up arms and unite under Sam Houston's leadership for a war that culminated in their decisive victory on the sun-baked plains of San Jacinto in April 1836.

23
SIR GEORGE GORE, BUFFALO SLAYER

Fort Union, North Dakota, 1857. A frenzy of red flames crackled into the night sky while the men from the Fur Company watched in awe from the safety of their trading post. Through the haze they could see the silhouette of Sir George Gore's yellow carriage emblazoned in a halo of fire. All around the carriage, the inferno raged, consuming the Conestoga and freight wagons that had served Gore and his men for nearly three years. The fire engulfed nearly everything that the Irish peer owned. His violin, his library of classic novels, guide books and journals, his chronometer and sextant, his tents and his commode, the French carpets and rubber mats from his chamber, his pillows and blankets and the bedstead upon which he slept. Everything was reduced to ash.

It is not known what Sir George Gore was thinking as he watched the destruction of his worldly possessions. Perhaps the stout, balding, bewhiskered aristocrat was already regretting his actions. After all, he was the man who had started the fire. One thing was for sure – this was a dramatic finale to perhaps the most extravagant private hunting trip ever made. The tally of animals Gore killed is not something that would have impressed his young cousin Eva Gore-Booth, an early supporter of animal rights, or Eva's older sister, Constance Markievicz, later to become an ardent Irish Republican. Nor is his portrait likely to grace the wall of another kinsman, environmentalist and former US vice president Al Gore. Every family has its black sheep. If the Gore family had one, Sir George would have probably shot it.

St George Gore, as he was christened, was born in Sandymount on the south side of Dublin City on 28 April 1811. He descended from Sir Paul Gore, a wily Londoner who settled in Ireland in the early seventeenth century and was created Baron Gore, of Manor Gore (or Magherabegg) in the County of Donegal in 1622. One of Sir Paul Gore's great-grandsons served as Speaker of the Irish House of Commons in the 1730s. A generation later, the fabulously wealthy Sir Ralph Gore, a distinguished military commander (and prominent member of the Kildare Hunt), became Earl of Ross. When Lord Ross died without a son, his wealth and baronetcy passed to his nephew, another Ralph Gore. This young man married Lady Grace Maxwell, daughter of the 1st Earl of Farnham, and in 1842, their only son George succeeded as the 8th baronet.

Prior to this, the Oxford-educated Sir George Gore had managed the family estates in Ireland, which amounted to over 2,800 hectares (7,000 acres), including fifteen townlands in County Galway as well as other lands in Donegal, Limerick and Offaly. One of Gore's first moves after inheriting these lands was to abandon Ireland. Indeed, he was one of the worst types of absentee landlord, showing little mercy for his tenants when hunger and disease ravaged Ireland during the 1840s (p. 132). On Gore's orders, his agent Charles Cage continued to demand high rents throughout the famine period, which were completely disproportionate to the value of the land. Cage was also instructed to evict anyone unable to pay, felling their ramshackle abodes and clearing the lands. Some tenants were given money to pay their passage on an emigrant ship to America; others were simply herded off the estate to join the thousands of other dispossessed and famished souls wandering the countryside.

The collected rents were forwarded to Gore who, now living in England, used it to sustain a lavish lifestyle of fox hunting, fishing, shooting and hare coursing. He had his own pack of staghounds and bred several champion greyhounds; he won the prestigious Waterloo

Cup coursing classic two years in a row. He spent the long winter months fishing and duck shooting in Scotland, where he armed himself with a 2-m (7-ft)-long gun of exceptionally large bore. In the summers, he returned to the Scottish Highlands for grouse shoots and deer stalking; a loner, he was a lethal shot. Over three days in 1847, he killed twelve deer, six in a single day.

In October 1849, Charles Cage was assassinated as he rode his horse through Ferbane, County Offaly, and Gore was compelled to leave his hounds midway through the hare-coursing season to attend the funeral. This was a rare visit to his Irish lands and possibly his last.

Over the next five years Sir George Gore befriended Scottish hunter Sir William Drummond Stewart, who regaled him with stories of hunting buffalo and wild bear in the American prairies. Gore was seized with what the explorer Sir Richard Burton called 'prairie fever'. Accompanied by his valet, his personal servants, his gunsmith and his ghillie, he set sail for America. His party also included fifty of his finest hounds, who yapped all the way to the Mississippi, as well as their handler. When they reached St Louis, Missouri, Gore checked into a hotel, cashed a number of large Barings Bank drafts and began to buy wagons and provisions for his coming adventure.

His initial travelling companion was the future Earl of Fitzwilliam, one of the wealthiest men in Britain or Ireland, who frequently resided at his Irish home, Coolattin, in the southern foothills of the Wicklow Mountains. Fitzwilliam relished his relative anonymity in the Americas. In his homeland, deference to nobility was par for the course but, as Fitzwilliam later wrote, in the Far West, 'it does not matter what trade or profession a man is here.... Everybody is equal.'

Some were more equal than others. By the time Sir George Gore's entourage set off along the Oregon Trail a few weeks later, he had assembled twenty-one bright-red, two-wheeled carts – sixteen for his personal baggage – each hitched to six horses. There were also six heavy wagons pulled by oxen. One contained his armoury of seventy-five guns, including rifles, shotguns, revolvers and pistols manufactured by Joe Manton, Purdey, Westley Richards and other celebrated makers. Another held 3 tonnes of ammunition, while a third carried his fishing rods, lines, nets and hooks. Gore's own transport was a bright-yellow carriage that could be converted into a bed for sleeping. His private residence was a circular white and green striped tent, with a rubber mat unfurled beneath a French carpet on the ground. Heating was provided by a pair of stoves, one of which stood close to the fur-lined commode where he took a bath shortly after he arose at ten or eleven o'clock each morning.

As well as 50 servants (which by now included secretaries, a steward and several cooks) and his 50 hounds, there were 112 horses, 18 oxen, 40 mules and 3 milking cows. It must have been a staggering sight for the indigenous warriors who watched him coming. For the next three years, this enormous hunting party roamed through Wyoming, Colorado, Montana and the Dakotas as Gore laid waste to any wildlife he passed along the way.

After a late breakfast, he hunted nearly every day, accompanied by a small retinue of servants who carried his guns. If he was shooting fowl, a gunbearer stood close by, feeding him a continuous circle of fully loaded shotguns so he could blaze away without distraction. He became a master at killing, or 'running down', buffalo, for which he earned the name 'Buffalo Slayer'. He would often not return until ten o'clock at night and it was a rare occasion that he did not then instruct his servants to track down the beasts he had shot the following day in order to retrieve their skins, horns or antlers.

Despite being the only gentleman within several hundred miles, he was chary about making friends with any 'commoners'. The one exception was his American scout Jim Bridger who, generally suspicious of the upper classes, seems to have enjoyed Gore's company, commending him as a social companion and an agreeable gentleman. Bridger, who often dined with Sir George Gore, told how, after guzzling a couple of glasses of French wine, the aristocrat would pluck a book from his library – generally Shakespeare – and read some passages aloud, before asking Bridger his verdict on the tale. Bridger later surmised his thoughts on Falstaff to a journalist as follows: 'That thar big Dutchman Mr Full-stuff was a leetle bit too fond of lager beer.' Once he and Bridger had their fill of Shakespeare, Gore would turn in, sleeping snugly upon the down-feathers of his brass bedstead, breathing in the air that Sir Richard Burton eloquently described as 'brisk as a bottle of Veuve Clicquot'.

In the spring of 1857, Gore took a small hunting party some 480 km (300 miles) into the Black Hills in South Dakota. One morning they found themselves surrounded by a war party of 180 Lakota Sioux, who were by now fed up with Gore's ceaseless bloodlust. Their disdain for Gore echoed that of Alfred Vaughan, the Indian agent at Fort Union, who wrote to the Superintendent of Indian Affairs in St Louis decrying the 'killing and scattering of game vital to the sustenance of the red man, merely so the nobility might enjoy itself'.[1] The Lakota Sioux offered Gore a choice – remove your clothes and run away, or die immediately. He sagely stripped and ran, abandoning his remaining supplies. Along with his party, he spent the next five weeks plodding back to base, living on plants and the few animals they managed to trap en route.

When they reached the Fort Union trading station, he commissioned the construction of two boats, in return for which he offered his wagons and livestock. However, he became paranoid, perhaps correctly, that the boat builders were trying to overcharge him. Gore's anger brewed into a veritable rage and it was at this point that he assembled his caravan into one place and ordered his men to burn it all; rather than allow anyone at Fort Union to get hold of his animals, he simultaneously instructed his men to distribute his horses, oxen and cows among a number of white vagabonds and Native Americans living in the vicinity. When this was done, he boarded a flatboat with a handful of followers and made his way back to St Louis.

Among those who met him there was the military travel writer Randolph Barnes Marcy who, like Bridger, found Gore 'affable and communicative', although he was staggered by the 'enormous aggregate' of animals the aristocrat had slaughtered. Marcy concluded that Gore 'was one of those enthusiastic, ardent sportsmen who derived more real satisfaction and pleasure from one day's successful hunting than can possibly be imagined by those who have never participated in this exhilarating and healthful amusement'. He also considered that Gore was returning home much the better for his trip with 'a renovated constitution, good health and spirits, and a new lease of perhaps ten years to his life…he had seen something of life out of the ordinary beaten track of the great mass of other tourists'.

Gore managed to fit in one last fishing trip on the Saguenay in Quebec before the journey back to England. A social columnist for *Harper's Magazine*, who met him at this time, noted that they were 'received with great politeness at the door of the tent, and invited in to partake of some refreshments, after a huge dog and a ponderous stove had been expelled to allow free ingress [access] for the ample skirts of the ladies'.[2]

By the time he sailed east across the Atlantic, it is estimated that Gore had spent over $100,000, or about €5 million in today's currency. After his return, he does not seem to have spoken much of his time in America and never published any account of it. Nonetheless, the story of his three-year killing spree became the stuff of legends on both sides of the Atlantic, with the number of animals he is said to have killed being needlessly exaggerated. Gore's own tally listed 2,000 prairie buffalo, 1,600 deer and elk, as well as thousands of mountain sheep, coyotes and timber wolves. On a later visit to Florida, his prey would be birds and alligator.

Running low on funds, he placed his 3,600-hectare (9,000-acre) Irish estates up for sale in 1872. He died six years later, aged sixty-seven, and was succeeded in the baronetcy by a cousin. While the trigger-happy bachelor may have had no sons to carry his name onwards, he is nonetheless widely recalled in Colorado today, where Gore Pass, Gore Range, Gore Canyon, Gore Mountain, Gore Lake, Gore Creek, Gore Wilderness Area and, for a brief period, Gore City, were all named for him.

24

MARGARET OF NEW ORLEANS

New Orleans, Louisiana, 1862. Benjamin Franklin Butler is widely acknowledged to have been one of the most fearsome generals to serve in the Union Army during the American Civil War. However, even he had to concede that he might have met his match when a stocky, no-nonsense Irishwoman stormed into his tent in New Orleans. Since its capture on 1 May, General Butler's forces had secured the fallen Confederate city and yet somehow this lady had slipped out, taken a boat across Lake Pontchartrain and returned with a large cargo of flour for her bakery. Summoned to explain herself, she argued that the flour was to make bread for all of the hungry souls in the city, Confederate prisoner and Union soldier alike. Impressed by her defiance and resolve, the general granted her a pass to journey through enemy lines for the remainder of the occupation.

So runs one of the most popular legends about the woman variously known as 'Margaret of New Orleans', 'The Mother of Orphans', 'The Angel of the Delta' and 'The Bread Woman'. Whatever the truth of her breakout from the city, she was undoubtedly one of the most astounding characters to emerge from the Deep South during the long nineteenth century.

Margaret Haughery's story began in Tully, a lakeside townland near Carrigallen on the Leitrim-Longford border. She was born on Christmas Day 1813, the fifth of six children. William Gaffney, her father, juggled farming with tailoring and was, by one account, 'an uncompromising foe of Saxon rule'. Her first few years were spent sharing a mattress made of Leitrim rushes with her siblings and, most likely, a goat or a sow in the corner of the room.

In 1818, her father took the plunge and bought five tickets to America for himself, his wife and their three youngest children, including Margaret. The older siblings were to remain in Leitrim with an uncle until William Gaffney had made enough money to pay for their passage to join them. Circumstances would conspire to ensure that money never arrived.

After a hideous journey of nearly six months on board an overcrowded, typhus-riddled ship, the Gaffneys finally reached Chesapeake Bay, Maryland, but sadly baby Kathleen died shortly after they arrived in Baltimore, where William found work as a dockside carter. Further tragedy followed when both parents died of yellow fever in 1822. Margaret's older brother Kevin also disappeared at this time, never to be seen again. Everything that her family owned vanished too, incinerated in a bid to prevent yellow fever spreading.

Nine-year-old Margaret Gaffney was orphaned, alone and utterly destitute. Taken in by Helen Richards, a Welsh woman, she was put to work as a domestic servant. Almost nothing is known of the next thirteen years of her life, but in 1835 she married Charles Haughery, an immigrant from Cork. Suffering from poor health, possibly tuberculosis, Charles was advised by doctors to live near water. Two months after the wedding, he brought his bride south to New Orleans, by then one of the biggest port cities in the world.

The Haugherys were among more than 25,000 Irish that emigrated to New Orleans during the 1830s, but there had been an Irish presence in the city since its early days. With its French and Spanish colonial heritage, it was one of the few places in North America that genuinely welcomed Catholics. It became an especially attractive destination for Irish émigrés after the failure of the United Irishmen's rebellion of 1798. By 1806, there were enough Irish in New Orleans to justify a St Patrick's Day parade through the streets. True to form, the organizers raised seventeen 'official' toasts to mark the event.[1]

Margaret Haughery had been in New Orleans for less than two years when her life was again filled with sorrow. Her husband had sailed home to Cork, only to die soon after his arrival. She was left with their baby Frances, who appears to have succumbed to yellow fever soon afterwards. 'My God!', lamented the twenty-three-year-old to a family friend. 'Thou hast broken every tie: Thou hast stripped me of all. Again I am all alone.' And yet she was not someone who revelled in misery. On the contrary, this illiterate young widow slowly but assuredly channelled her time and energy in a direction that would convert her into one of the thriftiest entrepreneurs – and philanthropists – of her generation.

She was working as a laundress at the city's splendid new St Charles Hotel when she met with Father Mullen, the Irish priest who had officiated at Frances's funeral. She told him that all she wanted to do in life was to look after children. He brought her to see an orphanage run by the Sisters of Charity and introduced her to Sister Regis Barrett, the Mother Superior, who became a lifelong friend. Haughery instantly offered her services as a volunteer. When she subsequently learned that the orphans had gone without dinner the night before due to lack of funds, she promptly spent her washer-woman's wages on a lavish breakfast for all. Thereafter she donated most of her weekly pay to the orphanage. She also began pushing a rickety wheelbarrow around the streets, store to store, house to house, seeking donations of food, clothing and medical supplies for the youngsters. To complete this Dickensian picture, the orphans were often seen scampering alongside and helping to push her cart.

Over the coming decades, Margaret Haughery would be intricately involved in raising funds for the city's orphanages. New Orleans had many orphans, often the children of Irish immigrants who had flooded into the city following the Great Hunger (p. 132). By the early 1850s, the Irish constituted almost a quarter of its population. There was another spike in 1853 when yellow fever tore through New Orleans, killing over 8,000 and leaving many more dangerously ill. A sizeable number of those taken in by the orphanages actually had a surviving parent but were placed in care as a temporary measure while that parent sought to clamber out of economic crisis.

One of the Sisters of Charity's most remarkable fundraisers was a raffle in 1842 of a now-famous portrait of Margaret Haughery and two of the orphans by Neoclassical painter Jacques Amans. Having her portrait painted by such an eminent artist did much to boost Haughery's standing as a champion of charity among the citizens of the Big Easy. One prominent journalist applauded the way in which, despite all the 'milking…selling the milk, driving around the city on all kinds of errands, and performing most of the drudgery in the asylum besides', she was 'always cheerful, active and kind; beloved and respected by all who know her character and labors, as worthy and honest a woman as ever lived'.

Margaret Haughery may not have been able to read or write, but she was born with an innate entrepreneurial gift that was to prove the perfect complement to her growing flair for philanthropy. For instance, she deduced that the orphanage was spending a small fortune on buying milk for the girls. With memories of her Leitrim farm to the fore, she invested her money in two cows that she began milking herself. By 1852, she was running a forty-cow dairy on Seventh Street, selling milk directly to numerous households, as well as to the Catholic Church. The profits helped pay off a loan the Sisters of Charity had taken to build a new, larger purpose-built orphanage.

She began to buy property across New Orleans, and helped fund the construction of shelters for the indigent and homeless. More discomfiting, she appears to have concurred with the widespread practice of slavery in antebellum Louisiana and she bought at least six enslaved Africans.

Haughery also invested in a bakery on present-day South Peters Street. When the owner defaulted on numerous personal loans, she found herself taking up the reins. She renamed it 'Margaret Haughery – Bread and Cracker Baker' and, by 1868, she was running what is regarded as the first steam bakery in the South. She had an exceptional knack for the business, carefully ensuring that her ovens were always the most up-to-date and efficient models available. Assisted by Louise Jarboe, her intimate friend, she ensured the market price for her bread and biscuits stayed low, and also branched out into selling flour and macaroni.

One of her trump cards was working out how to keep her biscuits fresh for weeks on end, which greatly appealed to passengers preparing to embark on the long voyage from New Orleans to Europe. To seal the deal, she ensured her cakes, crackers and cookies were all tied up in beautifully presented packages. She was also astute enough to take out patents on her bake ovens and did not baulk at bringing lawsuits and injunctions against the male-dominated merchant community when they tried to encroach on her business.

Such savvy behaviour saw her bakery flourish into one of the largest in the United States and yet she always remained true to her humble roots. The Bread Lady, as she was now known, was often seen delivering bread to the city's poor. To prevent drunkards and crafty street-children from reselling it, she broke each loaf into pieces. This routine continued unabated until her flour supplies ran out during the Union Army's occupation of New Orleans in the Civil War, which is when she reputedly broke through General 'Beast' Butler's curfew to fetch fresh flour supplies. Whether she really shouted Butler down so brazenly is unknown, but she certainly did not shy away from asking his officers to donate some of their wages to her orphanages, which were at maximum capacity on account of the war. To the officers' credit, they appear to have contributed generously.

Margaret Haughery continued to be one of the best-loved characters in New Orleans until her death aged sixty-nine in 1882. 'No woman has been borne to the tomb within the limits of New Orleans who was more generally respected and loved,' declared *The Picayune*, the city's foremost newspaper, which put her obituary on the front page, bordered in black, beneath the heading, 'Our Margaret'. She was honoured with a state funeral and the city shut down for the day. Her pallbearers included two governors and the city mayor, who carried her coffin out of St Patrick's Church, the city's most prestigious Irish church completed just before her arrival in New Orleans nearly half a century earlier. In her will, which she signed with an 'X', she left an estate of $50,000 ($1.3 million today) as well as her share in the bakery to various orphanages and charities.

In 1884 she became only the second woman in US history to be honoured with a public monument. Located in a small park near St Theresa's orphanage, the life-sized Carrara marble statue was refurbished in the wake of Hurricane Katrina in 2005. Elevated skywards, it depicts her as a stout, elderly, bonneted woman with a motherly arm around an affectionate young girl. The plaque beneath it is inscribed with a single word, 'Margaret'. For the citizens of New Orleans in 1884, no further explanation was necessary.

25

CHILDREN OF
THE GREAT HUNGER

Before the emigrant is a week at sea, he is an altered man.
How can it be otherwise? Hundreds of poor people, men,
women and children, of all ages from the drivelling idiot
of 90 to the babe just born; huddled together, without
light, without air, wallowing in filth, and breathing a fetid
atmosphere, sick in body, dispirited in heart.

STEPHEN DE VERE, REPORT ON AN 1847 VOYAGE

Ireland, 1845–50. In 1845, a fungal blight of the potato crop triggered the Great Hunger, also known as the Famine, the most cataclysmic event in recent Irish history. A million Irish people are said to have died of disease and malnutrition over the next five or six years. However, the seminal legacy of this horrific era was encapsulated by the mass exodus of almost as many men, women and children from Ireland during the same time period. Nearly a quarter of a million people emigrated in 1847 alone.

Most fled to Britain, where the census recorded approximately 400,000 Irish-born residents by 1851, primarily living around the port cities of Liverpool, Glasgow and London. Huge numbers braved the Atlantic and set their sights on North America. The cheapest tickets were to the Canadian port of Quebec, although perhaps as many as 90,000 sailed on assisted-passage schemes, whereby their landlords effectively paid to get them away from the country.

Some of these schemes were deeply flawed, most memorably that of Major Mahon of Strokestown, County Roscommon, who arranged for 1,490 of his tenants to sail from Liverpool to America. The vessels on which they travelled became known as 'coffin ships' because they were overrun with typhus, or 'famine fever' (p. 146). Almost half of the passengers died aboard ship or in the quarantine sheds at Grosse Île, an island 32 km (20 miles) east of Quebec.

Major Mahon was held accountable for their deaths and shot dead with a blunderbuss near his home.

The fate of the Strokestown emigrants was by no means unique. One in five of nearly 100,000 emigrants who sailed for Quebec in 1847 died either on the voyage or at Grosse Île. Among those buried on the island was Clonakilty-born Thomasine Ford, who had sailed from Cobh in County Cork with her husband John and six children but succumbed to fever en route. John Ford made his way to Michigan and acquired a farm amid the pine forests of Dearborn, near Detroit. His oldest son Billy helped to run the farm and married an orphaned Belgian girl who had been raised by a neighbouring farmer, Cork-born Patrick O'Hern and his wife Margaret.

Billy Ford's firstborn son Henry is a man whose racist, anti-Semitic character does not hold up well in the present age. Nonetheless, he was one of the most influential figures in US history, not only establishing the Ford Motor Company but also pioneering the use of assembly lines in the mass production of cars. Indeed, he had the concept down to such an art that a Model T automobile could be built from scratch in ninety-eight minutes. He also raised workers' wages and lowered costs across the United States and, as such, is sometimes credited with creating the American middle class.

In January 1847, the population of Toronto was 20,000; by the close of the year it had trebled to 60,000. The vast majority of newcomers were refugees from Ireland, such as ten-year-old Mary Harris and her father, Richard, a railway labourer from Cork. She was to experience considerable hardship between 1867 and 1871 with the loss of her husband and all four of their children to a yellow fever epidemic in Memphis, and then the destruction of her seam-stress enterprise during the Great Chicago Fire. She survived and by the 1890s had become one of the most celebrated champions of socialism in America. Known as Mother Jones, she was especially popular in West Virginia, Colorado and Pennsylvania, where she organized mass rallies of women and children in support of strik-ing coalminers, as well as the mass delivery of farm produce to the strikers' camps. 'Pray for the dead, and fight like hell for the living' was her battle cry.

In 1903 she led a 'children's crusade' on a 145-km (90-mile) march from Philadelphia to President Roosevelt's summer home on Long Island in protest against child labour. Variously described as 'the most dangerous woman in America' and 'the grandmother of all agitators', she was arrested and imprisoned on numerous occasions but remained active in the labour movement until her death in her nineties in 1930. Steelworkers, textile workers, unskilled labourers and Mexican revolutionaries alike were among other downtrodden souls who benefited from her support. Her name is now enshrined as a symbol for feminists and the radical left, as well as in *Mother Jones* magazine.

Mother Jones was clearly made of tough material but arriving into Toronto seems to have offered a marginally easier route for Irish emigrants than that faced by the tens of thousands who streamed into New York during the famine years. A census of Manhattan taken in 1855 revealed that over 25 per cent of its population was Irish born, with an equal ratio of men and women. Many lived in the ramshackle tenements of Five Points, so violently depicted in Martin Scorsese's *Gangs of New York*. Among them was seventeen-year-old Catherine Devine, later recalled as a 'jolly Irish lady, full of fun and mischief', who arrived on board the *Devonshire* in 1846.

Two decades later, Catherine relocated via Indiana and Kansas to New Mexico with her young son Henry McCarty, his father being deceased, and married a silver miner by the name of William Antrim. When she died of tuberculosis in 1874, young Henry began to master the arts of cattle rustling, gambling and pistol-packing, as well as fluent Spanish and croquet. He shot his first man dead at the age of seventeen, a bar-room bully called Frank 'Windy' Cahill who was apparently from Galway City.

At about this time, Henry changed his name to William H. Bonney and so the legend of Billy the Kid was born. By the time he was gunned down by Sheriff Pat Garrett in 1881, he is thought to have killed eight men, although posterity often credits him with twenty-one, one for every year of his short life. Most of his victims worked for Galway-born James Dolan and Wexford-born Lawrence Murphy, the unscrupulous beef barons who had arranged the murder of John Henry Tunstall, a London-born rancher whom Billy the Kid had greatly admired.

Another son of Five Points was 'Big Tim' Sullivan, whose father Daniel emigrated from Kenmare, County Kerry, during the famine. Daniel served in the Union Army during the American Civil War but died of typhoid in 1867. Left to fund his family, young Tim started off shining shoes and selling newspapers. By the 1890s, he was one of the most powerful figures in New York. He served three years in Congress and two terms as a senator, all on a Democratic ticket, advocating shorter working hours for women, better conditions for workhorses and an act of gun control legislation that became known as Sullivan's Law.

Meanwhile, the Tammany Hall boss continued to rake in the dollars through his various real estate, theatre, boxing and horserac- ing ventures, not to mention his robust links with organized crime, the New York City Police Department, prostitution, gambling and high-ranking politics. He pumped a good deal of his wealth into looking after his constituents – handing out food, coal and clothes in winter, and hosting large picnics in the summer. His mental health declined in later life and he was found dead on a railway track in the Bronx in 1913. Over 25,000 people turned out for his funeral at St Patrick's Old Cathedral.

Daniel O'Sullivan, Big Tim's father, was one of nearly 200,000 Irishmen who fought in the Civil War. Like him, many had arrived into America during the Great Hunger era. Most fought for the Union Army but at least 20,000 served with the Confederacy, including Galway-born Dick Dowling, who grew up on a 38-hectare (93-acre) farm near Milltown, County Galway. When the farm was unable to provide a living for the family, his parents found themselves in the Tuam workhouse, but somehow they managed to send their eleven-year-old son and one of his sisters to New Orleans in 1846.

Dick Dowling later moved to Houston, Texas, where he started a property business, bought a half-share in a steamboat and ran 'The Bank of Bacchus', a popular hub for Irish dockers and railroad workers. He subsequently held shares in what is believed to have been the first oil company in Texas. During the Civil War, he became a hero across the South for his brilliant leadership when he utterly destroyed an attempt by the Union Army to invade Texas via the Sabine Pass.

Dowling was a sympathizer, if not a member, of the Fenian Brotherhood, a republican organization established by Irish exiles in New York in 1858 and named for a band of warriors from Irish mythology. The Fenians' primary objective was to establish Ireland as an 'independent democratic republic' – by armed revolution if need be. They were closely entwined with the secret, oath-bound Irish Republican Brotherhood (IRB; p. 221). In April 1866, the Fenians launched a series of raids against various army depots and custom ports in British Canada. The raids had petered out by June when Patrick Condon, inspector general of the IRB, visited Houston and stayed at Dowling's house. Indeed, Dowling may well have played a much greater role in the Fenian story had he not contracted yellow fever and died in 1867.

The citizens of Houston named a street in the Third Ward in his memory, while nearby Tuam Street was named after the Galway town where he had once lived. In 1905, he was commemorated with the first publicly financed monument in Houston – a white Carrara marble statue that was originally installed in front of the city's Market House but later moved to Hermann Park. Ultimately, his support for the Confederacy would serve against him: Dowling Street was renamed Emancipation Avenue in 2017, while his statue was removed in the wake of the George Floyd protests in June 2020.

By 1849, the Irish were the largest ethnic population in Boston, Massachusetts. Among the city's 'famine children' was Timothy Deasy, a six-year-old from Clonakilty, County Cork, whose family initially lived at nearby Lawrence. Having served with the Union Army during the Civil War, Deasy joined the Fenians and was sent to Ireland in June 1865 to help plan a rising in the island against British rule. He served on the IRB's military council and played a key role in organizing James Stephens's escape from Richmond jail in England that autumn. Upon his return to the United States, he offered advice ahead of the disastrous Fenian invasion of Canada in 1866.

Another Atlantic journey brought Deasy to England to serve as second-in-command during an abortive Fenian raid on Chester Castle in February 1867. His precise role in the Fenian Rising in Ireland the next month is unclear, but he was arrested in Manchester only to be freed by his fellow Fenians while in transit to the county jail. The killing of a police sergeant during the operation led to the infamous hanging of three of his rescuers, the 'Manchester Martyrs'. In later life, Deasy became less radical and sought to improve the status of the Irish in the United States as a politician, serving alongside P. J. Kennedy (p. 239) in the Massachusetts House of Representatives. He died, unmarried, in 1880.

One of Deasy's comrades in the Fenian Rising was Thomas Francis Bourke from Fethard, County Tipperary. In 1852, the twelve-year-old Bourke had emigrated to America with his family. A house painter by profession, the premature death of his father meant he was soon the Bourkes' principal income earner. Based in New Orleans when the Civil War broke out, he joined the Confederate Army, either for the pay or for the adventure, not because he was a big supporter of the cause. Badly shot in the thigh at the Battle of Gettysburg in 1863, he spent the remainder of the war in prison.

Bourke subsequently became foreman in one of New York's largest painting firms but quit to become a full-time recruiter, fundraiser and organizer of the Fenian Brotherhood in Manhattan. In 1867 he returned to Ireland to participate in the Fenian Rising but was captured and tried for high treason in Dublin. His speech from the dock was hailed by many as the best since that impromptu tour de force delivered by the Irish nationalist Robert Emmet the day before he was hanged in 1803 for leading his failed rising against the British authorities. Bourke's words may have been impressive but he, like Emmet, was nonetheless found guilty and condemned to death.

Following appeals from Cardinal Paul Cullen and the US president Andrew Johnson, his sentence was commuted to penal servitude for life. Released on amnesty in 1871, he returned to America where he played a key role in healing the divisions in Fenianism. He later transferred his allegiance to Clan na Gael, the spiritual successor to the Fenian Brotherhood, and was appointed a trustee of the Clan's 'skirmishing fund', which sponsored John Philip Holland's submarine (p. 161). He died in New York in 1889.

The impact of the Great Hunger was not only felt in Britain and North America. In 1848, for example, Earl Grey, Britain's Secretary of State for the Colonies, initiated an assisted emigration scheme that brought 4,175 Irish teenage girls on a 19,300-km (12,000-mile) journey to Australia over the next two years. Known to posterity as Earl Grey's orphans, most of these 'rosy-cheeked' girls had fetched up in Irish workhouses in the wake of the potato blight.

The scheme was partly conceived as a way to rescue them from those cold, overcrowded, disease-riddled death-traps. However, the principal purpose of transporting so many unmarried young women to Australia was to redress the imbalance of the sexes in the colony, where men heavily outnumbered women. A tour of workhouses duly commenced as Earl Grey's scouts sought out 'morally pure' girls aged between fourteen and eighteen, ideally with the skills of domestic service and the ability to read and write. As part of their travelling package, each girl was supplied with flannel petticoats, stockings, shifts, shoes and aprons, as well as a box with a lock, a key and their name painted on the front.

The voyage to Australia took between three and four months. Upon arrival, the young women were by no means welcomed with open arms. Many of the earlier Australian settlers were all too willing to accept the sweeping statement of a disgruntled surgeon who, having sailed into Sydney on a ship with 185 Belfast orphans, described them as 'barefooted little country beggars, swept from the streets into the workhouse...notoriously bad in every sense of the word.' As more of these fertile Catholic teenagers arrived on Australian shores, the colonial press became especially hostile. 'Hordes of useless trollops, thrust upon an unwilling community,' sneered the openly sectarian *Melbourne Argus*. 'We are being inundated with Irish paupers,' concurred the *Sydney Morning Herald*.

After the grim drudgery of the Irish workhouse, life in Australia was to prove no less horrific for some of these adolescents, who were subjected to sexual abuse and exploitation. At least one was murdered, while others committed suicide, succumbed to alcoholism or died in childbirth. And yet there were also those for whom the scheme afforded a lifeline to an infinitely better future than the workhouse. Ellen Parks from Belfast enjoyed a happy marriage to George Clarke, a prosperous, London-born oyster merchant and restaurateur in Sydney. Others also found themselves in a better world, rising into a middle class that thrived in the lengthy boom generated by the gold rushes of the 1850s.

Catherine Hart, who arrived from Galway aged seventeen in 1850 was married to a settler from Gundagai, New South Wales, within two years. She subsequently eloped with a well-to-do Tasmanian settler by the name of Cornelius Kerrison, with whom she had eleven children. It is thought that she and her sisters had been looked after by the Sisters of Charity in Clarinbridge, County Galway, before they left for Australia. If so, she never forgot the sisters and she donated to their convent in Ballaghaderreen, County Roscommon, from at least 1891. In 1899, Catherine became one of the few Earl Grey orphans to return 'home', visiting Ballaghaderreen, as well as the Lakes of Killarney and her home county of Galway.

Among the most successful descendants of the Earl Grey orphans is the singer and actress Mandy Moore, who was awarded a star on the Hollywood Walk of Fame in 2019 for her work in such productions as the Disney film *Tangled* and NBC's comedy-drama series, *This Is Us*. In 2018, she was the subject of an episode of *Who Do You Think You Are?*, in which I was recruited to reveal how her great-great-grandmother Ellen Flynn had been taken out of the workhouse in Cashel, County Tipperary, aged fifteen, and dispatched to Australia in 1849. She was understandably much moved to learn of such events.

26

LITTLE AL CASHIER

Mississippi, 1863. The men of G Company in the 95th Illinois Voluntary Infantry must have cheered loudly as 'Little Al' Cashier clambered up the tree, pulled off the tattered, gun-shot Union flag and hoisted a new one, or perhaps they held back their applause until he was down again, safely out of sight of the Confederate snipers. Either way, all were agreed that Little Al was as courageous a soldier as any of them.

A third of G Company were dead by the end of the American Civil War, killed in action or prey to the virulent diseases that swept the lines. Far fewer were still alive in 1913, nearly fifty years later, when word reached them that Little Al had been incarcerated in a state psychiatric institution. That might have been shocking enough but an infinitely greater surprise was in store; it transpired that Private Albert Cashier from Ireland had been born a woman.

Mary Hodgers was born in Clogherhead, County Louth, on Christmas Day 1843, the second daughter of Denis Hodgers, a tenant farmer, and his wife, Catherine Maguire. He appears to have spoken, or certainly understood, Irish in later life, indicating that the Hodgers were bilingual in Irish and English.*** Any further details about his early life are as yet unknown, but it is assumed that he was illiterate as he signed all identified documents with an 'X'. Nor do we know when Hodgers emigrated to America. It is believed he arrived as a stowaway, quite possibly direct from the port in Drogheda or via Liverpool. His emigration came in the wake of a long, lean period in and around Clogherhead. One theory holds that he went to work at an all-male shoe factory in Belvidere, Illinois, which was run by an uncle, and that it was from this point that he began identifying as Albert Cashier.

By the summer of 1862, the American Civil War was in progress and Congress authorized the drafting of a new militia for the Union Army. Over 144,000 Irish answered the call, including twenty-year-old Cashier, who went into the recruiting depot at Belvidere on 6 August 1862 and enlisted in the 95th Illinois under the name of Albert D. J. Cashier. Nobody suspected a thing; Captain Elliot Bush, his company commander, merely noted that the 1.6-m (5-ft 3-in) private was the smallest of the new recruits. Cashier was among at least 400 women who dressed in the baggy clothes of a soldier and served during the Civil War. He is also believed to be the only one who survived the entire war, undiscovered, and who consequently went on to receive a military pension.

***

*** As Albert Cashier (Mary Hodgers) identified as a man, male pronouns have been used throughout this account.

One can only speculate at Cashier's motives for joining the army: it offered a reasonable salary and the prospect of a decent pension. His motives for reinvention are likewise unknown, although several of his neighbours in later life maintained that he had been following a sweetheart who was subsequently killed.

'Little Al' Cashier, as his comrades nicknamed him, managed to keep his secret for fifty years. After the truth became known, surviving testimonies of fellow soldiers in G Company reveal that they just thought him aloof and a little feminine. 'We never suspected that "Albert" was not a man,' remarked Corporal Robert Horan of G Company. 'But we did think sometimes that she acted more like a woman than a man. For one thing, she always insisted on bunking by herself. And she did [lots] of washing for the boys – she used to wash our shirts. When the strangeness wore away she made a good comrade. She was a soldier with us, doing faithfully and well.'[1] Corporal J. H. Himes of the same company concurred: 'I never suspected anything of that kind…. Albert D. J. Cashier was very quiet in her manner and she was not easy to get acquainted with. I rather think she did not take part in any of the sports and games.'[2]

It was Charles W. Ives, his company sergeant, who recalled how Little Al Cashier hoisted the Union flag despite the high risk of being shot by a sniper. On another occasion, the blue-eyed, auburn-haired soldier leapt onto a fallen tree-trunk and began jeering at his Confederate opponents on the other side of the battlefield. 'Al did all the regular duties,' Sergeant Ives recalled. 'Not knowing that she was a girl, I assigned her to picket duty and to carry water just as all the men did. One time, we went into barracks…. All of the bunks were double, but over in one corner there was a single cot. Cashier asked me if he might have the cot. I consented and thought nothing of it.'[3]

Cashier often sat apart from the others, puffing on a pipe. On account of his short stature, he wasn't able to carry as much as other men, but his fellow soldiers never failed to help out, in return for which he looked after the laundry and mended their clothes. By the time he was discharged from the army on 17 August 1865, Albert Cashier had travelled nearly 16,000 km (10,000 miles), including 2,900 km (1,800 miles) on foot. He had seen action in forty different battles and skirmishes in states such as Mississippi, Louisiana, Missouri and Tennessee. This included the Red River Campaign, the Battle of Atlanta and the Battle of Guntown, Mississippi, in which Captain Bush and many other members of his regiment were killed.

He also served at the Siege of Vicksburg in 1863, where he was briefly captured by a Confederate soldier but somehow managed to grab his opponent's gun, knock him down and bolt back to his own lines. When Vicksburg fell, he was one of the first to victoriously march into the Mississippi city. Private Albert Cashier's name is among 36,325 Illinois soldiers immortalized on the bronze plaques at the elaborate Illinois victory monument in Vicksburg.

After the war, Albert Cashier continued to identify as a man for the remainder of his life. As such, he is considered one of the earliest examples of a transgender person in American history. By 1868 he had moved to the small village of Saunemin, Illinois, southwest of Chicago, where he worked as a general handyman, gardener, janitor, lamplighter and, later, chauffeur. As a man, he had the advantage of being able to open a bank account and vote, long before women had such a privilege; presumably, his military papers sufficed for identification purposes. He worked closely with the Chesebro family, who paid for the construction of his small timber home; a replica now stands on the site and is an increasingly popular tourist destination.

He also joined the Grand Army of the Republic, an organization of Union Veterans, enabling him to reunite with his comrades from the 95th, which he frequently did in ensuing decades. As one Saunemin citizen recalled: 'On Decoration Day [Cashier] always wore his uniform and led the parade, proudly carrying the big flag as slight as he was. He was in his glory when he did that.' Another neighbour appears to have been a little charier: 'Many times he came to our place to stay a while, and he could rock my baby daughter to sleep better than we could. He would go uptown and bring him the most beautiful things, such as dress goods. We always wondered where he got such a feminine taste.'

In 1911, Albert Cashier was fixing a car for former State Senator Ira M. Lish when the latter accidentally drove over him and fractured his leg. He was taken to the Soldiers' and Sailors' Home in Quincy, Illinois, where his anatomical sex was revealed. Father P. D. Curran, the retirement home's chaplain, was a native of Ballyconnell, County Cavan. When he went to see his wounded compatriot, Cashier began 'rambling' and confided that his name was 'Jennie Hodgers from Clogherhead, Ireland'. (It is unclear why he gave the name Jennie when he was christened Mary.)

Senator Lish, Father Curran and Dr Leroy Scott, the doctor at the home, agreed to keep the information secret but slowly it leaked out and by 1913 the extraordinary story had been disclosed to the world, including the Irish press. Father Curran did what he could to set the record straight, writing a letter that was published in the *Anglo-Celt*, a Cavan newspaper, in which he compassionately observed: 'She wanted to be a man, and because Nature cheated her of this privilege she did the next best thing, disguised as a man, so she could do a man's work, lead a man's life and be a man in everything, but sex.'

The news caused much astonishment among the surviving members of the battalion. They had frequently mocked Private Cashier for his lack of facial hair and compact height but none appear to have suspected the truth. More importantly, they were unanimous in their support, hailing his courage throughout the war and applying so much pressure that the Bureau of Pensions concluded that there was no option but to continue paying his $12 a month pension.

Sadly, Albert Cashier's mind was in rapid decline, possibly triggered by the trauma of the accident and the global fascination in his secret. In March 1914, the County Court diagnosed him with advanced dementia and sent him to reside at the Watertown State Hospital in East Moline, Illinois. He was placed in a female ward and ordered to wear a dress. The hospital recorded his condition on arrival as 'no memory, noisy at times, poor sleeper and feeble'.[4] Corporal Robert Horan was sceptical about the hospital's motives; 'they don't care for Cashier, it's his money there [sic] after'.[5]

When former Sergeant C. W. Ives visited, he remarked: 'I left Cashier a fearless boy of 22...when I went to Watertown, I found... a frail woman of 70, broken because, on discovery, he was compelled to put on skirts.' It is notable that his former comrades-in-arms, born in the 1830s, evidently had a much more open-minded and accurate understanding of Cashier's gender identity than the Watertown doctors who insisted he wore a dress during the last years of his life. When a correspondent from the *Hartford Republican* visited him, he described 'a face for a painter to dwell on; half a century of sun and wind had bronzed that face, sowed it with freckles and seamed it with a thousand wrinkles'.

Little Al Cashier died aged seventy-two on 10 October 1915. He was given a funeral with full military honours in East Moline before his body was shipped back to Saunemin, where he was buried in a space the Chesebro family had reserved for him in their plot. The headstone reads: 'Albert D J Cashier, Co. G 95 ILL. Inf, Civil War. Born Jennie Hodgers in Clogher Head, Ireland 1843–1915.'

His death was reported in the Irish press, with a request that stated: 'If there are any friends of the old lady still about Clogherhead, they should forward the particulars of their relationship to Mr J. E. Andrews, Superintendent of the Soldiers' and Sailors' Home, Illinois, as he left considerable property and money behind him.'

Despite this succulent offer, no relatives stepped forward.

27

THOMAS D'ARCY MCGEE, FATHER OF THE CANADIAN CONFEDERATION

Ottawa, Canada, 7 April 1868. Shortly after midnight on that ice-cold night, Thomas D'Arcy McGee, one of the brightest lights in Canadian politics, inserted his key into the door of Mrs Trotter's boarding house on Sparks Street. As he puffed on his cigar, the forty-two-year-old was looking forward to a good night's sleep after a particularly long day of parliamentary debates. At the very moment that he stepped through the door, there was a flash of light and a .32 calibre bullet slammed into his neck. McGee's cigar and dentures flew from his mouth and the 'Father of the Canadian Confederation' crumpled into the snow.

The assassination of McGee was to become the greatest *cause célèbre* in both Canada and Ireland in 1868. Regarded by some as the greatest Irishman in Canadian history, he had certainly achieved an enormous amount since his arrival in North America as a teenager. He had also been a household name – certainly in Irish nationalist circles – ever since a warrant was issued for his arrest during the Young Ireland rebellion of 1848.

Born in Carlingford, County Louth, on 13 April 1825, Thomas D'Arcy McGee moved to Garron Point, County Antrim, at the age of three to reunite with his father James, a Catholic, who worked as a tidewaiter with the customs and excise service in Cushendall. His early education was provided by his beloved mother Dorcas, the daughter of a Dublin bookseller who had been embroiled in the United Irishmen's rebellion of 1798. 'She instilled in my mind a love of poetry, and for the old legends of my native land,' he would later recall. The family were devastated by her untimely death in a carriage accident when McGee was only eight years old. By then, the family were living in Wexford, where his father was now working as an excise officer.

The income enabled James McGee to send his son to a pay-school run by Michael Donnelly, whose father had been hanged in 1798. Here the youngster became Donnelly's star pupil, soaking up further tales of British oppression and learning ballads about heroic Wexford rebels. Such education took place in an age when all talk was of Father Theobald Mathew's temperance movement and Daniel O'Connell's campaign to repeal the Act of Union, which had shifted the principal stage of Irish politics from Dublin to London in 1801. Meanwhile, there was further sorrow for McGee with the death of his older sisters Mary and Betsy in 1839 and 1841 respectively. His brother also died young.

In 1842 seventeen-year-old McGee sailed for the United States from Wexford on board the brig *Leo*. During the voyage he penned a number of poems about Ireland, which helped secure him work as an assistant editor of the *Boston Pilot*, one of the principal Catholic newspapers in America. By 1844 he was its lead editor, a remarkable position of responsibility given that he was still a teenager at the time. His articles focused on Ireland's right to self-determination, as espoused by O'Connell, while also insisting that Britain should cede control of Canada to the United States 'either by purchase, conquest, or stipulation'. O'Connell heartily applauded these 'inspired utterances of a young exiled boy in America'.

McGee returned to Ireland on the eve of the Great Hunger (p. 132), initially to work as parliamentary correspondent for the *Freeman's Journal*. He then joined the dynamic team who ran *The Nation*, Ireland's leading nationalist newspaper. He was one of its few writers who had not been educated at Trinity College Dublin and also one of its more moderate voices, a characteristic he shared with Charles Gavan Duffy, who would go on to become premier of Victoria, Australia. Such restraint earned the wrath of John Mitchell, the paper's most firebrand writer, who castigated both McGee and Duffy as 'rosewater revolutionists'.

In 1847, McGee married Mary Theresa Caffrey, a Dubliner, with whom he had six children. That same year he was present when the Young Ireland nationalists founded the Irish Confederation in Dublin, vowing 'to drill, seek arms, march and eventually attempt a rebellion', and McGee was appointed the Confederation's secretary. Horrified by the effects of starvation and disease that ripped into Ireland in 1847, he declared in a speech to the Confederation on St Patrick's Day, 1848:

> *My heart is sick at daily scenes of misery. The towns have become one universal poorhouse and fever shed, the country one great grave-yard. The survivors of the famine and pestilence have fled to the sea-coast and embarked for America, with disease festering in their blood. They have lost sight of Ireland, and the ships that bore them have become sailing coffins, and carried them to a new world, indeed; not to America, but to eternity!*

With these lines, McGee introduced the new term 'coffin ship' to the debates then raging about the state of Ireland (p. 132).

When Europe exploded into revolution in the spring of 1848, the Young Irelanders were swept up in the tsunami of rebellious passion.

On 14 July, McGee was arrested for making a seditious speech in Roundwood, County Wicklow. Released on bail, he went to Scotland to muster recruits, arms and ammunition. His plan was to bring these into Sligo Bay to ignite a rising in the northwest. However, the mission proved a dismal failure and McGee went on the run dressed as a priest. Meanwhile, the rest of the Young Irelanders launched their equally unsuccessful rebellion at Ballingarry, County Tipperary, on 29 July. Outlawed, with a £300 price on his head, McGee made his way to Tremone Bay, County Donegal, where he boarded a ship bound for Philadelphia. 'I am not at all ashamed of Young Ireland,' McGee would say in later life. 'Politically we were a pack of fools, but we were honest in our folly.'

By 1850, the 'short and stubby' young man was one of the best-known figures in the Irish-American community in the United States. He had established two newspapers, the *New York Nation* and Boston's *American Celt*, both of which he also edited. His disposition to promote social welfare was in full flow: he tried but failed to spearhead a campaign to move immigrants out from the 'big city' slums to new suburban villages and he developed a series of night schools to help people attain better education. As well as his poetry and pamphlets, he also found time to pen two pioneering works, *A History of the Irish Settlers in North America* (1850) and *The Catholic History of North America* (1855).

McGee's ambition had been to garner support for Irish independence from the Irish diaspora but, perhaps triggered by the failure of the Irish-American elite to rally behind him, a profound change of direction gradually took place within his mind. As a devout Catholic, he was increasingly dismayed at how Irish Catholics were clearly doomed to be eternal underdogs in the United States. The omnipresent red tape of bureaucracy also caused him considerable disillusion. He became an ardent critic of America with its aggressive expansionism, republican proselytizing and materialistic way of life.

His private life was also challenging. He was drinking heavily and three of his children died prematurely in the 1850s, but despite this, he managed to retain a tender relationship with his long-suffering wife. In 1857, fed up with the 'American Dream', McGee took his surviving family across the border into Canada, which was then made up of the British provinces of Ontario and Quebec. They settled in Montreal, where one-third of the city's 70,000 inhabitants were Irish Catholics, and he established another newspaper, the *New Era*. Through this, and accompanying pamphlets, he advocated his opinions, which, by now, had hardened into those of a Catholic Conservative.

Within a year, the journalist-turned-orator had won a seat as an independent MP in the Legislative Assembly of the Province of Canada (akin to Ireland's Dáil Éireann or the United Kingdom's House of Commons). He made his mark defending the rights of Irish Catholics in the face of Canada's powerful Orange Order and did much to promote reconciliation between the two sides. An enthusiast for modernization, he supported the manufacturing industry (through a high protective tariff) and railway construction.

A brilliant public speaker, McGee was the most popular lecturer in Canada during the 1860s, wooing vast crowds with his melodious voice and evocative language, and it brought him both wealth and fame. He generally spoke on uncontentious issues such as literature and Irish legends but sometimes Orangemen would protest at the presence of this 'Irish Papist'. On one occasion he hopped off a train only to be greeted by a group of men with drawn revolvers who suggested he hop right back on again.

His political beliefs were harder to pin down. Perhaps fatally, the man who had once opposed the British Empire urged Canadian settlers to stay loyal to British rule, largely on the basis that it offered them protection against the behemoth of the United States. 'The British flag does indeed fly here,' said McGee, 'but it casts no shadow.' He had long been of the view that the only way forward for the disparate colonies of British North America was to unite as one great nation. 'I see it quartered into many communities,' he declared, 'each disposing of its own internal affairs, but all bound together by free institutions, free intercourse, free commerce.'

In 1863, his dream of Canadian unity led him to abandon his Reformist colleagues in parliament and cross the floor to become Minister of Agriculture, Immigration and Statistics in a new Conservative government. As the most vocal supporter of the Canadian

Confederation, he was a key figure in the 'Great Coalition' that oversaw the creation of the new Canada in 1867. He had previously attended the conferences in Charlottetown (on Prince Edward Island) and Quebec, at which the Confederation was largely conceived. At the Quebec conference in 1864, he introduced a resolution that led to the guarantee of the educational rights of religious minorities in Canada.

McGee's failure to keep onside with Irish nationalism would cost him his life. In 1866, the Fenian Brotherhood launched two abortive raids from the United States on Canada (p. 136). McGee hotly denounced the attacks, furious at the backlash they caused to Irish Catholics in Canada. He caused further outrage by denouncing the 'Manchester Martyrs', three Irishmen who were executed for killing a policeman during a bungled attempt to rescue Fenians from prison. Such influential condemnation of the Fenians appears to have been his death warrant; the former Young Ireland rebel was accused of selling his soul in pursuit of political power. Castigated as a traitor, he was expelled from the St Patrick's Society of Montreal. As his popular support among Irish Catholics plummeted, the Canadian prime minister also withdrew his support. Nonetheless, he was elected as the Liberal-Conservative member for Montreal West when the first Canadian parliament met in the new capital of Ottawa in 1867.

On 6 April 1868, he delivered a powerful speech in parliament, urging the people of Nova Scotia to keep faith in the Confederation. His murder on the streets of Ottawa later that night caused widespread shock; it is considered Canada's first political assassination. McGee's funeral in Montreal was one of the largest in Canadian history – over 80 per cent of the city's population of 105,000 followed his hearse and he was interred in a crypt at the Notre-Dame-des-Neiges cemetery.

Within twenty-four hours of the murder, over forty men were in custody, primarily Irishmen. Among them was Patrick Buckley, a coachman to John A. Macdonald, Canada's first prime minister. He directed the authorities towards Patrick James Whelan, a tailor from Galway with well-known Fenian sympathies. Jim Whelan, as he was known, had served as assistant marshal of Ottawa's St Patrick's

Day Parade three weeks before the killing. He knew McGee and had watched his Nova Scotia talk from the parliamentary gallery that night. A police raid on his hotel room revealed a .32 Smith & Wesson pistol with six rounds in it. The eight-day trial that followed was notable for the number of questionable testimonies by people with one eye on the $2,000 reward up for grabs if Whelan was convicted.

The Galway man was found guilty and sentenced to hang. 'I am here standing on the brink of my grave,' he responded. 'And I wish to declare to you and to my God that I am innocent, that I never committed this deed.' He was publicly hanged in Ottawa on 11 February 1869. He reiterated his innocence to the 5,000-strong crowd but also stated that he knew the true identity of McGee's killer. 'God save Ireland and God save my soul,' he said, shortly before the trapdoor dropped. His spirit reputedly haunts the Ottawa jail where he died, now an unlikely but popular guest hostel.

28

THE RAILROAD MEN

Promontory Summit, Utah, 10 May 1869. A hushed silence descended as Leland Stanford, the former governor of California, stepped forward to pound home the golden spike, the final nail of the Transcontinental Railroad. This was the moment everyone had been waiting for since the late President Lincoln had green-lighted the project nearly seven years earlier. Among the large crowd gathered for the occasion were some of the many thousands of Irishmen who had helped lay the 3,069-km (1,907-mile) track that would finally connect the railway networks of the eastern United States with the Central Pacific line that came west from California.

As the American press photographers raised their cameras, Stanford hoisted the silver mallet above his right shoulder and aimed for the golden spike. Down came the mallet…and down it continued to come, slamming into the rail alongside the spike and nearly pummelling the ex-governor's ankles to pulp. 'What a howl went up!', recalled Alex Toponce, a leading wagon freighter who witnessed the event. 'Irish, Chinese, Mexicans, and everybody yelled with delight. "He missed it. Yee!" The engineers blew the whistles and rang their bells.' Nonetheless, by early afternoon, the news of the momentous connection had been telegraphed to towns and cities all over America.

The completion of the Transcontinental Railroad was one of the greatest game-changers in American history. Prior to the railroad, the only way to get from the eastern United States to the Pacific coast was either to take a steamship all the way around (with an optional overland trek across Panama) or to embark upon a long and arduous trail across the states by wagon. In both cases, the journey time was likely to be several months. With the 1869 connection, the time was reduced to just eight days. From that moment on, it became infinitely easier for emigrants seeking the American dream to simply board a train and 'go west'.

The Transcontinental Railroad was a collaboration between two railroad companies: the Central Pacific, laying a track eastwards from Sacramento, California; and the Union Pacific, which went westwards from Omaha, Nebraska. Irish emigrants played a key role in the construction of this industrial goliath from the outset: at least 3,000 Irish signed up to work with the Union Pacific and hundreds more were hired in New York and Boston and shipped west to worked for the Central Pacific. Some had fled Ireland during the Great Hunger; many more had served during the American Civil War, for the Union and Confederate armies alike.

The work was not particularly well paid – $35 a month – and large numbers would abandon the railroads to take their chances in the silver mines of Montana and Nevada, adding fuel to those who regarded the Irish as unreliable. Working on the railroad was a tough way to earn a living – as well as the inevitable construction accidents, the workforce had to contend with outbreaks of smallpox and the occasional attack by Native Americans who believed, quite rightly, that the railroad – the Iron Horse – would bring an end to their culture.

One of the most celebrated events took place on 28 April 1869 when nine Irishmen laid an astonishing 16.1 km (10 miles 56 ft) of track in less than twelve hours. In the annals of global railways, this feat has never been matched or surpassed. The record was achieved in response to a $10,000 bet wagered by T. C. Durant, vice president of the Union Pacific Railroad, after a team from his company laid just over 11 km (7 miles) in a single day; he believed the record could not be beaten. Charles Crocker, founder of the Central Pacific, thought otherwise and accepted the challenge. Step forward the Irishmen of the Central Pacific. Alas, little is yet known of the background of these muscular men bar their names. George Coley was the gang foreman, while the eight rail-handlers tasked with hauling all the iron rails into place were Mike Sullivan, Fred McNamara, Tom Daley, George Wyatt, Edward Killeen, Mike Kennedy, Pat Joyce and Mike Shay.

The men were at the forefront of a railroad army that numbered 14,000 at its peak. As well as the hundreds of Irish, there were large numbers of Mexicans, Native Americans, freed slaves and assorted European labourers. However, much of the greatest part of the labour force were Chinese immigrants, primarily refugees from Canton (present-day Guangdong) Province who had fled to California during the Taiping Rebellion (1850–64), in which at least 20 million people died. Crocker was a particular enthusiast for Chinese labour. 'Did they not build the Chinese Wall, the biggest piece of masonry in the world?', he remarked. The Chinese were also paid $5 a month less than their Irish counterparts. By 1868, more than 80 per cent of the Central Pacific's army was Chinese and sure enough, often working under Irish foremen, they proved an immense asset, blasting and tunnelling their way through the treacherous, snow-covered granite rocks of the Sierra Nevada.

Once they had cracked through the mountains, Crocker's men 'passed like a hurricane across the open country' of the Nevada and Utah deserts. And now, as they awaited the early morning whistle on 28 April, the Irish and Chinese were to unite again. The show began when Chinese workers unloaded enough iron rails, ties, spikes, fishplates, bolts and other material to complete the job. They did this in eight minutes, with a noise that the *San Francisco Bulletin* likened to 'the bombardment of an army'. Then came Coley and his team, working in two squads of four. The Irishmen worked 'with a will', at breakneck speed, for the next twelve hours, lifting and placing 3,520 rails, each weighing 254 kg (560 lb). In total, they shifted nearly 975 tonnes (960 imperial tons) of iron in a single day.

Once each rail was down, another unit of Chinese labourers moved into place, ensuring each bolt was screwed up and every spike driven home, laying a colossal 25,800 wooden ties and driving 28,160 spikes in that same twelve-hour period. Then came another wave of workers to level and fill in the ground, shovelling earth beneath the ties, tamping and moving on to the next rail. A senior US army officer watching the scene stated that he had never seen such organization: 'It was like an army marching over the ground and leaving a track built behind them.'

By the close of day, the combined efforts of the Irish and Chinese labourers had given the Central Pacific a record-breaking new track that was verified by two engineers from their Union Pacific rivals. And just to prove it was as good as any other stretch, one of their men leapt into a locomotive and chugged it back over the new line at a clip of 64 kph (40 mph). It was a huge triumph for the Central Pacific, and Charles Crocker won his bet.

Coley and his men were rewarded with four days' pay for their single day's work. It was also particularly good publicity for the Irish, who had been losing considerable ground to the Chinese ever since a strike action backfired two years earlier. Anti-Irish discrimination was widespread in the United States in the 1860s. General Dodge, the Union Pacific's chief engineer, was among their most vocal critics, remarking, 'The Irish labor, with its strikes, its dead fall whiskey shops and reckless disregard of all our interests, must be gotten out of the way.'

Less than two weeks after Coley's team broke the record, the link between east and west was completed when the Union Pacific's steam locomotive No. 119 met the Central Pacific's *Jupiter* engine at Promontory Summit, Utah. Alex Toponce spoke fondly of the celebratory party that followed the 'Wedding of the Rails': 'It was a very hilarious occasion. Everybody had all they wanted to drink all the time. Some of the participants got "sloppy," and these were not all Irish and Chinese by any means.'

After Stanford missed the spike, Durant had a shot at it and he also failed. Toponce was ecstatic:

> *Everybody slapped everybody else again and yelled, 'He missed it too, yow!' It was a great occasion, everyone carried off souvenirs and there are enough splinters of the last tie in museums to make a good bonfire. Both before and after the spike driving ceremony there were speeches, which were cheered heartily. I do not remember what any of the speakers said now, but I do remember that there was a great abundance of champagne.*

29

ELIZA LYNCH,
FIRST LADY OF PARAGUAY

Cerro Corá, Paraguay, 1 March 1870. The face of Eliza Lynch's lover was hard to recognize. His teeth had been smashed with rifle butts. Tufts of hair had been ripped out and his left ear had been hacked off. Elsewhere his fingers were also missing. It was, of course, the end of everything. Francisco Solano López, the president of her adopted Paraguayan homeland, the father of her six children, was dead. And so too was her firstborn son, whose body the Brazilian soldiers were now hauling to the same grave where López had been flung. Somehow she managed to find the strength to approach the soldiers, to plead with them to make the grave deeper. And then she began pulling at the earth with her own bare hands, determined to give López and their boy as decent a burial as possible.

Eliza Lynch was born in Charleville, County Cork, on 22 April 1834, the firstborn child of Dr John Lynch, a Catholic medic, and his Protestant wife, Jane Lloyd. Her father had studied at Trinity College Dublin, qualifying as a doctor shortly before his marriage in 1833. With property in Mallow and a university degree to his name, the doctor was clearly from a well-to-do background. One of his closest friends – and godfather to Eliza Lynch's younger brother John – was Daniel Clanchy, manager of the National Bank in Charleville and a particularly prominent supporter of Daniel O'Connell. Mary Ann Clanchy, her godmother, may have been Clanchy's sister. Eliza Lynch would have been too young to understand the political backdrop of her early childhood but Dr Lynch was also an enthusiastic follower of O'Connell, the man who secured the vote for Ireland's more prosperous Catholics in 1829.

As well as his general practice, John Lynch worked as medical attendant to the Charleville Dispensary and Fever Hospital. This frontline position was especially perilous during periods when contagious diseases were running rampant. On 18 August 1840, a little over two months after his appointment to the Medical Council of Ireland, Dr Lynch died of a fever contracted 'in the discharge of his professional duties'.

His widow came from a family with a strong nautical tradition and she certainly did not shy away from taking to the seas. In the wake of Dr Lynch's death, she brought her three small children – Eliza, John and baby Thomas – to France. Little is known of the next decade except that Eliza Lynch learned to speak fluent French and became a proficient pianist, while her mother married a man by the name of Clarke. It is thought the family lived in Boulogne-sur-Mer, a resort popular with former naval officers and Britain's rising middle class.

The blonde-haired Eliza Lynch grew into a woman of exceptional beauty and was thus something of a catch for Xavier Quatrefages, a French officer more than double her age, whom she married in Folkestone, Kent, in 1850. The doctor's daughter was only sixteen at the time but her mother evidently approved of the match, signing the requisite documents. Nonetheless, the marriage was not considered legal in France and it seems his wife's presence was kept undercover lest Quatrefages's military career be ruined by the revelation. Like the late Dr Lynch, Quatrefages was of a medical mindset, working in the army's pharmacy sector. Consequently, the couple spent the first two years of their marriage at the military hospitals of Val de Grâce, near Paris, and Bourbonne-les-Bains in northeastern France.

In June 1852, Quatrefages was posted to the military hospital at Constantine in the French colony of Algeria. His wife accompanied him but, according to her own account, the couple separated a year later. Having returned to France in poor health, she moved to Boulogne-sur-Mer to live with her mother's elder sister Eliza Crooke, and her husband, William Boyle Crooke, a British naval officer from Kinsale, County Cork. She seems to have moved to Paris towards the end of 1853, residing with the Strafford family and her widowed mother. The following spring, she would meet Francisco Solano López.

In the fifteen decades since López's death in 1870, the narrative of Eliza Lynch's life in Paris in 1854 has consistently cast her as a notorious concubine, an infamous whore or a 'lubricious harlot' who changed lovers 'as often as she changed her clothes', allegedly seducing a litany of English, Russian and French aristocrats, gentlemen and officers. That perspective changed in 2009 with the publication of *The Lives of Eliza Lynch* by Michael Lillis and Ronan Fanning, which debunked much of the mythology about Lynch's life. During the six months or so that passed before she met López, it is *possible* that she earned a living as a Parisian courtesan. The profession was enjoying a golden age in the French capital at this time and was considered perfectly acceptable. However, as Lillis and Fanning observe, there is not a single reference to 'Mademoiselle Lynch' in any diary, journal, letter or memoir from this entire period so, if she was a courtesan, she maintained a very low profile.

Contemporary accounts indicate that, at this stage of his life, the Paraguayan diplomat López was a smooth-talking, sharp-dressed, chain-smoking bon vivant with a passion for beautiful women, good food, singing and speaking French. Although he was probably illegitimate, he had been raised as a son of Carlos Antonio López, Paraguay's absolute dictator since 1844. Educated by a private tutor, Francisco Solano López was just twenty-six when he arrived in Europe with a considerable pile of gold and a brief to purchase as much weaponry, rolling stock and track as he could find, and to recruit as many preferably English engineers and doctors as possible.

It is unclear how or where or when he met Eliza Lynch. He had lately dined with both Queen Victoria and Emperor Napoleon III of France so he was evidently in excellent fettle. She was certainly with him by the time the Paraguayan Legation made its way south towards Rome in the spring of 1854. She journeyed with them as far as Marseilles before returning to Paris, where she penned a note to López, who she now described as 'my Panchito'.

By the summer, the Crimean War was underway, Paris was buzzing and Eliza Lynch was pregnant. López seems to have been so smitten that he bought her mother a house of splendour at 320 rue Saint-Honoré in the city's fashionable 1st arrondissement. He also hired her brother John as a crew member on board *El Tacuari*, the gunboat that he had purchased in Britain. The matter of her husband was also tidied up when Quatrefages effectively let her go in return for an unspecified payment. He would go on to hold the prestigious post of chief pharmacist at the military hospital of Les Invalides in Paris.

López and Lynch may have travelled to Dublin for a discreet visit on 27 July 1854. They certainly bought linen worth £41 from Irish Linen and Damasks of 41 Upper Sackville Street (now O'Connell Street). The affair deepened and Eliza Lynch found herself with great wealth. On 10 November 1854, armed with a tin box stuffed with £3,000 and another £1,000 in English gold, the twenty-year-old Irish beauty boarded a commercial packet at Bordeaux, destination Buenos Aires. López followed the next day on *El Tacuari*, with John Lynch as the ship's second-in-command.

Paraguay had been utterly isolated from the world for many decades before the López regime began. While the López family amassed a private fortune from the state coffers, they also made it the most technologically advanced country in Latin America, with a telegraph system, a railroad, a shipyard and other structures, which gave its industry and agriculture a solid backbone. Paraguay's multicultural colonial population was about 400,000 when Lynch arrived into the docks of Asunción, the capital city, following a three-week boat journey from Buenos Aires. Unique to Latin America, the majority spoke the language of the indigenous Guaraní population, a people depicted in the 1986 film *The Mission*.

Eliza Lynch is barely mentioned in the surviving records of the López government. Her name was either erased or simply never recorded, so piecing together what she did during the next fourteen years is difficult to verify. Her romance with López, whom she never married, reads like something out of an Isabel Allende novel. She bore him seven children, three of whom died of illness when young, while a fourth was fated to be shot dead in the coming war. López had several other mistresses, and children by those mistresses too, but Lynch was his firm favourite. She was also the recipient of a collection of his erotic love poems.

With her chic Parisian attire and jewelry, Eliza Lynch stood out in Paraguay from the outset. Within days of her arrival, she began establishing her credentials as a businesswoman, investing primarily in cattle and tobacco. She took a townhouse in Asunción, which was rapidly decorated and furnished in the most luxuriant Parisian style, complete with walls papered in green satin. It even had a private theatre, apparently modelled on La Scala in Milan. Frequented by poets, musicians and other members of the country's cultural elite, the parties she hosted were likened to Parisian salons. To boost López's career, she hosted dinner parties for people such as Sir Edward Thornton, Queen Victoria's Minister to the Argentine Republic, which did much to strengthen Paraguay's relationship with the British Empire. López also built her a new country palace, with its own railway station, about 48 km (30 miles) outside of the city. She introduced new fashions, hairstyles, cosmetics and cuisine from France, as well as champagnes and wines, and inspired a craze for photography, portrait painting and the polka dance. The latter is now so deeply entrenched in the Paraguayan folk music tradition that it is called the 'Danza Paraguaya' (Paraguayan dance). The 'London Carapé' was a particular favourite.

And yet there were plenty of people who despised her, some resenting her bond with López, who had become the frontrunner to succeed to the dictatorship after he negotiated an end to a long-running civil war in neighbouring Argentina in 1859. Others deplored her tendency to socialize with lower classes. Ultimately, she was an outsider from the interrelated families of Paraguayan society.

In 1862, the corpulent President López died and Francisco Solano López became the supreme power in Paraguay. To celebrate, Lynch hosted the biggest ball in Paraguayan history, a masquerade at the Club Nacional. López began building a new presidential palace and planned to continue his father's legacy of construction and innovation. However, tensions were brewing between wealthy Paraguay and its covetous neighbours in Brazil and Argentina. War seemed inevitable and Asunción was rife with spies and intrigues.

López appears to have staked his future on the possibility of a dynastic marriage to Princess Isabel, daughter of Dom Pedro II, emperor of Brazil. When the emperor scathingly snubbed the suggestion, López mobilized his 100,000-strong army and declared war on Brazil. The War of the Triple Alliance formally began on 4 November 1864. Not only would López's forces find themselves pitched against the combined armies of Brazil, Argentina and Uruguay, but also the war would become the bloodiest conflict in South American history.

In the decades to come, Eliza Lynch would be castigated as the Lady Macbeth who brainwashed López into squandering his country's position. However, she remained insistent that she had little if any role in his warmongering. López had clearly been planning for such a war for years, building up an extremely impressive and highly disciplined army, as well as the Paraguayan navy. Initially, the war went Paraguay's way; however, López's subsequent campaigns were so disastrously conceived that, by the end of 1865, a huge portion of his army had either been killed or captured, while the navy was also destroyed.

Eliza Lynch remained loyal to her 'Panchito', even as he became ever more paranoid, drink-addled and bloodthirsty. In the wake of a failed coup in 1868, he initiated a massive purge of his Cabinet, judiciary and army. Hundreds of the Paraguayan elite were executed, including his own half-brothers and one of Lynch's closest friends. Once again, hostile contemporaries depicted her as a lewd, sex-crazed woman who had induced this horrific behaviour, but she had no direct hand in it: 'I did not influence the President, or try to do it in the direction of severity,' she would later maintain. 'I had no ill-will to anyone, and did a good turn, when I could, to those who needed it.' Sir Richard Burton, the great explorer, was in Paraguay during the time of the purge and, while he loathed López, he also concluded that 'Madame Lynch' had done 'her utmost to mitigate the miseries of the captives and to make the so-called "détenus" comfortable'.[1]

Conversely, the international press, sympathetic to Paraguay and unaware of the purge, attributed considerable military prowess to Eliza. In July 1868, for example, *The Irishman*, a Dublin-based publication, declared her to be a cross between Grace O'Malley, the 'Pirate Queen' of Connaught, and Joan of Arc, misinforming its readers that 'Brigadier-General Eliza Lynch leads the female forces, the Amazonian army, of gallant Paraguay, fighting for its independence.'[2]

Although denying any involvement in the war, Lynch was by no means inactive at this time. By January 1870, she considered herself the owner of nearly 90,000 sq. km (34,750 sq. miles) of Paraguay, a holding larger than the entire island of Ireland, which would have made her one of the largest female landowners in the world. She also held an entire block of Asunción, as well as twenty-three other townhouses and her country palace.

Shortly before the Brazilians captured Asunción, Lynch, López and their children managed a narrow escape, canoeing through a hail of Brazilian cannon fire. Anticipating the end, López wrote a will leaving everything to her. He then presented the will, along with their four younger children, to Martin McMahon, the thirty-year-old US diplomatic representative to Paraguay, whose parents hailed from Waterford.

Lynch remained with López, as did their older sons Juan Francisco (known as Panchito) and Enrique. They were now the prime target of the Brazilian army, as Dom Pedro II had vowed to fight on until 'Marshal López' himself was dead.

In February 1870, the group reached Cerro Corá, a hill in northeast Paraguay, along with a couple of hundred soldiers, many of them children, elderly, starving or wounded. Two weeks later, they were surrounded and all but annihilated by a superior Brazilian force. López was fatally lanced and then shot dead; his body was mutilated by the enemy. Fifteen-year-old Panchito Lynch was also killed. Eliza Lynch and eleven-year-old Enrique preserved their lives by claiming to be English.

The Brazilian general ordered his men to dig a shallow grave for López and Panchito in the Paraguayan jungle. This was the moment that Lynch famously began to dig with her own bare hands, cutting locks from the hair and beard of her lover and their son. Their deaths marked the end of a war in which perhaps 65 per cent of Paraguay's pre-war population of 430,000 people had been killed, including almost 90 per cent of males over the age of seven.

Remarkably, Eliza Lynch made it back to Britain, where she would spend much of the next sixteen years trying in vain to reclaim ownership of her Paraguayan assets. Her cause was hampered by a series of salacious biographies, much of them fictitious, penned by those eager to vilify her. Barred from returning to Paraguay, she moved from London to Paris in 1882. She died of stomach cancer on 25 July 1886, aged fifty-two.

Initially buried in Paris, her remains were repatriated by General Alfredo Stroessner, the Paraguayan dictator, in 1961, after he proclaimed her a national heroine. She was subsequently reinterred at La Recoleta, the national cemetery in Asunción. Stroessner also named the main highway from Asunción to Paraguay's principal international airport 'Avenida Elisa Lynch' in her honour. Hundreds of schools and other institutions throughout the country are also named for the doctor's daughter from Charleville.

30

JOHN PHILIP HOLLAND, FATHER OF THE SUBMARINE

Paterson, New Jersey, 1878. The bespectacled, moustachioed man from County Clare must have sensed the positive response even before the vessel rose up from the riverbed of the Passaic River. He had been submerged underwater for an entire hour without problem, securely sealed inside a vessel no bigger than a rowing boat. On reaching the surface, he pushed open the hatch, clambered out of the tower and duly received the applause of those who had paid him to develop his battleship destroyer, namely the Fenian Brotherhood of America. Although he did not invent the submarine, John Philip Holland is renowned as the man who perfected the design in order for it to become the paramount, game-changing war machine of the early twentieth century.

Holland grew up by the ocean, raised in a humble cottage, still standing today, near the Cliffs of Moher in County Clare. Born on 24 February 1841, he was the second of four boys, the sons of a coast-guard, John Holland, and his second wife, Máire Ní Scannláin (Mary Scanlon), a native Irish speaker from nearby Liscannor. Holland was also raised as an Irish speaker and did not learn English until he attended St Macreehy's National School in the late 1840s. The potato blight had desecrated the countryside all around him by the time he went to study with the Christian Brothers in Ennistymon, 8 km (5 miles) from Liscannor. His father, younger brother and two uncles died during the appalling period of the Great Hunger. It is also thought to have caused his poor eyesight, which, in turn, thwarted his ambition to become a navigator so that, as he later put it, 'no one would trust me even to row a two-oared boat, much less navigate a ship'.

Following his father's death in 1853, the Holland family relocated to Limerick, where young Holland continued his education with the Christian Brothers, taking vows in 1858. He spent the next fifteen years as a sort of roving maths and music teacher at the order's schools in Armagh, Cork, Portlaoise, Enniscorthy, Drogheda and Dundalk. As a music teacher, he pioneered the solfège technique for sight-singing, later made famous when Julie Andrews taught the von Trapp children how to sing 'Do-re-mi-fa-so-la-ti-do' in the film The Sound of Music.

During his time at the North Monastery school in Cork, Holland read an account of the Battle of Ironclads, an inconclusive duel fought between two competing ironclad battleships in Virginia in the American Civil War. It occurred to him that the future of naval warfare was likely to be determined by vessels that could travel covertly underwater and surprise attack such mighty battleships. Having completed the first fledgling drafts of his submarine design, 'a clock-driven' model that he submerged in a wooden tub of water, he now began experimenting with scale models in the school's ornamental pond and, later, in the River Lee.

Submarines were still the stuff of science fiction in the 1860s. However, Holland already had people who believed in him, such as Brother Dominic Burke, an innovative science teacher at 'North Mon' school, who not only crafted Holland's wooden models but also encouraged his interest in science and aerodynamics. While at the Dundalk school, Holland would construct a sundial, design a form of aeroplane and teach his students astronomy with the aid of a telescope.

In May 1873, Holland left the Christian Brothers, citing ill health, and sailed across the seas to Boston where he joined his widowed mother and two surviving brothers, Michael and Alfred. Shortly after his arrival, the thirty-two-year-old slipped on an icy street and broke a leg. While recuperating, he returned to work on his submarine design, assisted by an Irish priest called Isaac Whelan. He then spent a period with an engineering firm before resuming his work as a lay teacher. For the next six years, he was based at St John's Catholic School in the manufacturing stronghold of Paterson, New Jersey.

In 1875 he submitted designs to the US Navy Department in Washington, DC for a one-man submarine powered by foot pedals. It was rejected as 'a fantastic scheme of a civilian landsman'.[1] He might have offered it to Britain's Royal Navy but he was not inclined to hand potentially powerful weaponry to the old enemy. Instead, he turned to his older brother Michael, a sworn member of the Fenian Brotherhood (later Clan na Gael), an Irish-American organization committed to the overthrow of British rule in Ireland (p. 136).

In 1877, Michael Holland lined up several senior Fenians to view his brother's submarine prototype at work on Coney Island. John Philip Holland proposed that, with the right funding, he would be able to invent a submarine capable of carrying three men, which could be carried into the vicinity of a British battleship by an innocuous merchant vessel, slipped into the water and unleashed to attack the battleship at close range. The Fenians were so enthusiastic that they offered to pay him a development fee of £6,000 from their 'skirmishing fund', a rather charmingly named bursary for anyone with a sound plan for attacking British interests in the United States. With money in the bank, the inventor set to work.

In 1878 he launched *Holland No. 1* in the Passaic River. Planned and completed in Paterson, the diminutive submarine measured 4.4 m (14½ ft) in length and was driven by a primitive 3 kW (4 hp) petrol engine. It carried a solitary man, namely Holland himself, but no armaments. After a few false starts, he made a series of successful dives, at one time spending an hour underwater on the riverbed. The Fenians were sufficiently fascinated to offer more money for him to complete a submarine 'suitable for war'.

Having now given up his teaching job, Holland started anew from the Delamater Iron Works in Manhattan, New York. The press was fascinated but Holland was cagey, suspecting most reporters of being British spies in disguise. A journalist for the *New York Sun* got to the nub of the project when he dubbed the vessel 'The Fenian Ram'. The name stuck and in May 1881, Holland launched his 9.5-m (31-ft)-long submersible *Fenian Ram* in the Hudson River. It was powered by a 11.2–12.7 kW (15–17 hp) Brayton petroleum engine with a large flywheel. Modelled on the streamlined form of a porpoise, the submarine could travel at 14.5 kmph (9 mph) over water and 11.3 kmph (7 mph) under water. It was also armed with an underwater 'dynamite gun', fired by compressed air.

While the launch was a success, Holland was to spend the next two years tinkering and improving the craft. Unfortunately, the situation with his Fenian sponsors was not so positive. A row ensued over the payment due to Holland, resulting in a lawsuit and a bitter split within the often-fractious organization. After the Fenians withdrew their funding, some disgruntled members stole Holland's prototype submarine, towing it through Long Island Sound to New Haven, Connecticut, where it was abandoned by the pier for many years.[2]

A furious Holland severed his ties with the Fenians, although he maintained his interest in Irish nationalism. In 1901, for example, he was a guest speaker at a banquet given in New York to honour Major John MacBride, commander of the Irish Brigade that had fought alongside the Boers against Britain during the recent war in South Africa.[3] MacBride would be executed by the British for his role in the Easter Rising of 1916.

The 1880s were lean years for Holland. The US naval authorities consistently dismissed his invention, writing him off as an eccentric dreamer. In January 1887 the forty-six-year-old married twenty-five-year-old Margaret Foley, the daughter of an Irish emigrant, with whom he settled in Newark, New Jersey. Later that year, he had a possible breakthrough when he won an open competition for a submarine design run by the US Navy Department. However, despite his victory, the department was still unwilling to invest in the project.

Desperately short of money and having lost their first child in infancy, Holland took a low-paying job as a draughtsman to support his wife and, in due course, four children. He continued to research submarines, as well as manned flight, and in 1893 he set up the John Holland Torpedo Boat Company. Two years later, he won a $350,000 contract from the US Navy to build a submarine, but he was plagued by experts from the department who insisted on major changes to his design. When it was launched in 1897, the submarine was a flop because, to quote Holland, it had been 'over-engineered'.

Meanwhile, Holland commenced work on what was to be his most successful submarine. Based on the *Fenian Ram*, the 16-m (53-ft)-long *Holland VI* took its first dive off Staten Island in New York Harbour on St Patrick's Day in 1898. Carrying a crew of fifteen with a torpedo tube in the bow, the *Holland VI* was the first submarine to travel a considerable distance while submerged, remaining underwater for 1 hour 40 minutes. It was also a pioneer of the hybrid engine, combining electric motors for submerged travel and gasoline engines for surface travel. The *New York Herald* hailed it as 'the most marvellous revolution in maritime warfare'.

It also caught the eye of Theodore Roosevelt, Assistant Secretary of the Navy, who recommended immediate purchase to boost the naval fleet when the United States declared war on Spain five weeks after the St Patrick's Day dive. However, the US government dithered, obliging an irritated Holland to state publicly that if the US Navy would transport his boat to the Caribbean, he would demonstrate the effectiveness of his submarine by single-handedly sinking the entire Spanish fleet holed up in Santiago de Cuba. He quickly received 500 applications from electricians, engineers and sailors willing to join him.[4] Still the navy stalled, ripely observing that when the boat was submerged it 'yawed like a drunken washerwoman'.[5] More trials were required but in 1899 the cash-strapped Holland was obliged to sell his firm to Isaac Rice, a German-born businessman, who renamed it the Electric Boat Company and retained Holland as general manager.

Following a demonstration on the Potomac River in Washington, DC in March 1900, Rice persuaded the US Navy to buy the submarine for $150,000 – nearly half of what it had cost to build. Commissioned on 12 October 1900, the *Holland VI* duly became the US Navy's first submarine. A further seven of these submarines were then built at shipyards in New Jersey and California. To Holland's dismay, the company also sold the designs to the Royal Navy – the original intended target of the *Fenian Ram* – who launched its own Holland-designed sub in October 1901. The Royal Netherlands Navy also bought the submarine while, during the Russo-Japanese War of 1904–5, Rice's company managed to sell submarines to the navies of both sides.

Medals were all very well, but Holland's financial reward was far less satisfactory. Rice had demoted the Irishman to chief engineer on a salary of $90 a week, while the submarines he invented were now selling for as much as $300,000 each. As Rice later put it, his company needed 'a naval constructor, not an inventor', and most of Holland's proposed 'improvements' were now rejected. Frustrated by the diminishment of his technical authority, Holland resigned in 1904 and set up a rival business to build submarines and flying machines. Addressing the La Salle Society in Newark in December 1906, he told how his new submarines were designed 'not to destroy, but to cripple and disable' all that they attack, without, he hoped, 'a single loss of life'. He concluded: 'I believe the new boat will startle the world.'[6]

However, Holland's attempts to secure sufficient funding were doomed when Rice's legal team sought to not only block his usage of the patent for overseas clients but also stop him using the 'Holland' name on any of his marketing. The company folded in 1907, its greatest success having been to sell a design to the Imperial Japanese Navy upon which two submarines were built in Kobe. The following year, Emperor Meiji awarded Holland the Rising Sun Ribbon for his work.

Holland spent the next few years battling in vain to remove Electric Boat's scurrilous monopoly on submarine construction. With the outbreak of the war in Europe on 28 July 1914, he anticipated the first real test of his submarines, given that almost every navy in the world now had one. However, beset with rheumatism and paralysis, the seventy-three-year-old was struck with pneumonia and drifted into unconsciousness at his home in Newton Street, Newark, where he died on 12 August 1914, with his wife, three sons and a daughter at his bedside. He is buried in Totowa, New Jersey, less than a mile from where he launched his first submarine.

Just over a month after his death, a German submarine sank three British cruisers in the North Sea with the loss of 1,459 lives. During the course of the war, the Electric Boat Company and its subsidiaries built 85 navy submarines and 722 submarine chasers for the US Navy, along with 580 motor launches for the British Royal Navy. The company Holland pioneered would evolve into the General Dynamics Corporation, one of the world's largest aerospace and defence contractors.

31

NELLIE CASHMAN,
ANGEL OF THE WILD WEST

The snows that are older than history,
The woods where the weird shadows slant;
The stillness, the moonlight, the mystery,
I've bade 'em good-by – but I can't.

ROBERT W. SERVICE, 'THE SPELL OF THE YUKON', 1907

Tombstone, Arizona, 1880. John P. Clum was twenty-eight years old when he founded the *Tombstone Weekly Epitaph*. A former Indian agent, he was highly regarded across Arizona as the man who had captured Geronimo without firing a single shot. He would also go on to become one of Wyatt Earp's closest friends. But of all the people that John Clum ever encountered, there was no one quite like Nellie Cashman. Since her arrival in Tombstone earlier that year, she had already set up a boot and shoe shop, a general store, a restaurant and a hotel in quick succession. Clum figured she was about his age, born in 1849, maybe 1850. In the decades to come, he became friendly with her nephews and nieces, the Cunninghams, who helped him piece together the background of a woman that his newspaper described as 'the only woman mining expert in the United States'.

Ellen 'Nellie' Cashman was born in County Cork, probably around Midleton, where a monument to her was unveiled in 2014. Nothing more is known of her until she and her sister Fannie boarded a ship at Queenstown, now Cobh, and sailed for America, arriving into Boston in about 1867. Legend holds that she was working as a bell-hop in a Boston hotel when she fell into conversation with General Ulysses S. Grant, who advised her to 'go west'. The Cashman sisters duly journeyed west on the newly completed Transcontinental Railroad (p. 150) to San Francisco, where Fannie married Tom Cunningham, an Irish bootmaker, in 1870.

Marriage was not for Nellie Cashman. Tall, brown-haired and dark-eyed, she was mesmerized by the rugged, anything-goes mayhem of the American West. Her eyes lit on Pioche, Nevada, a silver-mining boomtown about 900 km (560 miles) east of San Francisco. Life was so rough in Pioche that, as the town proudly claims to this day, the first seventy-two people buried in its cemetery were all shot dead in gunfights. This did not deter her and, by 1873, she was running a boarding house in the town.

Nellie Cashman was to live a remarkably nomadic life over the coming decades, but one of her greatest skills was knowing the right time to up stakes and move on. Sensing that Pioche's boom was coming to an end, she did just that in 1874 and headed way up north into the Cassiar Mountains of British Columbia, a nugget's throw from Alaska, where a new gold rush was underway. There is no record of her journey but, as the crow flies, the mountains are over 3,000 km (1,900 miles) from Pioche. Evidently, she possessed an exceptionally robust stamina.

She reached Telegraph Hill, a mining enclave on the Stikine River, where she set up another boarding house. Her timing was immaculate; by the end of 1874, the miners had prospected over a million dollars' worth of gold from the area. Cashman was undoubtedly motivated by money, but she was also a deeply compassionate woman. When miners were sick or wounded, she nursed them. When they were hungry and poor, she fed them. She also persuaded them to make donations for a new hospital that the Sisters of St Anne were building in Victoria, the state capital of British Columbia.

Cashman was in Victoria when the story broke that a group of miners had vanished following a snowstorm in the Cassiars. In an adventure that is hard to believe yet seemingly true, she rounded up six men and some mules and dogs, who she then led on a monumental journey into the mountains to track down the missing miners. The mules carried 680 kg (1,500 lb) of potatoes, lime juice, tea and other food and medical supplies. It was one of the severest winters on record and the party met various groups along the way, including some Canadian troopers who urged them to turn back. Cashman, however, was not to be dissuaded and, after seventy-seven days, she found the stranded miners and brought them home. Some had already died of scurvy and starvation. Others were riddled with sores, frostbite or blackened limbs. It is unclear how many men there were, with estimates varying from twenty-six to seventy-five, but either way, they called her the 'Angel of the Cassiar' after that.

Enchanted as she was by the Cassiars, she again anticipated the passing of a boom. As the camps of both California and Nevada were also in decline, she switched her attention to the hot sands of Arizona, where a new gold rush had kicked off. She pinpointed Tucson, a town that had been founded just over a century earlier by the Dublin-born governor of Spanish Texas, Hugh O'Conor. Again, it is astonishing to imagine how Cashman negotiated the journey south, but she arrived with sufficient energy and wealth to open the Delmonico Restaurant in Tucson in July 1879. Now aged about thirty, she was one of the few white women in the town, but she quickly commanded the respect of all, again distributing food and encouragement to the down and out.

The following year she moved 140 km (87 miles) southeast to Tombstone, a silver-mining boomtown that defined everything that was rough and raw about the Wild West, where she established herself as one of its leading lights. 'There are no cockroaches in my kitchen and the flour is clean' avowed one memorable advertisement for her restaurant. Local lore holds that an inebriated customer was in the act of grumbling about Nellie Cashman's cuisine when no less a soul than Doc Holliday drew his nickel-plated pistol and pointed it at him. 'Best meal I ever ate,' declared the customer swiftly. Doc Holliday would achieve his moment of fame in October 1881 when he and the Earp brothers outgunned their opponents in the gunfight at the O.K. Corral, just outside Tombstone.

At this time, there were an estimated 110 saloons and 14 gambling halls in the town, not to mention all the banks, parlours, dance halls and brothels. With more people pouring in daily, 'Miss Nellie' began collecting money for a miscellany of charities, as well as the Irish National Land League, which had lately been formed to end the quasi-feudal system of land ownership in her homeland. A devout Catholic, albeit ecumenical in attitude, she helped the Congregation of the Sisters of St Joseph find the funds to build a Roman Catholic church. She co-founded the town theatre, where the first play staged was a musical comedy called *The Irish Diamond*. She was also a volunteer nurse and branch member of the Miner's Hospital Association.

In 1884, the townsfolk of Tombstone were incensed when five outlaws were captured following a botched robbery in nearby Bisbee that had left four innocents dead. Many began braying for a public execution and journalists flocked in from all the big cities to cover the event. Nellie Cashman went to see the 'Bisbee Bandits', perhaps because three of them were from Ireland. Her compassion for the condemned men turned to fury when she learned that the execution was to be a ticketed event; a grandstand for 600 people was purpose-built to behold the scaffold.

Concealing her anger behind a good-humoured facade, she secretly liaised with some miner friends, who duly assembled by the grandstand with crowbars, sledges, saws and other tools at two o'clock in the morning. By break of dawn, the grandstand was no more. The men were still hanged on schedule but were spared the indignity of a public spectacle. When Cashman subsequently discovered that some students had plans to rob the dead men's corpses for medical dissections, she paid two armed men to keep watch over the graves for ten days.

By this time, Fannie was also in Tombstone – Nellie Cashman had heard about Tom Cunningham's death from tuberculosis and had returned to San Francisco in 1880 in order to bring her sister and her five small children to her home. Alas, Fannie also succumbed to tuberculosis in 1883 and so Cashman found herself foster mother to the five orphans. She and her associate Joseph Pascholy, a Swiss émigré, now had a string of restaurants and boarding houses across Arizona. However, faced with the care of her nephews and nieces, she sold her share and took them back up north.

She briefly ran a hotel in Kingston, New Mexico, where one of her dish washers was Edward L. Doheny, the son of a Tipperary emigrant. Doheny would go on to become one of the world's richest oil tycoons, inspiring the character of Daniel Plainview, so mesmerizingly played by Daniel Day-Lewis in the 2007 movie *There Will Be Blood*. By the mid-1890s, she had made her way back to San Francisco, via Wyoming and Montana, where she placed all the children in boarding school. There were no hard feelings for this decision; the Cunninghams remained devoted to 'Aunt Nell' for the rest of her life.

Unencumbered once more, Nellie Cashman felt a stirring in her heart for the cold mountains of the north. The Klondike Gold Rush kicked off in 1896, drawing 100,000 prospectors to Yukon in northwest Canada, not far from the Cassair Mountains where she had lived twenty years earlier. By 1897, she was running a grocery store in the newly founded town of Dawson City, listening to the miners talk of moose and grizzly bears and riding the rapids. A contemporary recalled how her habit of 'grub-staking prospectors' (giving food to those who had no money) left her low on funds until she would 'buttonhole' one of the wealthier miners to 'supply her with sufficient gold dust to put her back on easy street'.

When the gold rush petered out in 1899, she readied her pack of huskies and took a sled up through the perilous, frozen passes of Alaska in pursuit of further adventure. 'I plan to make a million or two before I leave this romantic business of mining,' she remarked to one startled prospector she met en route. Initially based in Fairbanks, she proceeded north again for a further 440 km (275 miles) to Nolan Creek, where she began looking after the miners working in the Koyukuk River Basin. 'There isn't a man in Alaska who doesn't take his hat off when he sees me,' she would later marvel. 'And they always stop swearing when I come around too.'

By 1908 she had settled in a cabin at Coldfoot, 100 km (60 miles) north of the Arctic Circle, where she remained, defiantly alone, for the next sixteen years. When her nephew Mike Cunningham invited her to come south and live with his family, she retorted, 'It'll be a long time before I reach the cushioned-rocker stage.'

Over the course of nearly six decades since her arrival in Boston, 'Miss Nellie' had become one of the most colourful icons of the pioneering age, blasting into the frontiers of Canada and Mexico. Always seeking to do the right thing, she had fed the hungry, sheltered the homeless and brought a little joy to the unforgiving reality of a miner's life. Born amid the heartache of the Great Hunger, she lived to experience a ride in an aeroplane over the mountains in the early 1920s. This astonishing woman was finally felled by a combined dose of pneumonia and rheumatism. She died on 4 January 1925 at the Sisters of St Anne Hospital in Victoria, the very hospital she had been raising funds for when she headed into the Cassairs to rescue the miners over half a century earlier.

32

THE GRACE BROTHERS: CONQUEST OF PERU

New York, 1 January 1881. Even as he was being sworn in as New York's first Catholic mayor, Billy Grace's attention must have occasionally wandered 5,900 km (3,650 miles) south to Peru. The land where he had made his fortune was already under siege from the Chilean army. Despite his best efforts to persuade the US government to back the Peruvians, the game was up. His younger brother Michael had wisely abandoned Lima, the Peruvian capital, which would fall to the Chileans on 17 January. Billy Grace would spend the next twelve months focusing on his mayoral duties in New York. One wonders whether he could have foreseen that Peru's defeat would ultimately provide the basis for a fortune that would seal the Grace brothers' position as two of the richest men on the planet.

William Russell Grace was born at Riverstown, near Glanmire, County Cork, in 1832. James Grace, his father, descended from Raymond Le Gros, an Anglo-Norman knight who settled in Ireland in the late twelfth century. A branch of this Catholic family settled between Ballylynan and Arles on the Laois–Kildare county border, where they lived in a once splendid mansion, Gracefield. Billy Grace liked to say of his ancestors, 'they're like potatoes – the best of them underground'. His father, being the descendant of a younger son, was not an especially wealthy man. He leased a 100-hectare (250-acre) farm on the Weldon estate near Gracefield, which included a lime kiln, a defunct quarry and an abandoned cotton mill. Horses and cattle predominated on the farm. James Grace, who also spoke Irish, earned additional income as an inland revenue supervisor.

Billy Grace was the third of his seven children by his wife, Ellen Russell. In his formative years, the blue-eyed, tawny-haired boy loved reading his father's newspaper, *The Nation*, which advocated a nationalist future for Ireland. In later life, he would help fund a monument to the Irish patriot Daniel O'Connell on what is now O'Connell Street in Dublin. His childhood dream was to join the Royal Navy but his father would not permit such a career. In 1846, the thirteen-year-old ran away from home and boarded a merchant ship bound for America. He spent the next two years in New York, initially as a cobbler's apprentice and later working for a printer and as a clerk.

In 1848, the prodigal son returned on a ship laden with Cuban sugar only to find his homeland devastated by disease and hunger. His family were by then living in Dublin at Brooklawn, a large house on Donore Avenue. Welcomed back into their fold, he was sent to the Jesuit school at nearby Belvedere House, now Belvedere College. Unsurprisingly, school was not for him. By 1850, the eighteen-year-old had moved to Liverpool and opened a passage broker business, William Russell Grace & Co., selling tickets for the US-bound packet ships.

In early 1851 his father led a group of 180 men, women and children to establish an Irish colony in Peru. Billy Grace closed his Liverpool business to join the venture. When it failed, he moved to the port city of Callao, where he found work with John Bryce & Co., a ship's chandler that supplied maritime provisions to American and European whalers as well as the clipper ships engaged in the guano trade.

Peru was the predominant global supplier of guano – dried bird or bat excrement that was used as one of the key ingredients in both gunpowder and fertilizer because of its exceptionally high levels of phosphorus and nitrogen. In 1855 Grace ingeniously equipped an old store ship and had it towed out to the Chincha Islands, the epicentre of Peru's guano bonanza. From this floating warehouse, he made his fortune selling ropes, sails, masts, turpentine, tar, hardware, salt pork and other supplies to the hundreds of clippers and square-riggers that arrived every week.

The store ship was also a lively party spot and the claret-swilling Billy Grace became renowned as an excellent host. Among his guests was George W. Gilchrest, a shipbuilder from Thomaston, Maine, whose beautiful, fun-loving daughter Lillius took a shine to the affable Irishman. She and Grace were married on 11 September 1859; their first child, Alice, was born on the store ship exactly nine months later.

In 1862, Billy Grace brought his wife and three daughters to visit his Irish homeland where, whenever opportunity knocked, he urged any young people that he met to emigrate to South America, assuring them they would find employment there. He expended some of his new-found wealth on improving the lot of his siblings in Ballylynan, but the trip was tragically marred by the illness and death of at least one, and possibly two of their younger daughters, who were buried in the family mausoleum in Arles.

Back in Peru, Lillius was tiring of the earthquakes and the constant stench of guano. A case of dysentery pushed her husband to the limit; by the end of 1866 the family had relocated to New York, where Billy Grace established the US offices of Grace Brothers & Company. The 'Brothers' in the name referred to both him and his youngest brother Michael, who had now joined the business and henceforth ran the Peruvian operations from Lima, where he and his wife Margarita were among the shining lights of society during the 1870s.

A flourishing trade in fertilizer, machinery, rubber, fabric and other products saw the Graces' profits soar, while Billy Grace also moved into real estate in New York. He acquired a 58-hectare (144-acre) farm at Great Neck, Long Island, which he renamed Gracefield after the ancestral estate in Ireland. It was a haven of swimming pools, tennis courts and polo playing fields to which he imported driving horses, saddle ponies, cows and sheep from Ireland. Pat Delaney, manager of the farm at Ballylynan, oversaw the transport of the animals and was then placed in charge of another Grace farm in Connecticut.

In 1880, Billy Grace was persuaded to stand as a Democratic Party candidate in New York's mayoral race by Honest John Kelly, the infamous boss of Tammany Hall. Grace's reputation among the city's considerable Irish community was first-rate at this time – following a particularly harsh winter in Ireland in 1879/80, he commissioned the American steamer USS *Constellation* to sail from New York to Ireland with 3,315 barrels of flour, potatoes, oatmeal and corn, as well as children's clothing and other relief supplies. Having triumphed at the election by nearly 3,000 votes, he was sworn in as New York's first Roman Catholic mayor on New Year's Day 1881. He devoted his term to stamping out organized crime, reforming the police's corrupt street-cleaning department, breaking up the Louisiana lottery and lowering taxes. However, his refusal to accept one of Kelly's men as a deputy set him on a warpath with Tammany Hall. 'No one can dictate to me, Mr Kelly,' he shouted, shortly before Kelly stormed out of City Hall.

Grace did not stand for re-election, but he did develop a friendship with young Theodore Roosevelt over the coming years. In 1884, with Roosevelt's support, he stood as an independent for a second mayoral term. Tammany Hall tried to take him down and failed miserably; he won by 10,000 votes. The highlight of this term was his acceptance of the Statue of Liberty from France on behalf of the American people. He also led New York's successful campaign to hold Grant's Tomb, the final resting place of Ulysses S. Grant, after the president's death in 1885.

His focus was never far from Peru, where Michael Grace was now a major power broker. By the time the guano bonanza petered out in the early 1870s, the Graces had already diversified so that, for example, they were supplying all the ordnance material for the Peruvian navy and most of the pine lumber and iron for the state's railway projects. Indeed, the railroads of both Peru and Costa Rica were primarily built with timber supplied by the Graces. Supported by Baring Brothers, the London bankers, the Graces were also creditors of various guano, nitrate and sugar enterprises in Peru. As Peru's financial agent in both New York and San Francisco, Billy Grace developed a fruitful relationship with the political elite. He was private commercial creditor to General Manuel Prado, Peru's liberal president from 1876 to 1879, overseeing the purchase of the pure-bred horses that Prado raced at the Peruvian Jockey Club.

In October 1879, a feud over the nitrate-rich Atacama Desert triggered the War of the Pacific, pitching Peru and Bolivia against the marginally superior might of neighbouring Chile. The four-year-long war was a disaster for Peru. Although Chile's military and naval infrastructure was second-rate, Peru still lagged far behind. Indeed, the Peruvian navy's warships were largely manned by Chilean sailors who had to be dismissed when the war began. Moreover, the Chileans had much stronger international support.

Prado commissioned the Graces to arm and equip Peru's army and navy with torpedoes, torpedo boats, rifles, carbines and ammunition, all bought from US manufacturers. Meanwhile, Billy Grace's media empire, and his substantial networking base, began lobbying US diplomats and congressmen to back Peru. His motivation was further fuelled by the fact that his brother had lately secured the contract to distribute Peruvian nitrates to the United States. Michael Grace also developed a close friendship with Nicolás de Piérola who, having ousted Prado in a coup, bought large consignments of weapons and munitions from the Graces, some of which transpired to be defective.

All this was not enough to stop the Chilean conquest of Lima in 1881, however, after which the corrupt Piérola was deposed and fled to Paris. Michael Grace subsidized Piérola in exile, correctly predicting that this 'valuable friend' would return to power one day. Hedging his bets, he also oiled his friendship with the victorious Chileans and opened a branch in Valparaíso.

The war left Peru in debt by over £32 million to the London-based Committee of Foreign Bondholders. In the mid-1880s, Michael Grace and a 'charming' red-haired Irish aristocrat, John Hely-Hutchinson, 5th Earl of Donoughmore, began buying up these bonds. Michael then offered his services as a broker to negotiate a settlement. His motive may have been to protect the firm's railway and mining interests but, either way, he secured an extraordinary deal that made Grace Bros & Co. Latin America's first bona fide multinational, with 15,000 employees in Peru alone.

Under the terms of the Grace-Donoughmore Contract, ratified in January 1890, the Grace brothers and Lord Donoughmore took over Peru's national debt. In return, they secured control of the lucrative silver mines of La Oroya and Cerro de Pasco, and the lease on all of Peru's railroads for sixty-six years (on condition that they complete the lines, for which they would be paid separately). They were also granted 2 million hectares (5 million acres) of land, including the oil and mineral rich Perené Valley, and the rights to Peru's entire guano harvest.

The contract was signed in the face of widespread opposition from Peruvian nationalists, as well as miners and landowners who understandably interpreted this 'monstrous' scheme as a geopolitical move by an American firm seeking to monopolize Peru's trade and enterprise. To get it over the line, Billy Grace met with US president Grover Cleveland (having donated to both his successful White House campaigns) and reworked some of the finer terms. Perhaps more importantly, the brothers also handed out at least nineteen gold watches to borderline opponents. To cap it all, Michael Grace took home his brokerage fee, as well as a 3 per cent commission on the shares of the new corporation, which were distributed to the original bondholders.

In 1891 the Grace brothers established the New York and Pacific Steamship Company, which became the Grace Steamship Company. It was the first steamship line to run between New York and the west coast of South America, via the Strait of Magellan. Five years later, the Graces' interests were combined under a single American charter with the creation of William R. Grace & Company; John Grace, Billy and Michael's brother, joined as a vice president. The company now had offices in every Latin American country and by the close of the century, it controlled light, traction and power in Chile, as well as significant stakes in the country's sodium, nitrate, cotton and sugar industries. Billy Grace was also involved with a failed attempt to build a canal in Nicaragua.

In 1897, Billy, Lillius and Michael Grace co-founded the Grace Institute in New York to help train women, primarily immigrants, in dressmaking, stenography, typewriting, book-keeping and domestic science.

When Billy Grace was debilitated by a stroke in 1898, his brother Michael took charge of the firm, along with their Dublin-born kinsman, Edward Eyre. In December 1903, Billy was assailed by pneumonia but he continued to transact business from his bed. At the time of his death on 21 March 1904, the seventy-one-year-old tycoon was actively promoting the America-led construction of the Panama Canal. When it opened a decade later, a Grace steamer was one of the first ships to pass through. Six of Billy Grace's eleven children predeceased him, but he was survived by his wife, two sons and three daughters.

Michael Grace also lived on, passing away at his home in Battle Abbey, Sussex, in 1920. In 1901, his daughter Elena Maria had married Lord Donoughmore's son and heir. Another daughter Elisa married the Hon. Hubert Beaumont, a Liberal Member of Parliament in Westminster; their son Michael bought the old La Touche home of Harristown House, County Kildare, after the Second World War and served as Master of the Kildare Hunt from 1948 to 1958. Another of the Grace daughters, Margarita, married John Shaffer Phipps, the American philanthropist and steel magnate.

In 1945, Billy Grace's grandson J. Peter Grace became chairman of W. R. Grace and Company. Over the course of his forty-seven-year term, Peter Grace – who was also head of the Knights of Malta – built the firm into a multi-billion-dollar corporation. As well as its fleet and fertilizer business, it boasted an airline (Panagra), two massive sugar plantations, a paper mill, a chemical works, three textile mills, a confectionery factory, numerous import and export companies and major interests in everything from packaging and fishmeal production to banking, mining and industry. Based in Columbia, Maryland, the company continues today as one of the world's biggest speciality chemical businesses.

33

ANNIE MOORE, THE FIRST
EMIGRANT THROUGH ELLIS ISLAND

Ellis Island, New York Harbour, 1 January 1892. The burly German had one foot on the gangplank, poised for take-off, when an Irishman named Mike Tierney grabbed him by his coat collars, hollered 'Ladies first' and ushered Annie Moore ahead of him. 'Step out, little girl,' added Mike Tierney. And so, with her two small brothers walking behind her, she walked down the gangplank towards the glistening new immigration station. The Statue of Liberty towered over the city of New York to her south. It was New Year's Day 1892 – and the day that seventeen-year-old Annie Moore from Cork City became arguably the most famous emigrant in American history.

The 1890 census for the United States recorded 483,000 Irish-born settlers, of whom 260,000 were living in Massachusetts (primarily Boston), 190,000 in New York City and 124,000 in Illinois (primarily Chicago). By the end of the century, the Irish comprised 2.12 per cent of the United States population. However, the population of Americans born to Irish parents constituted a further 6.53 per cent.

All of this made it eminently suitable that Annie Moore should find herself centre stage for the US government's public relations event of the year when they opened the immigration station on Ellis Island, which lies just off the New Jersey coast. This was the first serious attempt by the American government to control immigration into the United States and it wanted to ensure that all of America's major newspapers were there to capture the event. By design or by chance, the first person to register was a sweet, young Irish girl, described variously as 'bareheaded' and 'buxom' with a 'woolly sack buttoned closely about her'. Annie Moore's name was telegraphed down the wire from Los Angeles to London and a legend was born.

Annie Moore was born in the spring of 1874 in a cottage on the Old Youghal Road, near present-day Collins Barracks, in Cork City, where her father Matthew Moore worked as a labourer. In about 1885, he sailed for New York with his wife, Julia Cronin, and two of Annie Moore's older siblings, while she and two younger brothers went to live with relatives elsewhere in Cork City. At length, her parents raised the necessary money to pay for their three younger children to join them in New York.

On 20 December 1891, the trio departed from Queenstown (now Cobh) aboard the Guion Line's SS *Nevada*. Offering 'superior accommodation for all classes at low rates', this was the same ship on which Kate Coll, Éamon de Valera's mother, had sailed to New York twelve years earlier. The young Moores' ten-day voyage across the Atlantic was not an easy one. As steerage passengers they slept in bunk beds near the bottom of the triple-deck steamship. The stench of vomit must have been unbearable, for this was a period of severe weather, heavy gales and high seas. On Christmas Day, an enormous wave broke over the ship, smashing the bridge and fracturing the captain's leg.

The *Nevada* arrived in New York at 3.50 p.m. on Thursday, 31 December 1891 and docked at the Hudson pier, from where the first- and second-class passengers disembarked for a cursory customs inspection. However, the steerage – or third-class – passengers were kept on board until the following day, then taken by barge to Ellis Island for a legal and medical examination.

Normal inspections would later last between three and five hours but, given the high-profile nature of this first day, Annie Moore's case was studied with greater haste. Having being so courteously ushered down the gangplank by Mike Tierney, the teenager was greeted by the superintendent of immigration Colonel Weber, who doffed his large sombrero hat, before she was subject to a light questioning by Charles M. Hendley, former private secretary to the US Secretary of the Treasury. With 'a festive din of bells and steamer whistles' resounding overhead, she was officially registered, presented with a $10 gold piece and 'set free in the land of opportunity'. A *New York Times* journalist reported that Moore told him 'she will never part with [the gold piece], but will always keep it as a pleasant memento of the occasion'. (Alas, there has been no sighting of the gold piece in modern times.) Father Callahan of the Mission of Our Lady of the Holy Rosary in New York then blessed the young Moores before they were reunited with their parents.

Later that afternoon, three more large ships docked in New York and a further 700 European immigrants were registered at Ellis Island. By the close of the first year, nearly 450,000 people had passed through the station. The fate of Annie Moore vanished into the melee.

Over the ensuing decades, her story became emblematic of the Irish-American experience. She was hailed as a symbol of all that was courageous, self-sacrificing and noble about Irish emigrants. In truth, few knew what had really become of the Moore siblings. It was widely believed that they left New York shortly after their arrival and went west to fulfil the American dream. Moore was said to have reached Texas and married a descendant of Daniel O'Connell, the Liberator. That story became all the more dramatic in 1923 when an Annie Moore from Texas was run over by a streetcar and killed at the age of forty-six.

In the early 2000s, American genealogist Megan Smolenyak discovered that Annie Moore of Texas was, in fact, born in Illinois and thus could not have been the Annie Moore who arrived at Ellis Island from County Cork. Intrigued, Smolenyak offered a $1,000 reward for any further information on Moore. To her delight, this yielded the naturalization certificate for Moore's brother Philip, who was listed in the 1930 census as a chauffeur in Brooklyn. From this detail, Smolenyak was able to establish contact with his grandson.

It transpired that after their arrival on Ellis Island, the three Moore children went to live with their parents in a five-storey tenement on Monroe Street in Lower Manhattan's Fourth Ward, the rough-and-tumble Lower East Side tenement area where the bloody gang wars and draft riots of the 1860s took place. Annie Moore later married Joseph Augustus Schayer, an employee at Manhattan's Fulton Fish Market. Five of their eleven children died young, while a sixth only lived to the age of twenty-one. Moore remained in the Fourth Ward until her death at the age of fifty in 1924 and was buried in an unmarked grave at Calvary Cemetery in Queen's, New York. A decade after her death, her home was incorporated into the Knickerbocker

Village housing development that was built between the Manhattan and Brooklyn bridges. One of her granddaughters lived there until her death in 2001.

Anthony Moore, who had accompanied his sister on the *Nevada*, died aged twenty-four in the Bronx and was buried in New York's City Cemetery, a 'potter's field' for people who couldn't afford private funerals. Philip, the youngest of the siblings, was hit by a car and killed in 1941, at which time he had a job as a sweeper.

In 2006, prompted by Smolenyak's discovery, Cork historian Tim McCoy and a team of eleven-year-old students from Cork City's Scoil Oilibhéir made a short film about Annie Moore. While researching the film, they found the Moore family's original home in Cork City and Annie Moore's baptismal records. This in turn led Cork City Council to unveil a plaque to Moore's memory at Rowland's Lane, the only house still standing among the various places that she lived.

In 2008, Annie Moore's small grass-covered grave in New York was marked with a monument of Irish Blue Limestone by master carver Francis McCormack of Tubber, County Clare. The Irish tenor Ronan Tynan performed at the ceremony, singing 'Isle of Hope, Isle of Tears' by Irish composer Brendan Graham. New York's County Cork Pipe and Drum Band also performed at the ceremony. Moore's memory is today recalled by two bronze statues by the late West Cork-based sculptor Jeanne Rynhart – one at her port of departure in Cobh and the other at Ellis Island, her port of arrival, holding her hat in the harbour breeze.

Between 1892 and 1954, more than 12 million immigrants entered the United States via Ellis Island. Annie Moore from Cork City was the first of them. Like the Moores, the vast majority of the Irish people who passed through Ellis Island never returned to their homeland.

34

MARGARETTA EAGAR,
THE LAST TSAR'S GOVERNESS

London, 1906. Margaretta Eagar needed to set the record straight. The rumours were becoming ridiculous. Some said she had been caught stealing from the Tsar of Russia's study. Others claimed she had been dismissed for mistreating his sickly young son and heir. Still more called her an 'English spy'. In any event, it was time for the Irishwoman who had spent six years as governess to Tsar Nicholas II's beautiful, ill-fated daughters to address the situation.

Margaretta Alexandra Eagar was born in Limerick on 12 August 1863, the fifth of eleven children of Francis McGillycuddy Eagar and his wife, Frances Margaret Holden. Shortly before Margaretta's birth, her father became governor of Limerick County Gaol. (He had previously been governor of Naas Gaol in County Kildare and deputy governor of Spike Island, Cork.) Her mother was the daughter of Francis Smollet Holden, a prominent composer of military music who ran an instrument shop on Parliament Street in Dublin.

Margaretta Eagar, or Margaret as she sometimes called herself, was seventeen years old when her father retired as governor in 1880. He and his wife then moved to the West End, Kilkee, County Clare. This was the popular seaside resort where Eagar had her first encounter with royalty when the young prince of Siam (later Rama VI, king of the country now known as Thailand) stayed with a friend at Kilkee in the 1890s.[1]

The Shannonside town was also abuzz in the wake of a visit by Prince Louis of Battenberg, whose wife was an older sister of the Russian tsarina. Prince Louis, a naval officer, called by Moore's Hotel in Kilkee one night when his ship was anchored in the Shannon. Not realizing who her guest was, Mrs Moore shovelled him into a twin room with a passing commercial traveller. When the prince requested a room of his own, Mrs Moore grumpily directed him to an empty cottage nearby. After the prince signed the visitor's book the following morning, Mrs Moore finally realized her error and apparently spent the remainder of her days convinced that she would be arrested at any moment for her discourtesy. Many years later, Margaretta Eagar met Prince Louis, who confirmed the tale.

During her twenties, she trained as a medical nurse in Belfast, worked as a matron at an orphanage and learned how to cook, as well as needlework and housekeeping. In 1898, family friend Emily Loch was working as a lady-in-waiting to the German royal family when she heard that Tsar Nicholas II of Russia and his German wife, Tsarina Alexandra, required a nanny for their young daughters. Loch wrote directly to the Tsarina recommending Eagar, who soon found herself on a train headed east from Berlin to the snowy, sunlit streets of St Petersburg.

Arriving on 2 February 1899, she advanced to the Winter Palace where, after a short rest, she was summoned to the Tsarina's boudoir to meet her new boss. Alexandra was clad in a mauve dress and Eagar recalled her as 'the handsomest woman I had ever seen – tall, statuesque in appearance, with very regular features and a high complexion'. She was also introduced to the Tsar's toddling daughters, the Grand Duchesses Olga and Tatiana, and the newborn baby, Maria. Her charges would increase to four with the birth of Anastasia in 1901.

Her principal base was the Winter Palace, then the largest building in Europe, and her memoirs record in great detail an interior stuffed with Fabergé eggs and gilt furniture, Rembrandts and Rubens, tortoiseshell doors, glass cabinets full of precious jewels, stuffed horses that had once been ridden by Peter the Great and a massive aviary stocked with hundreds of canaries. The imperial nursery, where the children learned to dance, was apparently 'large enough to hold a "mountain" down which the children toboggan'. Margaretta Eagar adored her four 'dear little charges': 'Olga has grace, wit, and good looks; Tatiana is a regular beauty; Marie [sic] is so sweet-natured, good and obliging, no one could help loving her; but little Anastasie [sic] has personal charm beyond any child I ever saw.'

The Irish governess was certainly a hit with Tatiana, who 'thought me a marvel of education, and confided in her music master that no one in the whole world knew so much as I did; she thought I knew everything, except music and Russian'. (When she read Lewis Carroll's *Alice in Wonderland* and *Through the Looking-Glass* to the girls, Tatiana was horrified at the manners of the queens. 'No queens', she said, 'would be so rude.') Olga took a little more work. When she espied a policeman arresting a drunken woman on the street one day, she urged her governess to stop him from hurting her. Eagar explained that the woman had been 'very naughty', after which there was a marked improvement in Olga's behaviour.

It is said that the girls began speaking English with a soft Limerick accent. Eagar hinted as much when she recounted how Maria, hitherto hailed as a virtuous angel, polished off a tray of her mother's *biblichen* (vanilla-flavoured wafers) when no one was looking. When Margaretta Eagar found her, the child remarked: 'Dere! I've eaten it all up.' Her governess ordered her straight to bed but the Tsar, who was especially fond of Maria, intervened. 'I was always afraid of the wings growing,' he said, 'and I am glad to see she is only a human child.' As Eagar observed: 'When she was barely able to toddle, Maria would always try to escape from the nurseries to go to papa, and whenever she saw him in the garden or park she would call after him. If he heard or saw her, he always waited for her, and would carry her for a little.' At length, the Tsarina called upon the services of Sydney Gibbes, an English linguist, to rid her daughters of their Irish brogue.

Ireland was never far from Margaretta Eagar's mind. In her memoirs, she frequently alludes to the common threads in Russian and Irish folklore and superstitions: 'The Russian fairy, like its Irish prototype, is, as a general rule, a malignant being, always ready to do some mean or nasty trick.' Moreover, the 'unaccountable bruises [that] appear on one's body' are supposed to be 'the work of evil spirits who wish to get you out of the house'. In Ireland, she noted, such bruises are called 'dead men's pinches'. She also observed how the Irish and Russians both consulted cards to interpret dreams and have their fortunes told.

Maria's baptism at the Great Palace at Peterhof was one of the first events Margaretta Eagar attended; the exceptionally elaborate ceremony lasted nearly three hours. However, the royals were often on the move on state visits or attending weddings, shooting parties or other events with their royal cousins in Europe. Eagar always went with them, tasked with keeping watch over the four grand duchesses. The Tsar's yacht was 'as large as an ocean liner' and carried a crew of 500 men.

She spent the winter of 1900–1 with the Romanovs in the Crimea, visiting several of the sites where the bloody battles of the Crimean War had been fought nearly half a century earlier, including the Alma, Inkerman and Sevastopol. The royal yacht then crossed the Black Sea to Yalta and the party made its way to the Tsar's coastal estate at Livadia. The Christmas spirit was considerably dampened when the Tsar was stricken with a five-week bout of typhoid fever.

Margaretta Eagar was sailing back for St Petersburg with the family in late January 1901 when a telegram arrived announcing the death of the Tsarina's grandmother, Queen Victoria. Such proximity to Europe's intimately entwined imperial elite meant that she had plenty of royal encounters during her time in Russia. In 1903, she was at Darmstadt, the Tsarina's home city in Germany, to attend the wedding of Princess Alice of Battenberg (a niece of the Tsarina) and Prince Andrew of Greece, the parents of Prince Philip, the present Duke of Edinburgh. In Potsdam, she met the Kaiser, who would all too soon plunge Europe into the First World War. In Denmark, she met Edward VII, the new king of England, who 'frequently spoke to me…and called me "My Irish subject"'. (After the birth of the Tsar's son Alexei in 1905, the English king sent her a green enamel brooch. 'He has very winning manners and great tact,' she wrote. 'They say he never forgets anything, and I know he never forgets to be kind.')

One of her favoured hideaways was at Subswina Datcha, a rococo villa located about 8 km (5 miles) outside Peterhof, where the Romanovs lived the farm life, playing amid hayricks, feeding hens, gathering apples and helping milk cows. The children rode Shetland ponies or were driven around in a cart, feeding bottles of warm milk to newborn kittens. Otherwise she was in St Petersburg, where she often accompanied the deeply religious Romanovs to church. They worshipped in the Greek Orthodox Church, which, noted Eagar, was 'in ritual and doctrine' more Catholic than Protestant. (She was baptized into the Church of Ireland.) Every Good Friday, she and the girls would colour hundreds of eggs in the nurseries: 'It was a great pleasure to the children, but rather dirty work.'

There were random meetings with fellow Irishmen, such as a priest from Limerick who she met out shopping and who happened to know some of her family. The priest worked in the docks of Glasgow, where many of the poorest workers were Poles. Frustrated by his inability to communicate with the Poles, he had undertaken a mission to Poland, to unite with Polish priests and source 'a supply of prayer-books, catechisms, and other religious books' that might offer solace to the Glaswegian Poles. Eagar was greatly impressed, as was the Tsarina when she relayed the encounter. Margaretta Eagar's memoir reveals that she was not immune to Russia's horrific social problems, not least the cramped cabins she saw as the royal carriage trotted through the countryside. Overcrowding, she said, caused a death rate of 35 per cent among children. She maintained that the Tsar was determined to improve the lot 'for his poorer subjects' but such destitution was difficult for his daughters to stomach. In Poland, the 'very sensitive' Olga was horrified by the sight of people kneeling in the road whenever the children's carriage approached: 'She used to look at them with tears in her eyes and beg of me to tell them not to do it.' The Tsar spent 'hours each day' in his study, located next to the Tsarina's boudoir, 'working hard for the advancement of the great empire committed to his charge'. She decried the various attempts to kill him but passed no comment on Grand Duke Sergei Alexandrovich, the Tsar's uncle, who was assassinated by a terrorist bomb in early 1905.

She mused upon Russian industry: 'linen is almost as good as that produced in Ireland, but cottons and woollen materials fall very far behind our own productions'. (When a friend from County Cork posted her some Irish crochet lace, it was stolen by someone in the post office.)

Current affairs were a topic of much interest to her. She deplored the barbaric massacre of Bessarabian Jews at Kishinev (the capital of present-day Moldova) in 1903, blaming the local governor. Grand Duchess Olga Alexandrovna, the Tsar's younger sister, observed that Margaretta Eagar was once so absorbed discussing the Dreyfus Affair with a friend that she didn't notice when Grand Duchess Maria escaped from her bath and began scampering up and down the palace corridors naked.

The curtain began to fall for Eagar with the outbreak of war between Russia and the Empire of Japan in January 1904. The girls went to work knitting: 'Even little Anastasie worked at frame knitting. They made scarves for the soldiers, and Olga and Tatiana crocheted caps indefatigably.' That said, Margaretta Eagar wrote, 'It was very sad to me to witness the wrathful vindictive spirit that the war raised in my little charges.' One day she heard Olga say: 'I hope the Russian soldiers will kill all the Japanese; not leave even one alive.' Eagar gave her a stern lecture, explaining how the Japanese were 'people like ourselves'. After that, she wrote, Olga 'never again said anything about being pleased to hear of the deaths of the Japanese'.

Alexei, the long-awaited heir (known as the Tsarevich), was born on 12 August 1904. It was also Margaretta Eagar's forty-first birthday. When she called in to see the Tsarina, the new mother said: 'You see what a nice birthday present I have given you.' However, her term with the Romanovs ended just over six weeks later on 29 September 1904: 'I was very sorry and grieved to say good-bye to the dear children whom I love so well.' A rumour that she had been dismissed for stealing papers from the Tsar's study was so serious that she wrote to the press, emphatically denying the charge. She was also obliged to refute a story that she was sacked because the Tsar disapproved of her treatment of the baby Tsarevich; as she explained, Alexei 'did not, as a matter of fact, come under my charge'.

She insisted she had left for 'purely personal and private reasons' and remained on excellent terms with the royal family. *The Gentlewoman*, a weekly British socialite magazine, stated that she had 'quitted the Imperial service, owing to her father's illness (since terminated in death)'.[2] However, it seems her criticism of the anti-Japanese sentiment voiced by the grand duchesses may have been the source of her undoing. It is certainly notable that the Tsar's diary specifically refers to her causing 'trouble and dissension' at court with her penchant .

for tackling such xenophobia. Nonetheless, the Tsarina rewarded her with a 'handsome money present', while she was also granted a pension for life from the Russian government. She was to maintain correspondence with the Tsarina and her 'dear little charges' for many years afterwards.

In 1906, Margaretta Eagar penned a short and fascinating memoir called *Six Years at the Russian Court*, which recounted her intimate experience of the Romanov dynasty. She maintained that the Tsarina 'encouraged me to do so, saying so many untruths had been published that it would be a relief to have an account of the Russian Court which was absolutely true'. She is assumed to have gone to Ireland for a stint to see her mother who, widowed in 1902, was now living on the Main Street of Baltinglass, County Wicklow, with her daughter Grace and her bank manager husband Alister MacLeod. By 1908, Eagar was running a boarding house at 27 Holland Park Gardens, Kensington, London. At the time of the 1911 Census of Ireland, she was staying in Belfast with her sister Frances and her husband, Rev. George Hanson, Presbyterian minister for Duncairn.

Meanwhile, the Romanovs were on a devastating road. A year after Margaretta Eagar left, desperate to cure their haemophiliac son, the Tsar and his wife turned to the healer Rasputin. His rise and fall was followed by the catastrophic loss of life for Russia in the First World War and a series of revolutions during which the Winter Palace was stormed. The Russian royal family was shot and bayoneted to death by drunken Bolsheviks at Yekaterinburg on the night of 16/17 July 1918. Margaretta Eagar's four grand duchesses were all killed. Maria and Anastasia, who had loved blowing balloons with her, were the last to die, huddled against a wall covering their heads in terror, as the savage bullets rained upon them.

The sole survivor was Joy, Crown Prince Alexei's blind spaniel. Eight days later, a White Russian force arrived at Yekaterinburg commanded by Colonel Paul (Pavel) Rodzianko, one of the Tsar's former personal equerries who was serving with the British Expeditionary Force in Siberia. The spaniel appeared, wagging his tail hesitantly, and stumbled straight into Rodzianko's leg. He assumed care of Joy and when he later fled to the United Kingdom, Joy came with him.

The dog is buried in a garden in Windsor, his gravestone ironically marked by the line 'Here lies Joy'. Rodzianko later went to Ireland, married Anita Leslie of Castle Leslie and became manager of a triumphant Irish show-jumping team in the 1930s.

Margaretta Eagar's Russian pension stopped after the royal family's murder, but one can only imagine how appalled she was as the news of their death emerged. In 1922, a woman named Anna Anderson claimed that she was Anastasia; she was shown photographs of Anderson and swiftly declared it a falsity. Eagar died aged seventy-three at the Grange Nursing Home at Keynsham, near Bristol, on 2 August 1936.

35

THE MOORE BROTHERS, HOLLYWOOD STARS

Jersey City, New Jersey, 7 January 1911. Their ship was due to set sail for Havana the day after the film star Owen Moore tied the knot with his leading lady. She wore a sealskin coat to the courthouse wedding, along with a dress, a train and awkwardly high heels. The marriage was a closely kept secret, attended by neither friend nor family and certainly not the bride's mother. Indeed, as the bride later recalled, 'that was the first time I was ever disobedient to my mother'. Nonetheless, she returned home that night to share a bed with her sister, as she had always done.

The next day she reunited with her new husband and they sailed to Cuba, where they would spend the first weeks of their married life. They were filming a curiously prophetic short called *The Dream* about an abusive husband with an alcohol problem. By the time of their return to the United States, Owen Moore must have felt confident that his career was about to enter a golden age. What the Meath-born actor did not yet know was that he would soon be utterly eclipsed by his wife. Her name was Mary Pickford.

In the Roaring Twenties the Moore brothers – Owen, Tom and Matt – were household names across the United States, racking up more than 600 movie credits between them. They were descendants of a Catholic farming family who had lived in County Meath for as far back as records allow. Their grandfather Tom Moore was born in 1795 and lived at Fordstown, midway between Kells and Athboy. He died at the age of eighty-seven in 1882. His wife Elizabeth Farrelly was one of seven sisters who had inherited a lock of land at Seymourstown, some 15 km (9 miles) northwest of Fordstown.

Shortly before old Tom's death, his son John Moore married Rosanna Carey, daughter of Fordstown farmer Owen Carey, or Carry, for whom they named their second son, Owen Moore. They grew up in a modest, clay-walled farmhouse that has long since sunk back into the earth and been ploughed under, although the laneway to the house still exists.

John Moore was almost sixty years old when he and Rosanna decided to start anew in the United States. In early 1896, they crossed the Atlantic as steerage passengers on the SS *Anchoria*, accompanied by their five sons, thirteen-year-old Tom, ten-year-old Owen, eight-year-old Matt, two-year-old John and nine-month old Joe, and their seven-year-old daughter Mary. Having passed through Ellis Island, they made their way to Toledo, Ohio, where John found work as a farm labourer and janitor. He remained in Toledo until 1912, when he appears to have returned home to die. He passed away at Balrathboyne, near Fordstown, on 22 July 1912, aged seventy-six. Rosanna was also in Ireland at this time, but she returned to the United States on the SS *Carmania* in June 1913 and moved to Los Angeles, where she died in 1924.

Meanwhile, fed up with the penny-pinching lifestyle in Ohio, Tom and Owen Moore ran away in their teens and joined a travelling theatre company. They were both seasoned stage performers by the time the motion picture industry kicked off in 1908. Both made their movie debuts in New York that year, with films from Biograph Studios directed by D. W. Griffith, the son of a Confederate colonel from Kentucky – Owen in *The Guerrilla* (Griffith's first Civil War film) and Tom in *The Christmas Burglars*.

Bernardo O'Higgins Director Supremo de la República Chilena, Capitan General de exto Primer Almirante de sus Esquadras, Presid.^e del Consejo de la Legion de Mérito, y Grande Oficial de ella &c &c.

4 Bernardo O'Higgins was Supreme Director of Chile from 1817 until 1823. He is also hailed as the founder of both the Chilean Military Academy and the Chilean Navy.

LEFT **15** Margaret of New Orleans was the second woman in US history to be honoured with a public monument. First erected in 1906, the life-size Carrara marble statue was refurbished in the wake of Hurricane Katrina in 2005.

BELOW **16** The Alamo Mission in San Antonio, Texas, where the Battle of the Alamo took place in 1836. At least fifteen of those who died in the famous battle were Irish.

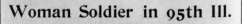

Woman Soldier in 95th Ill.

ALBERT D. J. CASHIER
OF
COMPANY G, 95TH ILLINOIS REGIMENT

Photographed November, 1864

ALBERT D. J. CASHIER
OF
COMPANY G, 95TH ILLINOIS REGIMENT

Photographed July, 1913

ABOVE **17** Andrew J. Russell's epic 'champagne photo' captures the celebrations at Promontory Point, Utah, marking the completion of the Pacific Railroad on 10 May 1869.

LEFT **18** Albert Cashier pictured as a solider with the 95th Illinois Infantry in 1864 and, on the right, at the Soldiers and Sailors Home in Quincy, Illinois, nearly fifty years later.

19 John Philip Holland,
the Clare-born engineer,
climbing out of the hatch
of the submarine in about
1910. Holland developed
the first submarine to be
commissioned by the
US Navy.

ABOVE **20** Nellie Cashman, *c.* 1880, shortly after her arrival in Tombstone, Arizona. The portrait is based on a photograph taken by her Chinese cook. Nellie was to become a household name for mining communities from Alaska to Mexico.

LEFT **21** Eliza Lynch, the Cork-born mistress of Francisco Solano López, president of Paraguay, was about twenty-one years old when this photograph was taken in 1855.

ABOVE **22** Billy Grace, the Irishman who became New York's first Catholic mayor in 1880, made his fortune supplying ships coming to collect dried bird droppings from the Great Guano Heap, pictured, in Peru's Chincha Islands in the 1850s.

LEFT **23** Margaretta Eagar, pictured with the Tsar of Russia's four daughters, the Grand Duchesses Olga, Tatiana, Maria and baby Anastasia, to whom she was governess from 1898 to 1904.

RIGHT **24** In 1929, Tom, Matt and Owen Moore starred in a crime caper called 'Side Street'. The brothers, born in County Meath, all have stars on the Hollywood Walk of Fame.

BELOW **25** Louis Brennan stands alongside his new Gyroscope monorail, shortly after it made its debut at the Mayo-born inventor's home in Gillingham, Kent.

ABOVE LEFT **26** Better known as Lord Haw-Haw, William Joyce had become the English voice of Hitler's Germany by the time this photo was taken in March 1940. He was also known as Scarface on account of his scar, the consequence of a brawl with a Communist a few years after he moved from Galway to London.

ABOVE **27** Violet Gibson photographed near to the time of her attempted assassination of Benito Mussolini in 1926.

LEFT **28** Winston Churchill considered Tipperary-born Brendan Bracken one of his closest friends and wept when he learned of his death. This photo was taken at about the time that Churchill appointed Bracken as Minister of Information in March 1941.

In 1909, Owen was cast as Sandro in *The Violin Maker of Cremona*, another Griffith movie, in which he falls in love with the violin maker's daughter, Giannina. The role of Giannina was played by a seventeen-year-old Canadian girl of Irish roots by the name of Gladys Smith, who made an astonishing fifty-one short movies in 1909 alone. As she later said, 'I decided that if I could get into as many pictures as possible, I'd become known, and there would be a demand for my work.' Since 1907, the enchanting, pint-sized Gladys Smith had acted under the stage name of Mary Pickford, a nod to her mother's father, John Pickford Hennessy of Ballyduff, County Kerry.

The chemistry between Mary Pickford and Owen Moore was obvious to all when the two collaborated on *Their First Misunderstanding*. The film was released on 9 January 1911, two days after their marriage. The ten-minute film was thought lost until found in a New Hampshire barn in 2006, and is now carefully preserved at the Library of Congress. Mary Pickford would earn the wrath of her mother, Charlotte Hennessy, for her clandestine marriage. However, the actress's meteoritic rise to stardom had by now commenced. By the close of 1915, the 'Girl with the Curls' was not only 'America's Sweetheart' but arguably the most famous woman in the world. She commanded a salary of $10,000 a week, with a $300,000 bonus, plus her own production company.

Her marriage to Owen Moore did not survive, however. There was a rumoured abortion or miscarriage and her husband's sense of being overshadowed metamorphosed into intense jealousy. With alcohol on board, he was prone to mental – and possibly physical – abuse of his wife. When she invited him to direct her movies, he ruined it by bullying and humiliating her in front of the crew, and then, in 1916, Douglas Fairbanks swashbuckled into the plot. Pickford filed for divorce and married Fairbanks in 1920.

Owen Moore married again in 1921 to the New York actress Katherine Perry, with whom he appeared in six movies. A star performer throughout the 1920s and early 1930s, Moore's biggest hit was *She Done Him Wrong*, a 1933 rom-com in which he played the nasty, unhinged boyfriend of Mae West's hip-swishing Lady Lou. Alcohol ultimately got the better of him in June 1939 when the fifty-two-year-old Meath man suffered a fatal heart attack in Beverley Hills.

Meanwhile, his older brother Tom Moore was married in 1914 to the Missouri-born silent star Alice Joyce, best known for *The Green Goddess*. They had a daughter Alice Moore, with whom Tom co-starred in six films during the 1930s. In 1920, the newly divorced Tom Moore met the beautiful Renée Adorée, the daughter of French circus artists, and married her six weeks later; she was to wow the world with a very short nude swimming scene filmed in 1928. After their marriage collapsed, Tom married a third time to Eleanor Merrie, with whom he had a son, Tom Moore Junior.

In November 1922, Tom Moore returned to Ireland for the first time in twenty-seven years. With a nod at a new word called 'fan', the *Freeman's Journal* observed: 'The popular cinema artist who, with his artistic sense, his dramatic ability and his merry smile, has won thousands of "fans", as they call admirers in America, has arrived in Ireland to visit the place of his birth.' With the Irish Civil War in full flow, the press were eager to get his opinion but he would not be drawn. 'I'll talk about anything but the "movies" or politics,' he said, with his famous smile. 'I'm on a holiday from one, and as far as politics is concerned, I'm Irish – and that's all.'

His visit to his home county of Meath was a highlight of his trip, including a day out with the Meath Hunt (filmed by Pathé News) and a reunion with some of his Fordstown relatives. Prior to his arrival, Tom Moore told the press that he could still remember the place clearly from his childhood: 'I have heard so much from [my father] that I am sure I can walk up to some of the oldest inhabitants and call them by their first names. And I can find the boreen that led off the main road to the old home with my eyes shut.'[1] With the economic recession of the 1930s, Moore quit the silver screen although he was later to return in minor roles. Struck with cancer, he died in Santa Monica, California, in 1955, aged seventy-one.

Tom and Owen Moore's younger brother Matt followed them from Toledo to New York and made his film debut in 1912 starring alongside Owen and the Canadian actress Florence Lawrence (whose mother was Irish) in the silent short, *Tangled Relations*. The

Los Angeles Times hailed him as 'one of the screen's finest and most facile young comedians'. He proved particularly popular with boxing fans after his performance as a screen fighter in the 1924 hit, *Fools in the Dark*. Five years later, he played opposite Mary Pickford, his brother's ex-wife, in the drama *Coquette*. It was Pickford's first talkie and, having shorn off her famous curls for the role, she was rewarded with her second Oscar.

Matt Moore eschewed the spotlight, making sure he had steady work but deliberately never setting the stage alight. 'I'm afraid of flares', he remarked, 'and never want to be one. Actors usually flop after a flare.' In 1928 he starred opposite Mary Astor in *Dry Martini*, a Paris-based silent film based on a book by John Thomas, whose maternal grandparents came from County Wexford. Matt continued to act until 1958, racking up 221 motion picture appearances and concluding with a B-movie horror film called *I Bury the Living*. He died aged seventy-two in 1960.

The Moores' only sister Mary also became a silent movie star, appearing in thirteen films between 1914 and 1917, including *The Adventure at Briarcliff*, directed by her brother Tom. She was serving with the Red Cross in France in 1919 when she was fatally stricken with the Spanish flu. Joe Moore, the youngest brother, also took to the screen, starring in thirteen films between 1914 and August 1926 when he tragically had a heart attack and drowned in Santa Monica, California, aged thirty-one.

Owen, Tom and Matt Moore only appeared together in one movie, a 1929 crime caper called *Side Street* (or *Three Brothers*, as it was known in the United Kingdom), in which they starred as the O'Farrell brothers alongside Owen's wife, Katherine Perry. The three Moore siblings were also united when they each had a posthumous terrazzo and brass star laid down on the Hollywood Walk of Fame in 1960. They are the only hat-trick of siblings to have been awarded such an honour.

36

LOUIS BRENNAN,
THE WIZARD OF OZ

London, 4 November 1910. Winston Churchill, David Lloyd George and Herbert Asquith step into a train driven by a man from Mayo. It sounds like the makings of a joke but this is precisely what happened in the Exhibition Grounds at Shepherd's Bush on that lovely autumnal day. As well as the sitting prime minister and two future prime ministers, the party in the carriage included Violet Asquith (later a British Liberal politician and grandmother of actress Helena Bonham Carter), Augustine Birrell (the new Chief Secretary of Ireland) and the fabulously wealthy merchant banker, Ernest Cassel.

It made sense that Churchill, then Britain's colonial secretary, should lead them. After all, he had already opined that this system would 'revolutionize the railway systems of the world'. He now grinned broadly as they whirled around and around the circular track, occasionally travelling in reverse. Afterwards the group dutifully gathered for an explanation of the Brennan Gyro Monorail from its moustachioed inventor, Louis Brennan.

Over the next three years, Churchill would do his very best to ensure that Brennan's gyroscopic monorail would become the must-have transport system of the twentieth century. He did not succeed but nonetheless, with a torpedo and a helicopter also under his belt, Louis Brennan must surely rank as the most remarkable inventor ever born in Ireland.

Louis Philip Brennan was born on Main Street, Castlebar, County Mayo, on 28 January 1852, the tenth of eleven children. Thomas Brennan, his father, was a merchant in the town who sold everything from hardware and bee colonies to wine, tea and condiments. Thomas and his wife, Bridget McDonnell, had endured great sorrow before Louis's birth, losing five children between 1842 and 1847.

By the time of Louis's fourth birthday, their eldest son Patrick had moved to Australia and found work as a teacher in the new gold rush boomtown of Melbourne. Michael Brennan, the next-oldest brother, was then working as a journalist and caricaturist with the *Connaught Telegraph*. He was to remain in Ireland when his parents and younger siblings, including nine-year-old Louis, joined Patrick in Australia in 1861. Over the next decade, Michael Brennan became a landscape and subject artist of considerable merit. His career was cut tragically short when he succumbed to consumption aged thirty-two in Algiers in 1871. Two of his 1866 paintings hang in the National Gallery of Ireland, namely *A Vine Pergola at Capri* and *In the Church of San Costanzo, Capri*.

Meanwhile, the family had arrived in Melbourne, where young Louis Brennan completed his schooling before going on to master the art of engineering through evening classes at Collingwood Artisans' School of Design. His genius was apparent by 1873 when the twenty-one-year-old dazzled the crowds gathered for the Juvenile Industries Exhibition in Victoria with inventions such as a window safety latch, a mincing machine and a billiard marker. His work also caught the eye of Alexander Kennedy Smith, a wealthy Scot who ran the biggest foundry in Melbourne and who became the city's mayor in 1875.

Encouraged by Smith, Brennan let his mind run wild with the possibilities of creation. The story runs that the young Irishman was toying with a cotton reel one afternoon when he devised a concept that would ultimately lead him to invent the world's first successful guided missile. The conceit was simple: if you pull the thread on a reel from underneath, the reel moves away; the faster you pull the thread, the quicker it moves. Over the ensuing weeks, he tried to think of things that needed to go away at speed and never come back. Introduced to someone from the Victoria Torpedo Corps, he stroked his chin and thought 'Eureka!'. Fast forward to the spring of 1879 and Brennan, now twenty-seven, was to be found striding around the shores of Melbourne's Hobson Bay, addressing the state governor and an assorted collection of senior army and navy officers. This was to be the first exhibition of the new wire-driven Brennan Torpedo, which he patented on 1 February 1878.

According to one rather morbid officer, the torpedo was shaped 'like a child's coffin', a square box tapering to a sharp bow and stern.

It contained two internal reels, each holding 3 km (just under 2 miles) of wire, connected to two propellers. As the crowd watched, a steam-driven machine – located on the shore – extracted the reel-wires at breakneck speed. The cogs spun, the propellers whizzed, the wires stretched and the torpedo shot into the air. A gunner steered it towards a small target boat 366 m (1,200 ft) away using left- and right-hand guide wires, keeping track of its positioning with a small mast that jutted above the waves. The torpedo ran for just over a minute at a speed of 11 knots before striking the boat. The flight pattern had been unnervingly erratic and it plunged with alarming regularity but it had struck the target. The military highbrows were impressed – the Royal Navy headquarters in London were informed and Brennan was invited to give a demonstration in Britain.

He was not a natural presenter. A correspondent for the *London Evening Standard* would later remark how he spoke 'hesitatingly… with a touch of an Irish brogue; and anybody less like an inventor introducing an eighth wonder of the world to an incredulous public could hardly be imagined'.[1] Perhaps in consequence of this, it took four years to convince the British that his torpedo was an essential weapon. The Royal Navy were understandably wary of a device so cumbersome that it required a railway system to move it, as well as observation points, engine houses and giant steam winchers. The missile itself weighed 3 tonnes and, as well as 100 kg (220 lb) of explosives, each reel required 1,030 m (3,375 ft) of wire in order to achieve a run of 320 m (1,050 ft). However, Brennan was fortunate to find favour with Sir Andrew Clarke, a former surveyor general of Victoria and close colleague of Alexander Smith. Clarke, who was raised in Donegal and educated at Portora Royal School, Enniskillen, was now Britain's Inspector General of Fortifications and he urged the War Office to show greater faith in Brennan's invention.

On 13 February 1883, Louis Brennan signed an agreement with the British government, under which £5,000 was paid to the Brennan Torpedo Company to cover all expenses incurred to date. The inventor was simultaneously given a three-year contract on a 'mutually agreed fixed remuneration'. The government also provided him with a workshop at the School of Military Engineering at Chatham in

England, and plenty of skilled labour. This investment paid handsome dividends. By 1885, the missile could be guided all the way to its target, with a range of 3 km (just under 2 miles), travelling at 40 kmph (25 mph) and cruising 3 m (10 ft) below the surface of the sea. It was to remain the most vital cog in Britain's coastal defence system for the next twenty years until it was phased out and replaced by the new 9.2-inch gun.

Precisely how the original torpedo was modified is unknown because everything was carried out under procedures of extreme secrecy. For instance, any team working on the project was kept in complete ignorance of what every other team was doing. Such mystery may have been part of an elaborate strategy to bluff Britain's overseas adversaries. No foreign power ever succeeded in copying Brennan's torpedo but perhaps no foreign power felt it was worth copying. To date, certain details of the torpedo's internal workings remain classified knowledge.

Louis Brennan was handsomely rewarded for his work. In 1887, Lord Salisbury's Conservative government paid him a lump sum of £30,000 (or close to €3 million today), to be followed by a further £80,000 (about €8 million today) over the next five years. He was also appointed superintendent of the new Brennan Torpedo Factory at Gillingham in Kent at a salary of £1,500 per annum (€185,000). 'It is not only your torpedo we want to buy,' explained Edward Stanhope, the war minister who brokered the deal. 'We want to buy your brains as well.'

Between 1884 and 1894, a series of brick and stone 'Brennan's torpedo forts' were erected over harbours along the coast of Britain, as well as at strategic naval bases like Malta and Hong Kong. The only station to be built in Brennan's native Ireland was at Fort Camden (now Fort Meagher), positioned to defend Cork Harbour, which was completed in 1895 at a cost of £9,225 (almost €1 million today). A source of much delight to twenty-first-century industrial archaeologists, its tracks and tunnels are still visible at the Cork fort today.

Meanwhile, Brennan was enjoying the high life in London, becoming a regular at royal levees, dinners and other soirées in a city of extraordinary confidence. At Queen Victoria's birthday honours in

May 1892, the thirty-nine-year-old Irishman was made a Companion of the Most Honourable Order of the Bath. Eight months earlier, he was married in Mount Argus Passionist Church, Dublin, to his childhood sweetheart, Anna Mary Quinn, eldest daughter of Michael Quinn, a butcher and cattle dealer based on Ellison Street, Castlebar.

Brennan used his fortune to build his bride a large family home called Woodlands, complete with a long, rambling garden, on a site beside the torpedo factory overlooking the River Medway. This is where the Brennan's three children enjoyed their childhood. As his wife had a heart condition, Louis Brennan invented what he called the 'Helping Hand' stair lift to help her ascend the stairs. He also built a recess into the floor of the main hall into which a billiard table could be lowered when not in use, thus enabling the room to be used for dancing. Among some forty inventions that he patented were a pocket-sized recording machine, a two-wheeled 'Gyrocar' and the Brennanograph, a five-key silent typewriter similar to those used by stenographers in law courts.

However, Brennan's greater dream was to create a gyroscopically balanced monorail. He had been obsessed by the concept ever since he purchased a wind-up toy from a street pedlar for his son in 1896. Nine years later, he announced that his new invention was ready and, with one eye on his bank balance, stated it was ideally suited to military use, confidently declaring that it would soon supersede the double-track railways of the Victorian Age.

In May 1907 he invited a group of Britain's most eminent scientists and engineers to view his extraordinary contraption in action at Woodlands. A wooden locomotive, held upright by a pair of giant gyroscopes, wended its way through the Brennans' extensive gardens, gliding past stately oaks and buoyant rhododendrons, swooping over lily ponds and mossy riverbanks, tilting as it rounded bends, like a motorcyclist leaning into a curve. In the back of the locomotive sat a young boy, dressed in plus-fours and a peaky cap, who held his nerve even when the train turned sharply just as it appeared to be about to plunge into a brick wall. To ensure that the 800-m (2,600-ft) track simulated reality as much as possible, Brennan had included a section where the track was bent sideways, as if by earthquake damage. The locomotive also journeyed over a chasm on a single steel cable, a manoeuvre that would have required a viaduct or bridge for a conventional train.

The press loved it, dubbing it the 'Blondin railway' after the famous tightrope walker. 'If Mr Brennan's hopes for his invention are realised,' noted one reporter, 'we are all to travel with the maximum of comfort and safety in cars which may be as large as a ship, running on wheels along a single line with beautiful smoothness, and at the rate of 100 to 150 miles hour.'[2]

With Churchill's support, Brennan persuaded the War Office to let him use the vacant torpedo works to develop his monorail. Churchill also bullied the India Office into giving him a secret grant of £5,000. The Maharajah of Kashmir, convinced that a monorail would be the perfect way to traverse the Himalayan foothills, put up another £5,000. Such investment was vital to Brennan, who had already sunk the bulk of his fortune into the venture and was now paying his workers out of his own increasingly empty pocket.

In 1910, ever wise to the power of spectacle, Brennan demonstrated his updated monorail at the Japan-British Exhibition in London with such aplomb that Prime Minister Herbert Asquith joined Churchill and Lloyd George for the much-publicized ride. Brennan received the exhibition's coveted Grand Prize and there was no doubt that the monorail could offer a cheaper, faster and smoother method of travel to the conventional railway. But was it safe? What would happen if his spinning train broke down? Would it simply keel over and crash? Facing bankruptcy, Brennan faltered, replying that his system could never break down. His answer was unsatisfactory and, one by one, the War Office, the India Office and the Kashmiri government rejected his gyroscope. So too did Major John E. Ballaine, who had been considering it for an extension to the Alaska Central Railroad. As the world tumbled towards the First World War, Brennan's monorail was abandoned. It would be another seventy years before people could ride on tilting trains.

Having invested so much of his time and money on the endeavour, Brennan was forced to sell his home at Woodlands and return to work. During the war, he moved to the Royal Aircraft Establishment factory at Farnborough in Hampshire, where he served in the munition's inventions department. In 1919 he convinced the Air Ministry to commission him to invent the world's first helicopter. His experiments took place in a closely guarded aerodrome, making it one of the greatest talking points in post-war engineering circles. Could one really devise an aeroplane that would hover? The British government spent vast sums on the project and, by the summer of 1922, it looked like the Irish septuagenarian was about to gain fresh laurels. With a pioneering use of rotor technology, his new 'helicopter' very briefly rose into the air, complete with a pilot and 113 kg (250 lb) of ballast. The *New York Times* giddily described the event as 'one of the most important and far-reaching steps yet made in the history or aeronautics'.

However, those within the bolted aerodrome knew that all was not so rosy: Brennan's helicopter was not quite right. Three years later, it had still not been launched and there were ominous reports that serious damage had been caused to the superstructure when it crash-landed during a take-off. In 1926 the Air Ministry closed down the operation, reasoning that progress was simply so slow that it could no longer be afforded.

Brennan was devastated but vowed to continue with his experiments. Inevitably, he poured his last remaining shillings into his doomed enterprise. On 26 December 1931, just months after the death of his beloved wife, Louis Brennan was knocked down by a car at Montreux, Switzerland. He died a few days short of his eightieth birthday on 17 January 1932. Nine days later, following a requiem mass at Westminster Cathedral, he was buried at St Mary's Roman Catholic Cemetery in London's Kensal Green. Although he was buried in an unmarked grave, a group from his hometown of Castlebar arranged for a headstone to be erected above his grave in 2014.

37

VIOLET GIBSON:
KILLING MUSSOLINI

How lucky it is we are to be judged by God instead of man.

VIOLET GIBSON, 1925

Rome, 7 April 1926. '*Giovinezza, giovinezza, primavera di bellezza*' bellowed the students gathered in Piazza del Campidoglio as they sang the official hymn of the National Fascist Party. At length, Il Duce himself stepped out from the Palazzo dei Conservatori to acknowledge his doting fans. It is not clear whether he spotted the bedraggled, fifty-year-old woman pointing a revolver at him. Maybe it was instinct, perhaps it was luck. Either way, Benito Mussolini turned his head just in time so that the bullet she fired at his temple scraped across the bridge of his nose. The woman pulled the trigger a second time but the bullet jammed. The would-be assassin was hurled to the ground, where she was kicked and punched by an incensed mob until the Carabinieri managed to push through and seize her. As the Italian dictator was hurried to safety, she was hauled across the Tiber to Regina Coeli prison and placed in a complex for female prisoners known as Le Mantellate. Within a few short hours she was identified as Dublin-born Violet Gibson.

The Gibsons were one of Ireland's most distinguished legal families, affiliated with counties Meath and Tipperary. Violet Gibson's father Edward enjoyed a particularly successful political career, becoming a darling of the Conservative Party in the age of Benjamin Disraeli and Lord Randolph Churchill. An exceptionally tall and command-ing man, with a shock of white hair and a booming voice, some thought he would make a future prime minister. Having come to prominence as Disraeli's principal advisor on Irish affairs, his most notable achievement was to oversee the passage of the Land Purchase Act of 1885, by which some 25,000 Irish tenant farmers borrowed money from a government fund to purchase their farms from their landlords. The Act marked a breakthrough in the bitter age of the Land Wars and Gibson was rewarded with a baronetcy (becoming Baron Ashbourne) and the lucrative office of Lord Chancellor, as well as a permanent seat in the Cabinet. When Gibson was made a baron, the courtesy title of 'The Honourable' was also bestowed on his eight children: four boys and four girls.

The Hon. Violet Albina Gibson, the second-youngest child, was born in Dalkey, a seaside suburb of Dublin, in 1876 and grew up at 12 Merrion Square, the family's Georgian townhouse. Childhood was not easy for Violet Gibson, known as Vizzy by her siblings. She was afflicted with near fatal bouts of scarlet fever, pleurisy and rubella. Her survival is all the more remarkable given that her deeply religious mother, an early convert to Christian Science, eschewed medical assistance, believing that her daughter's ailments were a penance for an unspecified sin.

Like most well-to-do Protestant women of her age, Violet Gibson was educated at home by governesses, primarily learning about music and art. She was also taught to speak French and Italian. The latter was especially useful when she accompanied her father, with whom she had a strong bond, on a visit to Italy as a child. She came out into society in 1896, attending balls and drawing rooms at Dublin Castle during the Season, and greeting the numerous guests who arrived at their Merrion Square home for the dinner parties that her parents hosted. She mingled with viceroys and duchesses, and met the Duke of York, later George V, when he visited the city in 1897.

Violet Gibson was always fascinated by religion. She tried her hand at Christian Science, her mother's faith, but then developed an interest in theosophy, a movement that was much in vogue with the upper classes at that time, which focused on karma and the emancipation of the soul. She attended theosophy lodges in Switzerland, France and Germany before concluding that it was not for her. Instead, to her father's intense dismay, she followed the lead of her oldest brother Willie and converted to Catholicism.

Willie Gibson was an unusual man. While studying at Trinity College Dublin he had taken to wearing Gaelic kilts and cloaks, a habit he would retain for life. Since his conversion at Oxford in

1891, he had become steadily more aligned with groups such as the Gaelic League and the Friends of Transvaal Committee. The latter were vehemently opposed to Britain's war against the Dutch Boers in South Africa, which was seen as a blatant land grab by the empire. Willie Gibson's politics were the complete opposite to his Conservative father. The Gibson family fell apart and he was disinherited, although he would still become the 2nd Baron Ashbourne when his father died in 1913.

There was further distress when Violet Gibson's favourite brother Victor returned from the Anglo-Boer War suffering from severe post-traumatic distress disorder, having narrowly survived an ambush in which many of his close friends were killed. He recovered, to an extent, and was present at Dublin's Rotunda in 1901 when a young Winston Churchill delivered a speech on the war; the future prime minister was introduced, on that occasion, by Violet Gibson's father. A pacifist at heart, she is unlikely to have supported such an imperial war. That said, she is thought to have attended an event at Farmleigh in Dublin's Phoenix Park to honour Queen Victoria when the elderly monarch came to Dublin in April 1900. Baron Ashbourne certainly met the Queen on various occasions during her three-week visit.

Ashbourne stopped speaking to his daughter after her conversion to Catholicism, unable to tolerate her modernist, Liberal views that land and power should be shared with the masses. She moved to London in 1902, and settled in the bohemian stronghold of Chelsea, where she was blighted by personal tragedy over the next seven years, including the death of an older brother, a beloved sister-in-law and, most cruelly, her fiancé. In 1909 she sailed to Italy to find solace among the holy sites and basilicas. She collapsed in Milan, exhausted by grief, necessitating a hasty visit by her younger sister Constance, who spent several weeks nursing her back to health.

When her father died in 1913, Violet Gibson made her final journey to Dublin, attending the internment of his ashes in the family vault at Mount Jerome Cemetery. Willie, now Lord Ashbourne, was increasingly embroiled in the fight for Irish independence. In 1914 he helped fund the purchase of German guns for the Irish Volunteers, a shipment that the spy novelist and increasingly nationalist Erskine Childers famously sailed into Howth harbour on the eve of the First World War.

Violet Gibson went to Paris at the start of the war to help those desperately trying to advocate peace, only to be diagnosed with cancer, requiring a left mastectomy. Two years later, suffering acute appendicitis and peritonitis, she was back under the surgeon's knife. She would be ever after stricken with abdominal pain and her mind was beginning to flicker. She became a devotee of Rev. John O'Fallon Pope, a Jesuit scholar from Missouri, who believed that self-flagellation, fasting and wearing hair shirts were key to spiritual enlightenment.

In 1922, she received the devastating news that her brother Victor had been found dead in a Surrey inn. She took to wandering outside in her nightdress and the police were obliged to bring her home on one occasion. The situation reached a crescendo when her housekeeper's daughter found her walking back and forth across a busy road and tried to intervene. Gibson lashed out with a knife and sliced the child's hand. Certified insane, she was taken to the Holloway Sanatorium in Surrey, where she reportedly tried to kill a fellow patient. Somehow her family removed her from Holloway and she went to live on her own in Kensington.

Always a voracious reader, she began to take a deep interest in Italy, frequently expressing her dislike of Pope Pius XI, a strong conservative and Fascist sympathizer. In 1924, the newspapers reported that Giacomo Matteotti, a charismatic Italian socialist, had been kidnapped and brutally murdered by the Fascists. Shortly afterwards, Violet Gibson sailed for Italy, accompanied by an Irish nurse, Mary McGrath. Upon arrival in Rome in November 1924, the two women went to Our Lady of Lourdes convent, from where Gibson sought an audience with the Pope. The request was declined, which was fortunate for the Pope as it seems her ambition was to kill him.

Three months after her arrival in Rome, Gibson shot herself with a revolver. The bullet missed her heart and lodged in her shoulder. She spent the next two months in a psychiatric clinic, after which she moved to the Convent of Santa Brigida. On 7 April 1926, she walked out of the convent with a Lebel revolver, a couple of bullets and a rock intended to smash any glass that might prevent her getting a clear shot at her target, Benito Mussolini, the Italian prime minister. Seeing Mussolini, she took her shot, but failed in the attempt and was apprehended.

Violet Gibson's motive for trying to assassinate Mussolini is a riddle that will never be solved. The Italian police were perplexed by her responses during the endless interrogations that followed. Initially, she insisted that she had done nothing. She then produced a number of possible motives – for the glory of God, to impress a handsome Italian aristocrat – before stating that she had no idea why she had tried to kill him. She could be mischievous, too: when asked if she had any accomplices, she confessed that she did and promptly named every saint she could think of. The story became ever more complex when the nuns at Santa Brigida weighed in with their thoughts: Gibson was often away from the convent but where did she go all day? And why was she so drained when she came back? Why was her room full of newspaper cuttings about Mussolini? How had she obtained a revolver? Why did she bring a rock?

One theory holds that she was put up to the task by Ernesto Buonaiuti, a dissident priest and philosopher who was based in Rome's poor Trastevere neighbourhood. As her politics were firmly aligned with the modernist anti-fascists, if Gibson interpreted her failed suicide attempt as evidence that God had another purpose for her, it is certainly plausible that she would have taken that purpose to be political. Conversely, the Vatican were of the view that her failure was a clear message that God was on Il Duce's side. Celebratory church bells resounded across Italy, but there was widespread violence, too, as Fascists seized the occasion to ransack and burn opposition newspapers. Another consequence was that Mussolini received a letter of support from a beautiful fourteen-year-old girl, Clara Petacci. He replied and a correspondence ensued; Clara became his mistress a decade later.

Whatever the truth about Violet Gibson's motives, Mussolini's propaganda team were eager to portray her as a religious fanatic who had acted on her own rather than a political assassin. Her earlier sojourn in Holloway was cited as evidence; she sealed her fate in July 1926 when, fed up with being taunted, she attacked a fellow inmate with a small hammer. She was transferred to a lunatic asylum where, after three weeks of intense psychological assessment, she was diagnosed with chronic paranoia. She was also subjected to an intrusive gynaecological analysis. She resisted as best she could, smashing a pottery jug over a prison guard's head and embarking on a hunger strike, before contracting a fever.

Neither her family nor the British government could see any good reason to dispute the Italians' view that she was insane. At this time, Britain and Italy were enjoying a relatively good relationship. In January 1927, Churchill arrived in Rome to meet Mussolini. He raised the matter of Violet Gibson – her father Baron Ashbourne, who had introduced young Churchill before his speech in Dublin over quarter of a century earlier, had been one of his own father's good friends. Mussolini had survived four assassination attempts in the past fourteen months but his view on Gibson seems to have been reasonably benign. He simply wanted her removed from Italy.

With the blessing of her other surviving siblings, Constance Gibson headed up the team who escorted her sister back to England where, in a veil of deception, she was incarcerated at St Andrew's Hospital for Mental Diseases in Northampton. This is where she would live for twenty-nine long, monotonous years before her death. It was, she observed, 'a kind of nun's life'. She did not want to be there and wrote a constant stream of letters to plead her case for release, especially when the British media turned against Mussolini after his vicious invasion of Abyssinia in 1935. However, her letters to people such as Churchill and, later, Queen Elizabeth II, were never delivered. The asylum authorities also appear to have withheld any post she received from supporters. Believing herself friendless and plagued by demons, she tried to hang herself in 1930.

In her twilight years, she found a degree of peace among the birds that flittered in the asylum gardens. She lived to hear of Mussolini's fall, and read about how the bodies of the dictator and his mistress, Clara Petacci, were hung upside down at a petrol station in Milan, the city she had gone to for solace in another age. She may also have met Lucia Joyce, daughter of James Joyce, who arrived at the hospital in 1951, having been diagnosed as schizophrenic.

Bedridden for her last five years, Violet Gibson died in 1956 aged seventy-nine. She had requested a requiem mass at her funeral, but this was not to be, and nor was there any mention of her passing in any newspaper. Neither friend nor family were in attendance as she was laid to rest in the asylum's non-denominational cemetery. So ended the wretched life of a woman who, but for a split-second, would have changed the course of history by assassinating Benito Mussolini. In 2022, a plaque commemorating Violet was unveiled at 12 Merrion Square, the site of her childhood home in Dublin.

38

DON PATRICIO O'CONNELL, BARÇA'S SAVIOUR

Barcelona, Spain, July 1937. The civil war was drawing ever closer to the Catalonian capital, and FC Barcelona – or 'Barça', as the world's richest football club in 2020 is better known – found itself teetering on the brink of extinction. Josep Sunyol, the club president, had already been murdered by Fascists and several Barça players were now serving in the Republican Army. La Liga had been suspended and the club's coffers were running empty. It was at this gloomy moment that Don Patricio, the club's Dublin-born manager, produced his ingenious plan to escort his endangered players out of Spain on a grand tour of the United States and Mexico.

Patrick 'Paddy' O'Connell was born in Drumcondra, Dublin, in March 1887, the fifth of ten children. His father, also Patrick, was born in County Kilkenny in 1839. His mother Elizabeth hailed from County Meath and had married O'Connell senior in 1875. The family initially lived in County Westmeath, where Paddy's three older sisters were born, but moved to Dublin in the 1880s, where his father found work as a clerk at Boland's Corn Mill in the Grand Canal Docks. By

1901, they were living at the corner of Fitzroy Avenue and Jones's Terrace, from where the fourteen-year-old went to work as a glass fitter, while three of his sisters were tailoresses. In 1908 he married Ellen Treston, a carpenter's daughter from nearby Bayview Avenue. Pregnant on their wedding day, she would go on to have four children, the first of whom was born in Belfast.

At the time of his wedding, Paddy O'Connell was a foreman at Boland's Mills where his father worked, but football was rapidly becoming his *raison d'être*. Having started with the Strandville Juniors on Dublin's North Strand, he went on to play for Liffey Wanderers. Shortly after his marriage, O'Connell was signed to Belfast Celtic, who were based on Donegall Road, not far from the Harland and Wolff shipyards where the famous ocean liner *Titanic* was then under construction. Another Belfast FC player at this time was Oscar Traynor, who would later lead the attack on the Custom House in Dublin during the Irish War of Independence and went on to become Ireland's longest-serving Minister of Defence.

In 1909, O'Connell crossed to England, where he played for Sheffield Wednesday and then for Hull City under Ambrose Langley. He earned his first cap for Ireland in 1912, but they were trounced 1–6 by England at Dalymount Park in Dublin. Although he only won five more caps for Ireland, he captained his home country when they defied the odds and won the British International Championship of 1913–14. The final game of the tournament was played at Belfast's Windsor Park in torrential conditions in April 1914. One Irish player left the rain-soaked pitch with a broken collarbone, while O'Connell also broke his arm. However, in the absence of any substitutes, he opted to play on, helping Ireland negotiate a 1–1 draw with Scotland, which won them the contest. For the rest of his life, he had trouble with the arm that he had broken in what became known as 'the match with 9½ men'.

The following month he was signed up by Manchester United for £1,000, a fee paid in three instalments. It is believed that this was the second-highest transfer fee in footballing history up to that time. Within six months, he had become the first Irishman in history to captain the team. It was by no means a golden era for the club, which avoided relegation by a single goal. O'Connell was a defender but managed to score two goals during his thirty-five appearances for the club.

His wayward inclinations emerged in April 1915 when he was named as one of a number of players from Man United and Liverpool involved in a match-fixing scandal. The players met in a pub the day before they were due to compete on the pitch for a Good Friday showdown. A series of bets were laid at odds of 8–1 that United would win 2–0. During the match O'Connell gave the game away, as it were, when he stepped forward to take a penalty kick and shoved the ball 'blatantly wide' of the goal. As the truth slipped out, the scandal brought considerable shame to O'Connell, but he escaped the life ban imposed upon seven of his fellow players and no criminal charges were brought.

He continued to play for Man United until 1919 and was also player-manager for Ashington AFC, a Third Division North club from Northumberland. However, he had become estranged from his wife Ellen and in 1922 he abandoned her and their four children in Manchester and sailed for Spain, where he had probably already secured his appointment as manager of Racing de Santander football club on the north coast. He remained with Santander for nearly seven years, doing much to boost the sport's popularity in the area. In 1928 he led the club into La Liga, Spain's new premier league, but perhaps his most memorable legacy was to teach his players the offside trap technique following the introduction of the offside rules to the game.

In 1929, Don Patricio, as he became known in Spain, began a two-year stint managing Real Oviedo in northwest Spain. However, he enjoyed his first real taste of greatness during his three years as manager of the small Seville club of Real Betis (then known as Betis Balompié) between 1932 and 1935. O'Connell not only helped these minnows to qualify for the Primera División – the first Andalusian team to do so – but then steered them to win the La Liga championship in April 1935. It was to be the club's one and only title clincher to date.

In order to beat Real Madrid to the title, Real Betis had to play one last match against Racing de Santander, O'Connell's old club.

According to one account, O'Connell met some of his former players for a drink beforehand. 'You've got nothing to play for tomorrow,' he reputedly said. 'You won't kill yourselves to beat us, will you?' To which one of the players replied, 'I'm sorry, mister, but Madrid wants us to win. Our president, José María Cosso, is a Madrid fan himself and is offering us 1,000 pesetas per player if we win.' Nonetheless, Real Betis went on to smash Racing de Santander 5–0.

The champion of Spanish football then returned to Ireland for a short holiday, quite possibly with his new bride Ellen O'Callaghan, from Midleton, County Cork. The handsome, flamenco-loving foot-ball manager had met her in Seville, where she was working as a governess. She was completely unaware that he was still wed to his first wife and that her husband was thus a bigamist.

In the summer of 1935 he was appointed manager of FC Barcelona, where he remained for the next five years. Several of his players joined the Republican forces when the Spanish Civil War broke out in July 1936 and the following month the club president Josep Sunyol was murdered by fascists. When La Liga was suspended because of the war, O'Connell was among those who established the alternative La Lliga Mediterrània (Mediterranean League), which Barça duly won. As O'Connell pondered what to do next, the club received an extraordinary, impeccably timed invitation from Manuel Mas Soriano, a prosperous former Mexican basketball player. If Barça would go on an exhibition tour of Mexico and the United States, Soriano would inject the considerable sum of $15,000 into the club's bank account.

For Ángel Mur, a young Barça groundsman, the options were stark: 'Stay in Barcelona and risk getting blown up or go on a foot-ball tour of America. It wasn't much of a choice was it?' Mur joined O'Connell and his team when they set sail for Mexico in the summer of 1937 – because the club's physio had been called up to fight before they set off, O'Connell had invited the youngster to take his place. When Mur reasoned that he knew nothing about physiotherapy, Don Patricio replied, 'Don't worry, I'll teach you on the way.' Given his personal experience of broken arms and legs, O'Connell evidently had plenty to say on the subject during the fourteen-day voyage, and he must have said it well because not only did Ángel Mur become a successful physio, both his son and grandson would also become physios to the Barça players.

The eight-week tour of North America was a major success, both for the team generally, which won ten of its fourteen matches, and for O'Connell specifically. Barça enjoyed a tremendous reception in Mexico, one of only two countries that had thus far offered its open support to the Spanish Republic. The journey from Veracruz to New York was a highlight. As Mur recalled, 'God knows why but there were several hundred women on the ship. Let's just say those women kept us busy. You had to be careful where you stepped when you went on deck because there were couples on the floor everywhere. We'd had a great time in Mexico but that boat trip was a four-day carnival. A few of the guys thought it was too much but we were young and I had a great time.'

However, news soon reached the team that the Franco regime had deemed the tour to be a political mission on behalf of the Republicans. Every player who participated was banned from playing football in Spain for two years. Rossend Calvet, the club secretary, was banned for eight. With such a future facing them, it was not surprising that when the tour ended in September 1937, twelve Barça players opted to quit the team and remain in exile rather than return to live in Franco's Spain. O'Connell must have had cause to reflect on the famous American Invasion Tour of 1888 when twenty of fifty-one Irish athletes on a tour of the United States sponsored by Gaelic Athletic Association (GAA) likewise decided not to go home.

At length, just nine men returned to Spain – O'Connell, Mur, Calvet, the club doctor and five players. Among the players he had lost were the striker Josep Escolà and the future Spain manager Domènec Balmanya, both of whom joined FC Sète in France. Calvet wired Soriano's $15,000 and other monies made on the tour to a bank account in Paris lest Franco's financiers laid claim to it. The war continued to ravage Spain; the Italian air force bombed Barcelona, killing 3,000 people and destroying, among many other buildings, the club's offices. There was no let up for the club when, following Franco's victory, the regime banned all exiled sportsmen from Spain for the next six years. That said, Enrique Piñeyro, the new Barça president, managed to get several players back from exile in 1941, including Balmanya and Escolà.

Meanwhile, O'Connell left Barcelona. By 1942 he was managing Sevilla FC, securing them second place in La Liga at the end of 1943 and third place the following year. He remained with them until 1945, memorably praising Seville itself as a city 'where people live as if they were to die tonight', then, coming in a near complete circle, he returned to Racing de Santander as manager from 1947 to 1949.

His later years are a source of ambiguity. An unhappy reunion with one of his four children from his first marriage appears to have compounded the break-up of his second marriage. The seventy-one-year-old was apparently penniless when he died of pneumonia on 27 February 1959. At the time of his death he was living with one of his younger brothers near St Pancras station in London. He was buried in an unmarked grave at St Mary's Roman Catholic Cemetery in London's Kensal Green.

In 2014, Martin O'Neill, Paul McGrath, Johan Cruyff, Franz Beckenbauer, Jamie Carragher and a number of other footballing greats united with GAA icons Paul Galvin and Brian Cody to raise funds to build a permanent memorial to mark his grave. In 2015, Paddy O'Connell was inducted into Barcelona's hall of fame when his portrait by Manchester-based artist Tony Denton was given to the FC Barça Museum at the Camp Nou stadium; its presence in Barca's hallowed grounds will surely enshrine the memory of the Dubliner who steered the club through the Spanish Civil War. Barça won La Liga in 2023.

39

LORD HAW-HAW,
THE VOICE OF NAZI GERMANY

Old Bailey, London, 19 September 1945. Judge Tucker placed the black cloth over his wig, cleared his throat and delivered his final judgment:

> *William Joyce, the sentence of the Court upon you is that you be taken from this place to a lawful prison, and thence to a place of execution, and that you be there hanged by the neck until you are dead; and that your body be afterwards buried within the precincts of the prison in which you shall have been confined before your execution. And may the Lord have mercy on your soul.*

The condemned was asked if he wished to speak but, for once, the famous voice was silent. Instead, he bowed stiffly and made his way back to his cell, throwing a cheerful wave at his brother and friends before he exited the court. In the months that followed, he would look back on his Galway childhood with immense nostalgia. His final letter to his wife Margaret listed the predominant features of the Galway landscape with an apology that he had never managed 'my cherished dream' to show her such sights himself. It would be another thirty years before his body was reinterred in his beloved Galway.

Known to posterity as Lord Haw-Haw, William Joyce had become a household name during the Second World War when he had hosted his own English language radio show, *Germany Calling*. Broadcast live from Hamburg, the show sought to persuade listeners across Britain, Ireland and North America to align themselves with the policies of Hitler's Germany.

He was a scion of one of the Fourteen Tribes, or leading merchant families, of Galway. Michael Joyce, his father, was born on a farm near Ballinrobe, County Mayo, in 1868 and raised as a Catholic. At the age of twenty, Michael emigrated to New York to work on the Pennsylvanian Railroad, becoming a naturalized American in 1894. During a return trip to Ireland, he befriended Emily 'Queenie' Brooke, the diminutive daughter of a Protestant doctor from Lancashire, England, who was on a fishing holiday in Ireland. They began a correspondence after his return to New York, which culminated in a marriage proposal that she received by post. In 1905, Queenie sailed for New York, where she married Michael Joyce at All Saints Church in Harlem, a prominent church for Irish Catholics in Manhattan.

They settled at 1377 Herkimer Street, a charming corner house in Brooklyn, where their son William Brooke Joyce was born on 24 April 1906. Although Joyce's New York business prospered, his wife felt the distance from home keenly. In 1909 the Joyce family returned to Ireland, where young William Joyce would spend the next twelve years of his life. For the first two of those years, the family lived on a farm about 8km east of Westport, County Mayo. Michael ran a pub in nearby Aughagower, which William recalled as full of dust and spiders. When Michael was appointed manager of the horse-tram system in Galway City, the Joyces moved to Salthill, settling at 1 Rutledge Terrace in Rockbarton Park.

This was the house where young Willie Joyce, as he was called, was raised alongside his four younger siblings, Frank, Quentin, Joan and Robert. From Rutledge Terrace, he walked to St Ignatius College on Galway's Sea Road, where his Jesuit teachers developed his considerable intellect. He became fluent in German and a commendable French speaker. A talented mathematician, he also learned the piano by ear, quoted Virgil and Horace at ease and spent many of his waking hours with his head buried in books. However, he was also an argumentative child and frequently ended up brawling with his classmates. In one such fight, his nose was broken. The Joyces' failure to reset it left him with the nasal drawl that would become so well known to listeners of *Germany Calling*.

His parents, one Catholic, one Protestant, were both devoted Unionists, but even they must have baulked at their fourteen-year-old son's brazen friendship with the reviled Black and Tans during the Irish War of Independence. His fellow classmates were appalled to see him seated in the front of a British army Crossley Tender as it powered through Salthill, pointing out buildings and chattering to the auxiliary officer seated alongside him. On another occasion, the teenager lunched at Lenaboy Castle where the Tans were based. Such behaviour was intolerable for Galway's nationalist community. After a series of threats, the Joyces' house was set on fire. Given that Galway's horse-tram system had by now been wound up, Michael Joyce decided to sell up and relocate his family to Lancashire in England.

William Joyce made his way to London, where he enrolled as a science student at Battersea Polytechnic. In 1922, the sixteen-year-old applied to join the London University Officer's Training Corps, stating that he had served 'in an Intelligence capacity, against the Irish guerrillas' during the recent war. The following year, he began working with the British Fascisti [sic], an organization which began as a right-wing branch of the Conservative party. He was by then a student at Birkbeck College, part of the University of London, where he was often to be found espousing his anti-Semitic views and dislike of Communists.

In 1924 he fought with a Communist, who leapt on his back and slashed him from mouth to earlobe with an open razor. Joyce maintained his attacker was Jewish and would ever after regard his facial scar as a grim reminder of 'the evils of international Jewry'. Over the ensuing years, he would instigate and lead numerous street fights with both Communists and Jews. He also became an extreme admirer of Adolf Hitler and joined Oswald Mosley's British Union of Fascists (BUF) shortly after its foundation in 1932. Both Joyce and Mosley were briefly arrested for hosting a 'riotous assembly' in Worthing, Sussex, in 1934. Among others with whom he worked at this time was the radical Dublin-born feminist Norah Elam, whose father had been an Irish nationalist.

By 1934, the thin, pale and intense young Irish-American was one of BUF's keynote speakers. His oratory was immense, his style immediately reminiscent of Hitler or Mussolini. When the novelist Cecil Roberts attended a rally at which Joyce spoke, he recalled how 'he had not been speaking many minutes before we were electrified by this man...so terrifying in its dynamic force, so vituperative, so vitriolic'. Mosley appointed him director of propaganda and later his deputy leader. For his part, Joyce praised Mosley as 'the greatest

Englishman I have ever known'. The duo planned to visit Hitler in Berlin, a project that involved Joyce falsifying his birth records to state that he was born in Galway rather than the United States in order to obtain a British passport. In the event, the Berlin trip fell through but his false passport would ultimately serve as Joyce's death warrant.

His first marriage collapsed when his wife tired of his extremist activities. In 1937 he was married a second time to beautiful Margaret Cairns White, a Fascist from Manchester with whom he had a tempestuous, drink-fuelled relationship. Mosley was by now finding Joyce's combination of alcohol and rabid anti-Semitism too distasteful for the BUF and sacked him. Joyce promptly co-founded the breakaway National Socialist League, an organization that became so pro-Nazi that by 1939 he was ending meetings with an impassioned 'Sieg Heil!'

With the inevitable approach of war in the summer of 1939, it became clear that the Joyces were on the shortlist to be incarcerated. They briefly considered escaping to Ireland but ran out of time when, at the end of August, Maxwell Knight, a friend at MI5, tipped them off that their arrest was imminent. (Knight would go on to become a major British spymaster and, more obscurely, a BBC naturalist, as well as the reputed role model for 'M' in the James Bond movies.) By the time the British police raided their London apartment, the Joyces were in Berlin.

Their arrival coincided with Hitler's invasion of Poland and the outbreak of the Second World War. After some weeks struggling to find employment, Joyce was invited to Berlin's Rundfunkhaus (Broadcasting House) by Dr Joseph Goebbels, Hitler's infamous Minister of Propaganda. Although radio was still in its relative infancy, Goebbels had a deft understanding of how to make use of the world's most powerful mass media tool. To this end, he recruited Joyce to work in the English language section of German radio.

Joyce's meticulously enunciated Shakespearean vocals were soon crackling through the airwaves of western Europe with extraordinary effect. Although nobody yet knew his name, 'Germany Calling, Germany Calling' became his introductory catchphrase as more and more households across Britain and Ireland tuned in to his evening broadcast of carefully scripted news updates. Many were convinced that every word he said was the truth; Irish listeners became particularly excited when he denounced British 'warmongers' like Churchill or spoke of places they knew well. On one occasion, he sent greetings to his old friends in Salthill. On another, he apparently remarked, 'When the Reich's Panzers roll through the Irish Free State, De Valera will have no more power to resist them than the tinkers of the Ballygaddy Road in Tuam.' It was certainly nothing like the traditional broadcasts on Radio Athlone.

However, his sardonic talk of Britain's 'precipitous and disastrous retreat' from Dunkirk and the 'military liquidation' of the Allied army also caused widespread fear among an audience that averaged 6 million but, at its peak, sometimes surpassed 16 million. Although the two men never met, the German Führer awarded him the War Merit Cross (First and Second Class) for his broadcasts.

Churchill's government was forced to counteract his influence, opting to ridicule him. By early October, the anonymous broadcaster had been rechristened 'Lord Haw-Haw of Zeesen'. On 17 December 1939, the *Sunday Mirror* revealed that the man 'responsible for Hamburg's nightly hymn of hate' was William Joyce. For good measure, the paper later alerted readers that another of his nicknames was 'Scarface Joyce'. Lord Haw-Haw would become the butt of musical hall parodies for the remainder of the war. He continued to broadcast right up until 30 April 1945, the day that Hitler killed himself, when, in a state of considerable intoxication, he concluded his broadcast by saying, 'You may not hear from me again for some months. I say, *ich liebe Deutschland*. Heil Hitler. And farewell.'

It is said that Goebbels enquired on the Joyces' behalf as to whether a submarine might be able to take them back to Galway. Instead, they were provided with false papers and bolted for the Danish border. Joyce was captured in the birch woods of Flensburg when he inadvertently struck up conversation with two British officers, one of whom recognized his voice. He was shot in the thigh while trying to escape and passed out unconscious. Margaret Joyce, who was also arrested, last saw him being carried through a frontier post on a stretcher. She rather incongruously shouted '*Erin go Bragh*' ('Ireland forever') before she was taken to a separate jail in Belgium.

William Joyce was brought to London to stand trial for high treason in what he described as 'the most flagrant hoax in the history of British Justice'. Given that the Irish-American had been naturalized as a German citizen in 1940, there was a strong argument that he should not have been tried in a British court. However, his false British identity papers were deemed reason enough to try him for the treasonous crime of aiding the king's enemies in a time of war and he was sentenced to death under a law that was nearly 600 years old.

Joyce remained cynical, and remorseless, to the end. In one of his last letters, written to his friend Ethel Scrimgeour, he wrote: 'As the days go by, it will become more and more obvious that the policy which I defended was the right one.... I cannot quite restrain my contempt for those who would hang me for treason. Had I robbed the public and impeded the war effort by profiteering on ammunitions, a peerage would now be within my reach if I were willing to buy it.'

At 9 a.m. on 3 January 1946, thirty-nine-year-old William Joyce became the last man to be hanged in Britain for high treason. He was buried in the prison yard at Wandsworth, London. In August 1976, his daughter Heather Rose had his remains reinterred beneath a simple white cross at the New Cemetery in Bohermore, County Galway.

40

BRENDAN BRACKEN,
CHURCHILL'S SPIN DOCTOR

Chartwell, England, 8 August 1958. It is no secret that Winston Churchill was prone to weep. The prime minister was often moved to tears by epic events such as Dunkirk and D-Day, or by the praise and cheers showered on him by his contemporaries. The deaths of old friends also set him off time and again. On this particular day, he learned of the passing of Brendan Bracken, the man who had engineered his accession to No. 10 Downing Street in 1940 and then served as his Minister of Information for the remainder of the Second World War. 'Poor, dear Brendan,' wept Churchill, who regarded Bracken as one of his closest friends. Shortly after their first meeting, Churchill applauded him as 'a brilliant young Australian of quite exceptional powers and vitality'.

Brendan Bracken was unquestionably brilliant. However, Churchill might have been astonished to discover that far from being Australian, his trusty comrade was the son of a Fenian from Tipperary, an identity that Brendan Bracken had done everything he could to shake off. His father Joseph Kevin Bracken was a sworn member of the Irish Republican Brotherhood (IRB), an oathbound society that was committed to the overthrow of British rule in Ireland by physical force.

Known as JK, the elder Bracken was a prosperous builder, monumental stonemason and road contractor. His company was especially busy building '1798' monuments (p. 83) in Irish graveyards to mark the centenary of the rising in 1898. He was also one of the seven founders of the Gaelic Athletic Association (GAA) in 1884 and, as its vice president, he was among the leading supporters of the 'Ban', which prohibited GAA members from playing 'garrison games' such as rugby, soccer, hockey or cricket. He also presided at the meeting that barred members of the Royal Irish Constabulary from the GAA.

JK Bracken was fifty years old when his pony and trap collided with a carriage belonging to Sir John Carden, the family's landlord, in 1902. When the local court found in Sir John's favour, a furious JK relocated his family to Kilmallock, County Limerick, where he died of cancer at Ardvullen House just two years later. He was survived by his six children by two wives, including a baby boy, Brendan. Born in Templemore, County Tipperary, on 15 February 1901, Brendan Bracken was JK's second son by his second wife Hannah Ryan, the 'hot-tempered' but apolitical daughter of a wealthy farmer-baker from Borrisoleigh.

In 1908, four years after JK Bracken's death, his wife moved to Dublin with her four small children, as well as two increasingly hostile stepdaughters. They initially lived on Iona Drive, Glasnevin, before moving to North Circular Road, from where young Brendan walked to St Patrick's National School, Drumcondra. He already stood out from the crowd, sporting what one of his teachers later recalled as 'a large red mop that stood out like a kind of halo'. In 1910 he transferred to O'Connell School on North Richmond Street. Run by the Christian Brothers, the school had an intensely nationalist ethos. Among Bracken's schoolmates were Emmet Dalton, who would be by Michael Collins side when the Irish patriot was shot dead in 1922, and future Taoiseach (prime minister), Seán Lemass.

Nationalism was not on the agenda for the red-headed mischief-maker from Tipperary. Bracken's teachers conceded that he had 'brains to burn' but his outrageous conduct and incorrigible scruffiness were to drive them and his mother to the brink. He was an absolute menace to the Glasnevin neighbourhood, chopping down trees, catapulting pebbles at the window of the parish priest's house, and popping hoses through open windows and turning the water on. At his stepsister's wedding in 1913, he pinched the celebrant priest's hat and ran away. Pranks aside, he was also an enterprising boy. When neighbours went on holidays, the thirteen-year-old offered to keep an eye on their bikes for a fee; the moment they had gone, he rented the bikes out. His stepsisters also paid him to assist with their nocturnal breakouts from home.

Young Bracken spent most of his earnings on newspapers, which he read voraciously. He produced his own version of a newspaper in his copybook and then charged people for the privilege of reading it. He also stood outside church and sold a news-sheet to his neighbouring parishioners, who were thrilled and startled in equal measure to see the content comprised gossip all about themselves. His mother, the source of many tales, was mortified.

Brendan Bracken was also head of 'Bracken's Gang', an unruly group who were constantly fighting the Manor Street Gang. After one such scuffle, an opponent was nearly drowned in the Royal Canal and the Dublin Metropolitan Police gave Hannah Bracken a sharp warning. Exasperated, she sent her son to board with the Jesuits of Mungret College near Limerick, where he was rapidly ranked as 'quite the cheekiest boy' in attendance. Although a teacher later claimed he could have 'charmed the birds off the trees', he made few friends. He ran away and stayed in a series of hotels in Foynes and Rathkeale under a false name, before finding work at a newspaper in Limerick, where he acquired a briefcase and a bowler hat.

Bracken could evidently not be tamed. In 1916 he took a ship to Australia, where he lived for nearly four years. He initially resided with the Brigidine nuns in Echuca, Victoria, devouring the contents of their extensive library. He then wandered far and wide across the continent, during which time he began to invent stories about his past. When he returned to Ireland in the latter half of 1919, he found his mother living at Dollardstown, near Navan, County Meath, with her new husband, Patrick Laffan, a nationalist supporter. Sadly, the prodigal son became embroiled in a bitter family row that prompted him to move to England. He maintained contact with his mother until her death in 1928 and thereafter he provided financial support to some of his siblings and other family members until his own passing three decades later.

In England, however, he was already very deliberately removing every trace of Irishness, nationalism and Catholicism from his past. Having perfected his Australian accent, he went for an interview at Liverpool Collegiate School, convincing them that he was Australian, four years older than he was, a former head-boy of an Australian public school and a graduate of Sydney University. He was given a job as a teacher. By September 1920, he had made enough money at the Liverpool school to enrol as a pupil at Sedbergh, a boarding school in present-day Cumbria. This time, the nineteen-year-old claimed to be a fifteen-year-old Australian orphan who had been willed enough money to complete his education when his parents died in a bush fire. Sedbergh's headmaster strongly suspected this was not true but permitted him to stay for one term, during which time he studied literature with aplomb, won a history prize and emerged as a perfectly British public-school boy, albeit one who spoke with an Australian twang. His Irish past was all but forgotten as he meandered through a series of teaching assignments before working at a London-based periodical called the *Empire Review*.

In the summer of 1923, J. L. Garvin, the editor of *The Observer*, invited the twenty-two-year-old Bracken to Gregories, his home near Beaconsfield, Buckinghamshire. The estate had once belonged to Edmund Burke, the famous Irish politician and orator. Winston Churchill, who had lost his seat at Westminster in the previous year's election, was among the other guests. Bracken is said to have caught Churchill's attention when he contradicted him during lunch. An unlikely friendship began thereafter as Bracken became one of Churchill's most devoted followers.

Bracken was closely involved in Churchill's unsuccessful attempt to win back a seat at Westminster as a Liberal candidate during a snap election in December 1923. Churchill had been a Conservative before he joined the Liberals. In 1924, he crossed the floor once more and rejoined the Conservatives. 'Anyone can rat, but it takes a certain ingenuity to re-rat,' he ruefully remarked.[1] The move transpired to be the making of the man. At the next general election in October 1924, Churchill triumphed as the Conservative candidate for Epping in Essex and was appointed Chancellor of the Exchequer by Stanley Baldwin, Britain's Conservative prime minister from 1924 to 1929. 'I shall never be so happy,' exclaimed Bracken in a letter to his mother when Churchill's appointment was confirmed.

Bracken was one of the few people who could shake Churchill out of his periodic fits of depression, the 'black dog' as he called it. Baldwin referred to him as Churchill's 'faithful chela', borrowing the Hindustani word for disciple from a story by Rudyard Kipling, one of Baldwin's cousins. Churchill himself seems to have continued under the false impression that Bracken was Australian. Clementine Churchill,

Winston's wife, was less convinced by the heavy-drinking young rogue who slept on her drawing-room sofa with his shoes on and addressed her as Clemmie. When strange rumours began to circulate that he was Churchill's illegitimate son, she challenged her husband, who mischievously said, 'I don't think so', and promised to check his diary as to his whereabouts nine months before Bracken's alleged birth.

However, there was a mysterious rift between Churchill and his chela at this time, which lasted until the general election of 1929. In the meantime, Bracken joined the London publisher Eyre & Spottiswoode, for whom he founded *The Banker*, a prominent finance journal. In 1928 he persuaded the company to acquire the *Financial News* (later merged with the *Financial Times*), as well as a half-share in *The Economist*.

In 1929 Bracken was himself elected a Conservative Member of Parliament for the London constituency of North Paddington, a seat he represented until 1945. During the first decade of his parliamentary career, Churchill was in the political wilderness, a lone voice urging rearmament in the face of the rise of Adolf Hitler. Bracken stayed loyal throughout, helped him out financially and continued to bring him good cheer during trying periods.

Brendan Bracken was now living the high life in Westminster, hosting lavish parties in a townhouse bedecked with period furniture, old masters and leather-bound books. Such a lifestyle provided the inspiration for Rex Mottram, Evelyn Waugh's social-climbing, name-dropping Canadian tycoon in *Brideshead Revisited*. Bracken never married, indulging in some brief but fruitless courtships with beautiful society women such as Penelope Dudley-Ward. There was a considerable flutter in the media when David Campbell published his memoir 'Minstrel Heart' in 2021 stating that, during the 1950s, Bracken liked to dress up as a schoolboy and hired teenagers to cane him as a punishment.

Bracken was a powerful political figure in his own right. Arguably the seminal moment in his career came when he masterminded Churchill's succession as prime minister in 1940, bringing to mind Dominic Cummings's role in Boris Johnson's ascendancy in 2019. Having ascertained that the Labour party would back him, Bracken convinced the sixty-five-year-old Churchill not to support Lord Halifax, his only rival for the leadership. When Churchill took control of Downing Street, Bracken was rewarded with a position on the Privy Council, the prime minister's inner circle. The tearaway from Tipperary was now central to the selection of Britain's wartime ministers, as well as its bishops and college masters. As his biographer Charles Lysaght put it, he was 'the most significant native Irishman in English political life since Edmund Burke'.

When George VI expressed concern at Bracken's lack of ministerial experience, Churchill wrote to reassure the king: 'He has sometimes been almost my sole supporter in the years when I have been striving to get this country properly defended.' In fact, Bracken played a vital role in winning US support for the war effort, securing the confidence of Harry Hopkins, President Roosevelt's most trusted advisor, when the American diplomat visited Britain to assess the situation in January 1941.

Five months later, Bracken was appointed Minister of Information, thus making him London's answer to Germany's Joseph Goebbels. He ran the ministry with exceptional and pragmatic skill for four long years, working closely with both the BBC and the print media. As well as his genius as a spin doctor, he held his own against Churchill when need be, opposing his attempts to curtail freedom of the press. 'They quarrelled and argued incessantly,' recalled future prime minister Harold Macmillan, 'just like a happily married couple.' Bracken also pointedly condemned Éamon de Valera, Ireland's Taoiseach, and 'those lousy neutrals', maintaining that people of Irish stock living overseas were heartily ashamed of Eire's wartime attitude. By the end of the war, even Clementine Churchill had developed a degree of respect for him.

After a brief spell as First Lord of the Admiralty in 1945, Bracken was ousted along with Churchill in a dramatic post-war election that brought Labour to power. He managed to win the Bournemouth seat at a by-election and spent his time in opposition criticizing high taxation, nationalization, the dismantling of the empire and any leftward leaning within the Conservative party.

When Churchill returned to office in 1951, many assumed Bracken would be part of the new Cabinet. Instead, he retired from politics and focused on his ongoing role as chairman of the *Financial Times*. He also founded *History Today*, one of the world's most respected popular history magazines. In 1952 he was elevated to the peerage as Viscount Bracken, of Christchurch in the County of Southampton. He never sat in the House of Lords, a chamber he referred to as the 'morgue'.

'I shall die young and be forgotten,' was a remark that Bracken uttered more than once. Increasingly reclusive, the fifty-seven-year-old chain-smoker was diagnosed with throat cancer in January 1958. 'Poor, dear Brendan' died on 8 August 1958. Unmarried and with no children, the viscountcy died with him. Churchill wept. 'The black-shirts of God are after me,' Bracken told a friend, when a nephew, a Cistercian monk, offered him the last rites; the nephew would have no success. Instead, Bracken decreed that his ashes should be scattered on Romney Marsh and asked his chauffeur to burn all his personal papers. As such, much about the man remains a mystery. And that is precisely what he wanted.

41

PATRICK GALLAGHER, VIETNAM HERO

Vietnam, 28 January 1967. The twenty-three-year-old Marine corporal finally plucked up the courage to write to his parents. It was nearly a year since he had visited them at their home in Ballyhaunis, County Mayo, and told them of his dream to join the United States Marine Corps. They had expressed alarm, as he knew they would, concerned that he might be drafted to fight in the Vietnam War. He had assured them that he would be fine; that he would have to spend his first year of training in San Francisco; that the war would surely be over by then. However, the truth was that Patrick Gallagher had already joined the Marines. He had signed up before he made that final visit to Ireland and he received his orders to make his way to Vietnam almost as soon as he returned to the United States.

'I hope you won't be too mad at me for the news I got for you,' he now wrote. 'I have been in Vietnam since last April, and I will be leaving here in 60 days. Now don't get worried. Everything is going just fine here and I am enjoying it very much.'

Gallagher would probably not have confessed his whereabouts to his parents if he had not just been singled out for the Navy Cross, the US Navy's highest medal of valour. It was to be awarded for an act of extraordinary heroism he had performed the previous summer. His commander in the Marines had warned him that the award would attract considerable media attention, not least in Ireland. His letter home was designed to soften the shock that his parents would feel when they found out that he had been at war in Vietnam for the past ten months. He ended on an upbeat note, assuring them he would come and see them just as soon his tour of duty was finished, and that he would bring his Navy Cross with him.

The people of Ballyhaunis were elated by the news that one of their own had been awarded such a prestigious medal. Plans were put in motion to celebrate Corporal Gallagher's homecoming with a street party on 14 April 1967. However, when the day finally came, the streets of Ballyhaunis were deathly silent. Patrick Gallagher returned as promised, but he came home in a coffin. He had been killed in an ambush two weeks earlier.

Patrick Gallagher was born on 1 February 1944, the second of nine children to Peter and Mary Gallagher. He grew up on the family farm at Derrintogher, about 5 km (3 miles) from Ballyhaunis. His older sister Margaret nicknamed him 'Bob' because she couldn't pronounce 'Patrick' when she was small. His grandfather Patrick, for whom he was named, had been a schoolteacher. The younger Patrick was educated by the Franciscans at Granlahan Monastery on the Roscommon-Mayo border. As well as being a fine footballer, he developed an interest in carpentry and cabinetmaking, studying at the vocational school in Ballyhaunis. He also won first prize for a vegetable plot at the school.

In 1962, the second year of the Kennedy presidency, the eighteen-year-old flew from Shannon to New York and moved in with his aunt, May Burns, on Long Island. He found a job in real estate and started studying at law school. However, with the escalation of the conflict in Vietnam, he found himself drawn to the Marine Corps, one of the world's premier fighting forces. He enlisted in late 1965.

At least 2,500 of the army personnel who fought in the Vietnam War were Irish, including several dozen women. Most fought for the US armed forces; others with the Australian and New Zealand forces.[1] There were also thousands of soldiers of Irish descent, such as the thirteen Irish-Americans who won Medals of Honor. The Irish writer, broadcaster and newspaper columnist Tim Pat Coogan recalled meeting a 'Shamrock Squadron' that served in Vietnam in which all twenty-two helicopters were piloted by Irish-Americans.

Irish-born soldiers were in the action from the moment the first US troops began arriving after a considerable escalation of the conflict in 1964. Among them was Michael Coyne of Jenkinstown, County Meath, who died in August 2020. He spent sixteen months patrolling the jungles and rice paddies in a Patton tank with 11th Armored Cavalry Regiment. Injured five times, he was decorated with five Purple Hearts and two Bronze Stars for valour, one for rescuing his comrades from a minefield in the middle of a firefight.

One of the most vocal supporters of the Vietnam War was Cardinal Francis Spellman, arguably the most powerful man in 1960s New York, whose father was a shoemaker from Clonmel, County Tipperary. On the other hand, Ireland's fight for independence from Britain had made a deep impression on a young Paris-based Vietnamese Marxist poet called Ho Chi Minh. Interested in the Easter Rising of 1916, Ho was particularly impressed by the hunger strike and death of Terence MacSwiney, the Lord Mayor of Cork, in 1920, remarking, 'A nation that has such citizens will never surrender.' Ho met the IRA veteran Seán MacBride at an anti-imperialist conference in Frankfurt in 1929. He also studied Tom Barry's book, *Guerrilla Days in Ireland*, first published in 1949, which he would put to good use himself when he led North Vietnam during its wars against the French and the United States.[2]

By the time Ireland was commemorating the 50th anniversary of the Easter Rising in April 1966, Patrick Gallagher was serving as a lance corporal in the jungles of Southeast Asia. Three months later, while stationed in Quang Tri Province in north central Vietnam, he performed the act that was to win him the Navy Cross. On 18 July, Gallagher and three other Marines were quietly manning a defensive, riverside post near the border at Cam Lo when a party of Viet Cong guerrilla fighters ambushed them with grenades. Gallagher managed to kick the first grenade out of the post before it exploded. A second grenade then landed on the ground between two of his comrades. The citation for his Navy Cross explains what happened next: 'Without hesitation, in a valiant act of self-sacrifice, Corporal Gallagher threw himself upon the deadly grenade in order to absorb the explosion and save the lives of his comrades.'

Remarkably, none of the Marines were wounded, despite the fact that two more grenades landed in the post and exploded. The grenade upon which Patrick Gallagher was lying had still not exploded – the squad leader ordered him to roll over and hurl the grenade into the river. The Mayo man did just that and the grenade exploded on impact with the water. Gallagher was rightly applauded for saving his comrades 'from probable injury and possible loss of life'. His action also chimed loudly with the Marines' code of 'Semper Fi' ('Always Faithful').

'It is a pleasure to pin this on your breast,' declared General William Westmoreland, deputy commander of the US army in Vietnam, when he awarded Gallagher his Navy Cross. Frank Erwin, one of his fellow Marines, later recalled him as 'the bravest Marine that ever wore the uniform.... He was so proud the day General Westmoreland presented him with the Navy Cross.'[3] At the ceremony, Gallagher was told that he would have been 'a shoe-in' for the Congressional Medal of Honor, the United States' highest military honour, if the grenade had exploded and killed him.

He was bashful when he told his parents the news in his letter of 27 January: 'It was not much, but they made a big thing of it.... I had planned on not telling you myself until I got back to the US.' When word of his award reached Ireland, there was considerable excitement. RTÉ News dispatched Seán Duignan to interview his family, while the Ballyhaunis Junior Chamber of Commerce began gearing up to light up the town for Gallagher's homecoming.

Twenty-eight Irishmen and one Irish woman were killed in action, died in accidents or perished of natural causes during the Vietnam War. March 1967 was the worst month of the war for Irish-born soldiers, four of whom were killed. The last of the four was Corporal Patrick Gallagher, who died on the morning of 30 March, just over two months after he wrote to his parents. He was one of eight Marines killed when their squad was ambushed by the Viet Cong during a patrol at Dai Loc, near the coastal city of Da Nang. Frank Erwin, who survived the attack, wrote, 'I crawled to him, rolled him over and saw that horrible stare of death on his face.' Erwin, who would later name one of his sons Patrick in honour of his Irish friend, described his death as 'a profound loss to our entire company, as everyone looked to Patrick for courage in battle'.

The news was wired to the American embassy in Dublin, who contacted Father Rushe, the parish priest in Ballyhaunis. Following Sunday Mass, he informed Patrick Gallagher's parents of the dreadful news. His younger sister Teresa Keegan was in her early teens when he died and clearly remembers her mother's desolate face when she learned the news. It was not yet twenty-four hours since they had received the letter in which Patrick had promised to bring his medal home.

On the day that had been marked to celebrate his homecoming, Patrick's casket was escorted to Ballyhaunis by a funeral procession that the *Western People* described as 'one of the largest ever to pass through the town'. Among those in attendance were the parents of Christy Nevin of Claremorris, County Mayo, who had been killed in Vietnam a year earlier, and Mary Freyne of Ballaghaderreen, County Roscommon, whose twenty-one-year-old son Bernard was another of the four Irishmen killed in March 1967.

Staff Sergeant Gerard Moylan laid a wreath on the grave on behalf of the US forces before presenting the American flag that had been draped on the coffin along with Gallagher's Navy Cross and citation to his mother. The Gallaghers also received a letter from US Senator Bobby Kennedy who wrote: 'Winston Churchill said, "Courage is rightly esteemed as the first of all human qualities because it is the one that guarantees all others." This courage, Corporal Gallagher gave to us all. To him and to his family are due the thanks of a humbly grateful nation.'

Patrick Gallagher's name is on the USA Memorial in Mayo Peace Park, Castlebar, as well as on Panel 17 East of the Vietnam Veterans Memorial in Washington, DC. In 2017, the community in Ballyhaunis finally hosted the celebration they had planned for Gallagher's homecoming fifty years earlier and unveiled a monument to the fallen soldier. However, his greatest honour was the culmination of a remarkable petition-led campaign that will enshrine the Mayo man's name on a US navy destroyer, the USS *Patrick Gallagher*. The ship's keel was laid in 2022 and, following completion and sea trials, it is expected to enter service in 2024.

42

THE IRISH AND
THE WHITE HOUSE

The Irish links to the White House run deep. The building itself was designed and built by the Kilkenny-born architect James Hoban (p. 76). At least twenty-two of its presidential occupants had Irish ancestry, including the last twelve bar Donald Trump. Three of them had a parent or parents born in Ireland. Since Kennedy's state visit to Ireland in 1963, six presidents have followed suit. Given the high profile of Biden and Kennedy's Catholic faith, one could be forgiven for thinking all these 'Irish American' presidents shared their religion. In fact, most descend from Scots-Irish Presbyterians.

In the 2017 American Community Survey, just over 3 million US citizens claimed to have 'Scotch-Irish' ancestry. The number of Scots-Irish, or Ulster Scots as they are sometimes called, is probably far higher but the historical distinctions between Irish and Scots-Irish have been lost along the way. The story of the Scots-Irish began in the seventeenth century when approximately 200,000 Scots moved west across the 13-km (8-mile) North Channel from Scotland to Ireland. These 'planters' were predominantly Presbyterians who settled in Ulster, the island's northerly province. In the early twenti-eth century, six of the nine Ulster counties were partitioned to make up Northern Ireland, while counties Donegal, Cavan and Monaghan would become part of the present-day Republic of Ireland.

During the eighteenth century, Ireland was a country in which those Protestants who adhered to the Established (Anglican) Church were top of the pecking order. Ireland's free-spirited Presbyterians, Methodists, Quakers and other non-Anglican Dissenters were con-sequently classified as lesser citizens, although their rights under the penal laws were still considerably better than those of Irish Catholics. Unwilling to tolerate such discrimination, vast numbers of Scots-Irish sailed for the Thirteen British Colonies in America, where they could practise their religion with greater freedom. Indeed, it is a curious statistical duplicate that, following the arrival of the afore-mentioned 200,000 Scots into Ireland in the seventeenth century, 200,000 Scots-Irish are said to have sailed for the colonies in the following century.

Many settled in New England and Pennsylvania but, with most of the prime land already snapped up by earlier settlers, others pushed onwards to the Appalachian frontiers. By the 1760s, this famously God-fearing farming community was a major force across Virginia, Kentucky, Tennessee, Georgia and the Carolinas, where it attempted to put manners on the wilderness and waged constant and brutal battles with the indigenous American tribes.

One of the key issues for Presbyterians was their inherent dis-taste for hierarchies. This set them at odds with the Protestant elite, whose very definitive colonial and ecclesiastical systems were both headed by the British monarch. As such, it is not surprising that most of the eleven Irish-born or Irish-American signatories of the US Declaration of Independence were from the Scots-Irish tradi-tion. So too was Charles Thomson, the secretary of the Continental Congress, who was born in Maghera, County Derry. The Declaration itself was printed by another Presbyterian, John Dunlap, who was born in Strabane, County Tyrone.

The financier Oliver Pollock, who was born just north of Strabane, not only helped bankroll the Patriots during the American Revolution but was also credited with inventing the $ sign for the US dollar in 1778. Another Irish claim on US heritage is the tune to 'The Star-Spangled Banner', which is metrically identical to a traditional melody called 'Bumper Squire Jones' composed in 1723 by the blind harpist Turlough O'Carolan, the last of the Irish bards.

Andrew Jackson, the seventh president of the United States, was the son of emigrants who were both born in Carrickfergus, County Antrim, as were his two older brothers. They emigrated shortly before Jackson's birth in 1767. The red-headed future president came to prominence in 1815 as commander of the US army that completely routed the British redcoats in the Battle of New Orleans. His victory was so resounding that Ned Pakenham, the Westmeath-born British commander, was among those killed. General Pakenham's body was pickled in a cask of rum and shipped back to Ireland for burial.

Jackson, who went on to serve two terms in the White House from 1829 to 1837, is frequently ranked as one of America's most successful presidents. Donald Trump had his portrait hung on the wall of the Oval Office shortly after he moved into the White House in 2016. The fact that Jackson's portrait has also been on the $20 bill since 1928, the centenary of his election, is considered a classic case of historical irony given that he was fervently opposed to paper money during his lifetime.

Jackson is perhaps the most controversial of the early presidents. He was the principal figure behind the relocation of some 60,000 Native Americans to Indian Territory (now Oklahoma), an event that would become known as the Trail of Tears. Jackson was also an ardent supporter of slavery, owning at least 161 slaves. In 1821, his wife complained that a house slave called Betty had been 'putting on airs' and washing their neighbours' clothes without 'express permission'. Jackson threatened to have Betty tied to a public whipping post and lashed fifty times if she repeated the offence.

During the Black Lives Matter campaign of 2020, Jackson's track record as a slave owner motivated protestors to target his equestrian statue on Lafayette Square, Washington, DC. A statue of John Caldwell Calhoun, Jackson's vice president, was removed from

Charleston in the same week, shortly after the city mayor decried him as South Carolina's 'most consequential defender of slavery and white supremacy'. Calhoun, who was also vice president to John Quincy Adams, was the son of a Donegal-born Scots-Irish immigrant.

James Buchanan, the 15th president (1857–61), was also the son of a Scots-Irish emigrant. Both his father and grandfather were born at Low Cairn, near Ramelton, County Donegal. His father sailed from Londonderry in 1783 and bought a farm near Lancaster, Pennsylvania. He must have felt peculiarly close to home, given that the surrounding townships had names such as Drumore, Antrim, Donegal, Letterkenny and Coleraine. Buchanan remains the only president who never married, leading to inevitable speculations about his sexuality. In his younger years he was engaged to Anne Coleman, the willowy, black-haired daughter of a wealthy iron manufacturer who had emigrated from near Castle Finn in County Donegal. Coleman's sudden death shortly after she broke off their engagement has also been the subject of much debate, with suggestions that she died of a laudanum overdose. Buchanan, who was unable to attend her funeral, wrote to his father, 'I feel happiness has fled from me forever.'

In 1858 the first transatlantic telegram was successfully sent via 4,000 km (2,500 miles) of underwater cable from Valentia Island off the coast of County Kerry to Heart's Content, Newfoundland. It was one of the most remarkable feats in the history of global engineering. An ecstatic Buchanan dispatched an eighty-eight-word message down the line to Queen Victoria, declaring the link to be 'a triumph more glorious and far more useful to mankind than any battle'. He also hailed it as 'a bond of perpetual peace and friendship between the kindred nations, and an instrument destined by Divine Providence to diffuse religion, civilization, liberty, and law throughout the world'. It took seventeen hours for Buchanan's message to be 'downloaded', but when his message was received, church bells rang in celebration from Killarney to London.

Two weeks later, everything went badly wrong when the Atlantic cable effectively burned out. Seven years would pass before the connection was re-established, during which time the United States fought its civil war, leaving perhaps 750,000 people dead. Buchanan was widely blamed for the conflict, which began five weeks after he left office, although he remained defiant to the end. The day before his death in 1868, he predicted that 'history will vindicate my memory'. Alas for him, history thus far disagrees and his name usually appears on the lower rungs when anyone compiles a list of 'Worst US Presidents'.

Following Abraham Lincoln's assassination in the wake of the American Civil War, the office passed to his vice president Andrew Johnson, whose grandfather hailed from the Mounthill, Larne, County Antrim. Johnson's finest hour was the acquisition of Alaska from the Russians in 1867.

The assassination of another president, James Garfield, in 1881 likewise propelled his vice president Chester Arthur into the White House. William Arthur, Chester's father, was born in Cullybackey, County Antrim, where his thatched homestead now serves as an interpretive centre detailing the story of the president and his Presbyterian forebears. William Arthur studied in Belfast before emigrating to Canada in about 1819. Prior to his nomination as vice president in 1880, Chester Arthur's political opponents began spreading rumours that he was born in Ireland and did not move to the United States until he was fourteen years old. Had that proved true, Arthur would have been constitutionally ineligible for the vice presidency. However, the 'birther' conspiracy failed to gather momentum.

Grover Cleveland – the only president to serve two non-consecutive terms, from 1885 to 1889 and 1893 to 1897 – was the grandson of Abner Neal, a Presbyterian Scots-Irish merchant from County Antrim. Arguably, Cleveland's best-known Irish connection came in the early 1870s when, as Sheriff of Erie County (Buffalo, New York), he pulled the scaffold lever that sent two condemned men – one Irish-born, the other Irish-American – to meet their maker.

Cleveland's successor in 1897 was William McKinley, who descended from a family from Dervock, near Ballycastle in County Antrim. His ancestral homestead was dismantled some years ago and is stored in numbered stones at the Ulster American Folk Park in County Tyrone, awaiting resurrection. Following McKinley's assassination in 1901, he was succeeded by his vice president Theodore

Roosevelt, whose forebears – and by extension the forebears of Franklin Delano Roosevelt, the 32nd president – came from the village of Glenoe, also in County Antrim. James Bulloch, Roosevelt's ancestor, emigrated from Glenoe to South Carolina in 1729 and was father to Archibald Bulloch, governor of Georgia on the eve of the British invasion of Savannah. Archibald Bulloch's sudden death at that time is generally attributed to poison. His great-granddaughter Mittie Bulloch was Theodore Roosevelt's mother.

Woodrow Wilson, president from 1913 to 1921, was the grandson of James Wilson, who grew up in a cottage near Strabane, County Tyrone, that is now owned by the Ulster American Folk Park. James emigrated to Philadelphia in 1807, having received a letter from his fellow printer John Dunlap, advising him: 'The young men of Ireland who wish to be free and happy should leave it and come here as quickly as possible. There is no place in the world where a man meets so rich a reward for conduct and industry as in America.' Shortly after his arrival in the US, James married Ann Adams, who is believed to have been born at Sion Mills, also in County Tyrone. Woodrow Wilson was a forty-four-year-old professor at Princeton University when he visited Ireland in 1899, although he did not seek out either of his grandparents' homes. A supporter of Gladstone's Home Rule campaign for Ireland, Wilson was not averse to playing up his Irishness to woo the 'green' vote when he began campaigning for the presidency. At a Democratic rally in Chicago in 1912, he affably declared: 'I get all my stubbornness from the Scotch [on his mother's side], and then there is something else that gives me a great deal of trouble, which I attribute to the Irish. At any rate, it makes me love a scrap…'.

That said, the 'grave menace of the Irish problem' brought growing pains to Wilson during the course of his presidency. After the Easter Rising of 1916, he turned a blind eye to requests that he intervene to save Sir Roger Casement, one of its leaders, from the hangman's noose. In 1918, his secretary wrote that Wilson 'did not intend to appoint another Irishman to anything [because] they were untrustworthy and uncertain'. Despite intense pressure from the Irish-American lobby, Wilson kowtowed to David Lloyd George, the British prime minister, and resisted putting the subject of Ireland's right to self-governance on the agenda for discussion at the 1919 Paris Peace Conference. On the other hand, he did meet with Hanna Sheehy-Skeffington, the Irish nationalist, pacifist and suffragette, who thus, in her own words, became 'the first Irish exile and the first Sinn Féiner to enter the White House, and the first to wear there the badge of the Irish Republic'.

In the White Anglo-Saxon Protestant (WASP)-dominated United States, it was hard for the Catholic Irish to make an impression in the political arena. Hostility towards them was exemplified by the infamous 'No Irish Need Apply' signs that first began appearing across America in the 1840s. Kilkenny-born Martin Renehan was one of the few Catholics to make his mark on the White House staff, where he served as attendant and doorman to five presidents from Andrew Jackson through to Zachary Taylor. Ed McManus, another Irish doorman at the White House, is said to have been the only man who could make Abraham Lincoln laugh. Lincoln's children had Irish nannies despite his wife's dislike of the Irish. However, James Buchanan specifically precluded Irish Catholics from working at the White House during his presidency. Theodore Roosevelt's diaries from the 1880s were also outrageously damning of the Catholic Irish population of New York, whom he denigrated as 'a stupid, sodden, vicious lot'.

The breakthrough against such bigotry commenced in 1880 when Billy Grace (p. 173) became the first Catholic to be elected mayor of New York. Hugh O'Brien, an Irish immigrant, was elected Boston's first Catholic mayor four years later. Grace was one of three Irish-born mayors of New York, the others being Sligo-born Thomas Gilroy (1893–94) and Mayo-born William O'Dwyer (1946–50). New York has also had at least eight Irish-American mayors, including Hugh Grant (the son of an Irish liquor merchant, and the youngest mayor in New York history), Al Smith (the grandson of immigrants from County Westmeath) and Robert Wagner Jr. (the city mayor from 1954 to 1965).

In 1928, Al Smith became the first Irish Catholic to run for president, losing to Herbert Hoover. He went on to oversee the building of the Empire State Building, the world's tallest skyscraper, which was conceived as a way to boost New York's morale in the gloomy aftermath of the Wall Street Crash. On Smith's request, construction of the project commenced on St Patrick's Day 1930.

John Fitzgerald Kennedy, the first Catholic president, descended from Patrick Kennedy, an emigrant cooper from Dunganstown, County Wexford. In 1849 Patrick married twenty-eight-year-old Bridget Murphy, who had grown up in a single-room cabin on a small farm near Gusserane, also in County Wexford. The Kennedys settled on Noddle Island in East Boston's docklands, where Patrick died of cholera in 1858, leaving Bridget to raise their four surviving children on her own. She established a grocery, a variety store and a bakery, while her three daughters became seamstresses. Her son Patrick Joseph 'P. J.' Kennedy initially worked as a docker but later bought several saloons, made a small fortune as a whiskey distributor and became a prominent ward boss and Democratic state senator in Massachusetts.

P. J. Kennedy's son Joseph proved very adept at stockbroking, commodity investments and real estate. As well as becoming a multi-millionaire, he served as US ambassador to the United Kingdom during the early part of the Second World War. In 1914 he married Rose Fitzgerald, the eldest daughter of John 'Honey Fitz' Fitzgerald, the son of famine emigrants from Limerick and Cavan, who became the first Irish-American Catholic to be elected mayor of Boston in 1906.

In 1961, Joseph and Rose's son John Fitzgerald Kennedy became the 35th president of the United States. Having already visited his ancestral family home at Dunganstown as a young man, JFK returned to New Ross during his superbly choreographed state visit to Ireland in 1963. He duly paid tribute to his plucky ancestors in a speech that aired all over the world. In that moment, he reshaped the narrative so that he was no longer simply a rich, Ivy League, urban brat. He was now the epitome of a rags to riches triumph, a worthy heir to the 'log cabin' frontier presidents of earlier days, a symbol of optimism for all those hard-working Ellis Island immigrants who had made America great. The Wexford trip was the only time JFK is known to have made the sign of the cross and publicly acknowledge his Catholicism. 'This is not the land of my birth,' he said later, 'but it is the land for which I hold the greatest affection.' During that four-day trip, he also became the first foreign leader to address the Houses of the Oireachtas (the Irish parliament).

The Kennedy presidency did much to put Ireland on the map for Americans. Indeed, there were so many Irish-Americans on Kennedy's core team that they were dubbed the Irish Mafia. Dean Rusk, his Secretary of State, was the son of a Scots-Irish Presbyterian minister. Bob McNamara, Secretary of Defense during the early years of the Vietnam War, was the grandson of a famine emigrant from Cork. Larry O'Brien, his presidential campaign manager, was the son of emigrants from Skibbereen and Dunmanway in West Cork. During the 1962 Cuban Missile Crisis, JFK's most trusted special assistants were Kenny O'Donnell, Bobby Kennedy's roommate at Harvard, and Dave Powers, the son of emigrants from the Beara Peninsula in West Cork. Powers and O'Donnell were in the secret service car following directly behind the presidential limousine when JFK was shot in Dallas. Dick Donahue, another of Kennedy's advisors, was the grandson of a Kerryman and went on to work on the presidential campaigns for both Bobby and Ted Kennedy (winning New York for the latter) before becoming president of Nike in 1990. Richard J. Daley, another vital cog in JFK's victory, was the longest-serving mayor in Chicago history – until his son Richard broke his record in 2011. Like the Kennedys and Bob McNamara, the Daleys descend from famine emigrants, originating in Dungarvan, County Waterford.

One of the highlights of the Kennedys' visit to Ireland in 1963 was watching a contingent of cadets from the Irish Defence Forces perform the Queen Anne military drill during a ceremony to honour the Easter Rising dead at Arbour Hill, Dublin. Later, at the request of the president's widow Jackie Kennedy, a contingent of twenty-six Irish cadets executed the same silent drill by the graveside during Kennedy's funeral in Washington, DC. The cadets came from the Curragh Camp in County Kildare and were accompanied by Éamon de Valera, president of Ireland.

Jackie Kennedy's 'Irish' pedigree was arguably as strong as her husband's. Her mother Janet Lee was the granddaughter of Thomas Merritt and Maria Curry from County Clare, and she also had connections to the Lees and Nortons of County Cork. One of Jackie Kennedy's closest confidantes was Father Joseph Leonard, a Dublin-born priest, who counselled her after JFK's death, a role that was played with gusto by Sir John Hurt in the movie *Jackie*, filmed shortly before the actor's death in 2017.

Jackie Kennedy visited Ireland with her children in 1967 and stayed at Woodstown House, County Waterford. During her six-week sojourn, she opened the John F. Kennedy Arboretum in New Ross, visited the Kennedy home at Dunganstown and Lismore Castle, toured the Waterford Crystal factory, attended the Irish Derby and joined her friend Sybil Connolly on a visit to Castletown House in County Kildare to show her support of the new Irish Georgian Society. Always keen on swimming alone, she was caught in a current in the seas by Woodstown House and would have drowned but for the keen eye of Jack Walsh, a muscular secret service agent. Walsh, whose forebears came from Kerry, was a pallbearer at her funeral in 1994.

Richard Nixon, US president from 1969 until 1974, had Irish blood on both sides. One of his parental forebears was James Moore of Ballymoney, County Antrim, while his mother descended from a Quaker family from County Kildare. Having lost the 1960 election to Kennedy, Nixon completely understood the importance of winning the Irish-American vote. He also recognized that his Ulster Methodist and Quaker roots were unlikely to appeal to Irish Catholics. And so, just as his re-election campaign got underway in 1970, the attention was deftly switched to his First Lady, Patricia Nixon, whose Catholic grandfather, Patrick Sarsfield Ryan, was born near Ballinrobe, County Mayo, in about 1834 and emigrated to America in 1855.

The story of Patricia Nixon's Irish roots was carefully fed to the press ahead of the president's state visit to Ireland in 1970. Shortly after his arrival, Nixon became enwrapped in an urgent and unexpected meeting at Kilfrush House, County Limerick, with Henry Kissinger and others about the ongoing Vietnam War. Meanwhile, his wife was escorted by helicopter to Ballinrobe, where she was greeted by a brass band, Irish dancers and cousins galore, some real, others drafted in to boost the sense of occasion. Photographs of her visit to her ancestral home were duly splashed across the world's newspapers the following day. That same morning, she accompanied her husband when he discreetly visited the Quaker graveyard near Timahoe, where some of his mother's forebears were said to have been buried.

Gerald Ford, Nixon's vice president and eventual successor in 1974, was twenty-two years old when he had his name legally changed in 1935. He had been christened Leslie Lynch King after his biological father, a descendant of Robert Lynch and his Scots-Irish wife, Marcella Martin, of Fayette County, Pennsylvania.

Ronald Reagan, America's 40th president from 1981 until 1989, was reputedly so anxious that his Irish Catholic roots would put people off voting for him that he commenced his bid for the presidency by pitching himself as a WASP. However, when his Irishness 'came out', he quickly began to appreciate how his genealogy might actually persuade some Catholic Irish Democrats to transfer their loyalty to a Republican. By the time he arrived in Ireland during his re-election campaign in 1984, he was all up for a visit to his ancestral home at Ballyporeen, County Tipperary, from where he proudly declared: 'Today I come back to you as a descendant of people who were buried here in pauper's graves.'

Among the best-known Irish-Americans of the Reagan era was Tip O'Neill, Speaker of the House of Representatives from 1977 until his retirement in 1987, the longest continuous run in US history. Bill Casey, Reagan's director of the Central Intelligence Agency (CIA), descended from a shoemaker from County Offaly. Then again, William 'Wild Bill' Donovan, the founding father of the CIA, was also the grandson of Irish immigrants, one from Skibbereen, the other from Galway. And indeed, in more recent times, John Brennan, director of the CIA from 2013 to 2017, is the son of a blacksmith from County Roscommon.

The Bush family are of Scots-Irish descent but George Bush and his son George W. Bush, 41st and 43rd presidents respectively, opted not to capitalize on their links to counties Cork and Down. By contrast, President Bill Clinton was very eager to establish his Irish roots despite the absence of any documentation. His mother was a Cassidy so, when he visited Dublin in 1995, he made sure to have a pint of stout in Cassidy's pub on Camden Street. Clinton, who was president from 1993 to 2001, made three state visits to Ireland. He traced his interest in Irish politics to Georgetown University in Washington, DC, where his roommate, his first girlfriend and his most charismatic lecturer were all members of the Irish Catholic community. Clinton was to play a vital role in the Irish peace process, not least when he agreed to Ted Kennedy's recommendation that Jean Kennedy Smith, sister of Ted and JFK, be appointed US ambassador to Ireland in 1993 (p. 247). Also important during these talks was Dick Riley, Clinton's Secretary of Education, a man proud of his Cavan roots, while one of the Clintons' closest confidantes is Thurles-born, Drogheda-bred Niall O'Dowd, the then publisher of the *Irish Voice* newspaper and *Irish America* magazine. O'Dowd is credited with swinging much Irish-American support behind Clinton's election campaign.

Barack Obama is perhaps the most surprising president to have Irish roots, given his connections to Hawaii, Indonesia and Kenya. When he came to Ireland in 2011, he enjoyed a famous pint of Guinness at the Ollie Hayes pub in Moneygall on the Tipperary-Offaly border, the village where his ancestor Joseph Kearney once worked as a shoemaker. 'My name is Barack Obama, of the Moneygall Obamas,' he told the assembled crowd, 'and I've come home to find the apostrophe we lost somewhere along the way.' While his visit would pave the way for Barack Obama Plaza, a multi-million-euro fuel and food services station named in his honour, the media homed in on his memorably named forebear Fulmoth Kearney. The impression generated was that Fulmoth was 'driven from Ireland' during the Great Hunger, but there was little mention of the fact that he sailed to America in order to inherit a sizeable farm in Ohio from his Irish-born uncle or that the Kearneys had become wealthy by making wigs for the landed gentry of Ireland during the Georgian age.

Also missing from the tale was John Kearney, a cousin of the shoemaker, who became the bishop of Ossory and provost of Trinity College Dublin. That Bishop Kearney was a professor of oratory at one of the world's leading universities in the age of Edmund Burke was surely a missed opportunity for showcasing the provenance of

Obama's speechmaking prowess. And yet, Protestant bishops and Ohio landowners did not quite fit the narrative. Rightly or wrongly, someone deemed it more appropriate to link Obama to the American dream of a poor, small town émigré who made good in the New World. Nor, for that matter, was there any talk of Michelle Obama's alleged descent from a union in Georgia between Charles Shields, the son of a Scots-Irish plantation owner, and an enslaved girl called Melvina. Whether the relationship was teenage lust, genuine love or sexual assault is unknown. A similar tale is told of the 2020 Democratic vice-presidential nominee Kamala Harris, whose father is believed to be the grandson of a congress, voluntary or otherwise, between a former slave and a son of Antrim-born Hamilton Brown, one of Jamaica's most prominent sugar planters and slave owners in the 1820s and 1830s.

Pulitzer Prize-winning author Samantha Power, who grew up in the Dublin suburb of Castleknock, served as Barack Obama's US Ambassador to the United Nations from 2013 to 2017. Loretta Lynch, who served as Obama's Attorney General, is thought to have descended from a Lynch of Galway who settled in the Caribbean. Denis McDonough, Obama's Chief of Staff, is the devoutly Catholic grandson of emigrants from the Connemara Gaeltacht. Paul Ryan, the former Speaker of the House of Representatives, kept a hurley stick in his office in honour of his ancestor James Ryan, who emigrated from Graiguenamanagh, County Kilkenny, in 1851.

Donald Trump has no Irish blood, although he owns the Trump International Golf Links & Hotel at Doonbeg, County Clare. By a remarkable coincidence, Doonbeg is the very same village from which two of Mike Pence's great-grandparents emigrated in the 1890s. Pence, Trump's vice president, is named for his grandfather, who emigrated from Tubbercurry, County Sligo, in 1923 and became a bus driver in Chicago. Steve Bannon, Trump's controversial former Chief Strategist, is the direct descendant of famine refugees. Sean Spicer, Trump's first press secretary, is the great-grandson of an immigrant from Kinsale, County Cork, who won a Medal of Honour for his service as a gunner's mate in the US Navy during the Spanish-American war of 1898.

The 2020 election saw Joe Biden elected as the 46th president of the United States. There's a good reason why Biden's favourite band is The Chieftains, the Irish folk band, and why he loves to recite verses from the Nobel Prize-winning Irish poet Seamus Heaney. With ten Irish great-great-grandparents out of sixteen, he is the most 'Irish' US president since JFK. Arguably the most important of these ancestors was Edward Blewitt, a brick-maker and civil engineer from Ballina, County Mayo. As well as being one of the civil engineers who helped map Ireland for the Ordnance Survey during the 1830s and 1840s, he was general overseer at Ballina Workhouse from 1848 to 1850. In 1851, having cut his teeth on the construction of the Catholic cathedral in Killala, Edward took his family to Pennsylvania, where he helped lay out the streets of Scranton, now twinned with Ballina. Edward's grandson Edward Francis Blewitt was also an engineer and oversaw the construction of the drainage system and water works at Guadalajara in Mexico. A president of the formidable Pennsylvanian branch of the Ancient Order of Hibernians for a decade, the younger Blewitt stood for the Democrats in 1907 and became only the second Irish Catholic senator in Pennsylvanian history. Two years later, his daughter Geraldine married Ambrose Joseph Finnegan, the son of a blind fiddler and grandson of a shoemaker from the Cooley Peninsula of County Louth. Geraldine and Ambrose were Joe Biden's grandparents.

Joe Biden came into the international spotlight when he served two terms as vice president to Obama, the descendant of an Irish shoemaker. Given that Biden is also the descendant of an Irish shoemaker, it was surely a golden hour for the Guild of Shoemakers when he emerged as the eventual winner of the 2020 presidential election.

REFLECTIONS ON IRISH IDENTITY

Only one world leader is guaranteed an annual audience with the US president at the White House. Since 1952, the Taoiseach (prime minister) of the Republic of Ireland has shared centre stage at the White House on 17 March every year bar 2020, when the planned St Patrick's Day reunion between Leo Varadkar and Donald Trump joined the infinite list of events that fell victim to Covid-19. Pandemics aside, the annual 'Shamrock Ceremony' offers a golden opportunity for the two leaders to discuss the economic relationship between their countries, a relationship that was valued at about $680 billion (€606 billion) in 2018.

As part of the broader phenomenon of the global St Patrick's Day celebrations, the world has seen scores of major landmarks 'go green' in honour of Ireland's patron saint over the last decade. As well as the Chicago River, which has been dyed green since 1962, the line-up of sites that have gone green to date includes the Sydney Opera House, the Great Pyramid of Giza in Egypt, the Great Wall of China, the Taj Mahal in India, Christ the Redeemer in Brazil, the London Eye, the Nelson Mandela statue in Johannesburg, the Leaning Tower of Pisa in Italy, the Palestinian Museum in Ramallah, West Bank, the 'Welcome' sign in Las Vegas and the new One World Trade Center in New York. Away from the greening, the crowds that the St Patrick's Day parades muster look especially astounding in the post-pandemic world – 2 million in New York, 1 million in Boston, half a million in Savannah, Georgia – while the Milwaukee Irish Fest, the world's largest Irish music and cultural festival, drew more than 100,000 visitors in 2018 and 2019.

St Patrick's rise to global stardom did not happen overnight. Indeed, the greening is arguably the culmination of at least fourteen centuries of travel by Irish men and women such as those profiled in the pages of this book. For instance, the earliest recorded St Patrick's Day parade outside Ireland took place in the then Spanish colony of Florida in 1601 and was organized by Ricardo Artur, the Irish-born vicar of St Augustine.

About 1 per cent of the world's population claim to be at least a little bit Irish. That percentage figure rises to perhaps as much as 40 in Australia, 20 in New Zealand, 12 in both Canada and the UK, and 10 in the USA. In 2019, Ancestry.com, the genealogy company, revealed that two-thirds of its 15 million members who took a DNA test were at least 5 per cent Irish. About 633,000 Irish-born citizens are presently living in Britain (England, Scotland and Wales) and 170,000 (including c. 50,000 undocumented) in the United States. Large numbers of Irish ex-pats also live in European cities such as Barcelona, Paris and Brussels, or further afield in places such as Beijing, Cape Town, Dubai and Abu Dhabi. As well as an estimated global diaspora of perhaps 80 million, there are presently 6 million Irish nationals living on the island of Ireland.

The Irish government is not immune to the economic boost of a successful charm offensive on the diaspora. A case in point is the Gathering of 2013, a tourism-led initiative that saw grassroots organizations across Ireland host almost 5,000 events that were, by and large, aimed at attracting and honouring the diaspora. The number of overseas visitors swelled considerably in consequence, with a 15 per cent increase in the US market, an economic boost that helped Ireland find its feet after the economic collapse five years earlier. It remains to be seen how the diaspora might help bring the country out of the economic downturn ignited by the Covid-19 pandemic, not least with the entire concept of globalization in a state of retreat.

The romantic notion that those of Irish blood would help the 'old country' has provenance. At the end of the First World War, Henry Ford ensured his Detroit-based automobile firm built its first tractor factory outside of Europe in Cork, the county from which his father emigrated. By 1930, its workforce had reached 7,000, making it the second-largest employer in the Irish Free State after the railway.

In the 1960s, the impact of John F. Kennedy's presidency, and his return visit to Ireland, had a profound influence on Irish-American relations. Thirty years later, his youngest sister, the late Jean Kennedy Smith, arrived in Ireland as the new US ambassador. She carved out her own place in the history books when she persuaded Bill Clinton to host Sinn Féin leader Gerry Adams in the White House, thus paving the way for the 1994 ceasefire and the start of the Northern Ireland peace process. In 2020, eager to perpetuate the connection to such an influential American dynasty, the relevant local councils voted to name Ireland's newest and longest bridge by New Ross in honour of the Kennedy matriarch, Rose Fitzgerald Kennedy.

Could similar ancestral links prove useful to Ireland in the future? With almost 900 US firms in Ireland in 2022, employing 190,000 people (or twenty per cent of the workforce), such connections can prove surprisingly tangible. When Twitter established its European headquarters in Dublin, it must have given a little genealogical thrill to Jack Dorsey, its former CEO, who reputedly descends from a family from Erry, near Clara, County Offaly. That Google is such a massive employer across Dublin's Docklands must likewise have gladdened the heart of Nicole Shanahan, the former wife of Google co-founder Sergey Brin, who is the great-granddaughter of emigrants from Ballylongford, County Kerry. Downpatrick-born Neville Isdell, the former CEO of the Coca-Cola Company, fulfilled a lifelong dream in 2016 when he funded and launched EPIC – The Irish Emigration Museum in Dublin. Telling the story of the Irish diaspora, the digital museum swiftly established itself as one of the most popular visitor attractions in the city, winning Europe's Leading Tourist Attraction at the World Travel Awards, the Oscars of the travel industry, three years in a row in 2019, 2020 and 2021.

Internal politics is another area in which the Irish diaspora has long sought to have an influence. In the United States, the hue has primarily been nationalist. The United Irishman patriot Wolfe Tone was not overtly fond of Americans, but he nonetheless honed several of his republican policies during his ten-month sojourn in Pennsylvania in 1795–96. Tone's close friend Thomas Addis Emmet, older brother of the doomed patriot Robert Emmet, became attorney general of New York in 1812. In the ensuing generations, many members of organizations like Young Ireland, the Fenian Brotherhood and the Irish Republican Brotherhood lived in the United States, where they found an audience keen to hear their dreams of ousting the British from Ireland and establishing an independent state.

That sense of nationalism was understandably strong among those whose American story began during the Great Hunger. In the context of the diaspora, the relocation of such a huge percentage of the Irish population in the 1840s was the biggest game changer in Irish history. Put simply, hundreds of thousands of Irish-born people were now living, and having families, outside of Ireland, primarily in the United States and the United Kingdom. Irish-American antipathy to the British intensified during the latter decades of the nineteenth century. Nationalist politicians Charles Stewart Parnell (who was himself half-American) and Michael Davitt raised a small fortune for the Irish Land League on fundraising trips to America in 1880–81. To Davitt's surprise, the biggest contributors after Chicago and Philadelphia were the citizens of Denver, which was home to a massive population of Irish-born miners (mainly from the Beara Peninsula) and railroad workers.

A generation later, the Easter Rising of 1916 would not have been possible without the funds raised in the United States by Clan na Gael, an Irish-American organization committed to the nationalist cause. In the spring of 1919, Éamon de Valera escaped from a British jail and was pronounced president of the fledgling Irish Republic. In May, he sailed for New York, the city of his birth. A month later, he hosted a 'Freedom Rally' at Fenway Park, the home ground of the Boston Red Sox baseball team, recently built by another Irishman. Over 50,000 people arrived to hear his emotional plea: 'If America fails the good people of small nations seeking to wrest themselves from tyranny and oppression, then, democracy dies or else goes mad.' A correspondent for the Boston Daily Globe was greatly impressed: 'In the vast audience you sensed this new dignity that has sunk into their consciousness, born of the knowledge that millions of men of Irish blood have been fighting the past four years for democracy as against autocracy and for the self-determination of Nations in the world.'

De Valera spent the next eighteen months in the United States drumming up support for the Republic, as well as critical finances for both his government and his armed forces during the Irish War of Independence. At the same time, the American Committee for Relief in Ireland was founded in New York 'to devise and consider ways and means of relieving the acute distress' in Ireland on account of the war. When the British government finally sued for peace and brought the war to a close, one reason it did so was because of pressure from the White House, which was in turn under pressure from the Irish-American block in Washington, DC. In 1924, the Irish Free State was formerly recognized by the US government as a state with autonomous control over its foreign relations.

During more recent times, Irish-Americans provided much of the financial support that enabled the Irish Republican Army (IRA) to wage its war during the era of the Troubles. Founded in New York in 1969, the Irish Northern Aid Committee (NORAID) raised €3.5 million for republicans and the families of IRA prisoners before it was wound up in the early 1990s. Friends of Sinn Féin, its heir apparent, raised €10.7 million between 1995 and 2014, with philanthropist Chuck Feeney as its biggest donor. Between November 2021 and November 2022, it raised over €1 million in donations, primarily from trade unions and construction companies in the New York area. In contrast, the loyalist opposition to Sinn Féin neither sought nor received any significant support from America.

Needless to say, the nuances of this are infinitely multifaceted, but it again illustrates the impact of the Irish-American community, which has always had considerable influence over political affairs in the 'old country' and continues to do so. In 2023, Joe Biden came to Ireland for four days, shortly before the Clintons and George Mitchel arrived for an event to mark the 25th anniversary of the Good Friday Agreement. Biden has long been an unequivocal supporter of the agreement, describing it as 'the bedrock of peace, stability and prosperity for all the people of Northern Ireland.' Another historic milestone was reached in 2023 when Michelle O'Neill, vice president pf Sinn Féin and former First Minister of Northern Ireland, attended the Coronation of Charles III, as did President Michael D Higgins, the first Irish head of state to attend a Coronation. Also in play was Ireland's seat on the 15-member UN Security Council, the most powerful body in the UN system, for the 2021–2022 term.

In many ways, the very fact these curiously connected outsiders are looking in and assessing Ireland from the perspective of their own adopted homelands means there has been an inclination to reassess what it means to be Irish. It has also allowed a degree of old-fashioned celebrity gossip as that ever-growing list of Irish-born people who have become household names in the global entertainment industry is contemplated. The silver screen has also been no stranger to Irish talent since the early days of the silent movies when the Moore brothers and Mary Pickford were in their element.

The year 2023 was an astonishing year for the Irish film industry, five of the twenty acting nominees at the Academy Awards in Hollywood were Irish. Fourteen other Irish actors have garnered 26 Oscar nominations between them since 1939, resulting in three wins for Daniel Day-Lewis, an English-born Irish citizen, and one each for Barry Fitzgerald and Brenda Fricker. Liam Neeson and Richard Harris were among the near victors, as was Belfast-born Kenneth Branagh, who won the Best Original Screenplay Oscar for 'Belfast' in 2022. The Oscar statuette, as it happens, was designed by the multi-Oscar winning Dublin-born art director Cedric Gibbons. Saoirse Ronan earned four nominations before the age of twenty-five. Hopefully, she will achieve victory quicker than Peter O'Toole, who was nominated eight times before he finally scooped a special Oscar in 2003 for his general contribution to the film industry.

So where does it go from here in the post-Covid world? More Irish people crossed the Atlantic by plane in 2018 and 2019 than sailed to the Americas during the entire era of the Great Hunger. The major difference, needless to say, is that most present-day transatlantic passengers come home again. Such travel dried up when the pandemic struck but plenty of Irish are traveling now. In May 2023, the Nomad Passport Index ranked the Irish passport as the fourth-most powerful in the world. Holders of an Irish passport are presently allowed to enter 187 nations around the world without a visa.

More than a million Irish nationals are living abroad today, including over a thousand missionaries who are running schools, clinics and sanitation schemes across Africa, South America and Asia. For those who return, the influence and experience of their global travels invariably brings a healthy, open-minded international flair to their future selves. And for those who opt to live their lives in latitudes far from their place of birth and family homes, they are but replicating the decision of many millions of Irish people who have gone before.

NOTES

1. Columbanus and the Merovingian Kings

1 Aidan Breen, 'Columbanus (Colmán, Columba)', in James McGuire and James Quinn (eds), *Dictionary of Irish Biography* (Dublin and Cambridge, UK: Royal Irish Academy and Cambridge University Press, 2009).

2. Virgilius of Salzburg

1 Quoted in Dagmar Ó Riain-Raedel, 'Ireland and Austria in the Middle Ages: The Role of the Irish Monks in Austria' (2002).

2 John Carey, 'Ireland and the Antipodes: The Heterodoxy of Virgil of Salzburg', Speculum, vol. 64, no. 1 (1989), p. 1.

3. The Carolingian Irish

1 Quoted in Ted Byfield, *Darkness Descends* (2003), p. 253.

2 Adrian Guiu, *A Companion to John Scottus Eriugena* (Leiden: Brill, 2019), p. 34.

7. Jacobo of Ireland and the Mongol Empire

1 Peter Jackson, *The Mongols and the West: 1221–1410* (2005), p. 171.

8. Luke Wadding and the Vatican Elite

1 Hugh Albert O'Donnell to Fabrizio Veralli, Cardinal Protector of Ireland, Louvain, 7 October 1619, in Brendan Jennings (ed.), *Wadding Papers, 1614–38* (Dublin, 1953), pp. 19–20.

2 Francis Harold, his nephew, wrote his life story. The surviving volumes of Wadding's work include his history of the Franciscan Order.

9. Don Guillén, the Original Zorro

1 Peter H. Wilson, *Europe's Tragedy* (2009).

2 Archivo Histórico Nacional (National Historical Archive of Spain), *Inquisición, 1731*, exp. 53, fol. 363v., quoted by Natalia Silva Prada in 'Irish News in the New Spanish Kingdoms' (March 2009). The Inquisition wrongly but deliberately denounced his 'claimed nobility, service and grandeur of himself and his kin' and castigated him as 'an unfortunate lowly character' and 'a person of [no] account'.

10. Lord Bellomont's Piratical Venture

1 *Shields Daily Gazette*, Saturday 23 August 1879.

11. George Berkeley, the 'Irish Plato' and Bermuda College

1 Patrick Kelly, 'Anne Donnellan: Irish Proto-Bluestocking', *Hermathena*, no. 154 (1993), pp. 39–68.

2 E. Edwards Beardsley, *Life and Correspondence of Samuel Johnson D.D.: Missionary of the Church of England in Connecticut, and First President of King's College, New York* (New York: Hurd & Houghton, 1874), p. 77.

12. Richard Brew, Slave Trader

1 'Richard Brew to Richard Miles, 22 February 1776, Castle Brew', Public Records Office (PRO), National Archives, Kew, UK, T70/1534, quoted in Rebecca Shumway, *The Fante and the Transatlantic Slave Trade* (2011), p. 83. One wonders whether he might be the 'John Quamina' mentioned in Nneka M. Okona, 'How a West African Woman became the "Pastry Queen" of Colonial Rhode Island', Atlas Obscura, 13 May 2020, https://www.atlasobscura.com/articles/duchess-quamino.

2 'Richard Brew to Mr Gwyther, 7 May 1776', PRO T70/1534, quoted in Rebecca Shumway, *The Fante and the Transatlantic Slave Trade* (2011).

3 John Woolman, 'Considerations of the Keeping of Negroes: Extracts from a Collection of Voyages' (1774), p. 313.

4 Anon., *A Treatise Upon the Trade from Great-Britain to Africa* (1772).

253

5 Margaret Priestly, 'Richard Brew: An Eighteenth-Century Trader at Anomabu' (1959), p. 40.

6 James Sanders, 'The Expansion of the Fante and the Emergence of Asante in the Eighteenth Century', *The Journal of African History*, vol. 20, no. 3 (1979), p. 362.

13. The Abbé de Firmont

1 Quoted in Joseph Guinan, 'Henry Essex Edgeworth' (1913), p. 283.

2 Quoted in 'Louis Blanc's French Revolution', *The Edinburgh Review, Or Critical Journal*, vol. 118 (July–October 1863), p. 137.

3 Patrick M. Geoghegan, 'Flood, Peter', in James McGuire and James Quinn (eds), *Dictionary of Irish Biography* (2009).

4 Quoted in Joseph Guinan, 'Henry Essex Edgeworth' (1913), pp. 283–84.

14. Hercules Mulligan, Washington's Spy

1 M. J. O'Brien, 'Hercules Mulligan', *Journal of the American-Irish Historical Society*, no. 15 (1916), pp. 142–46.

15. James Hoban, Architect of the White House

1 *Dublin Evening Telegraph*, Saturday 18 May 1907.

2 William W. Warner, *At Peace with All Their Neighbors* (2004).

17. Pat Watkins, Crusoe of the Galápagos

1 *Royal Gazette of Jamaica*, 8 November 1817, p. 11.

18. Chile's Irish Patriots

1 Claudio Gay, *Historia física y política de Chile (1749–1808)*, vol. IV (1848), p. 506.

19. John Field: A Muscovy Nocturne

1 *Dublin Evening Post*, Tuesday 27 March 1792.

2 Franz Liszt's preface to his edition of Field's nocturnes, 1859 (trans. Julius Schuberth, 1859).

3 Hummel obituary, *Morning Post*, 1 November 1837.

4 *Belfast Commercial Chronicle*, 13 June 1831, p. 4.

21. Dr James Barry, Caesarean Pioneer

1 *The Gentleman's Magazine*, vol. 76 (1806), p. 303.

23. Sir George Gore, Buffalo Slayer

1 Peter Pagnamenta, *Prairie Fever* (2012), p. 105.

2 'The Saguenay', *Harper's New Monthly Magazine*, vol. 19 (Jul. 1859), p. 159.

24. Margaret of New Orleans

1 Laura D. Kelley, *The Irish in New Orleans* (2014).

26. Little Al Cashier

1 'Remarkable War Veteran: Woman Fought Three Years in Civil War', *Hartford Republican*, 6 June 1913.

2 'Deposition of J. H. Himes' (24 January 1915), quoted in DeAnne Blanton, 'Women Soldiers of the Civil War', *Prologue Magazine*, vol. 2, no. 1 (Spring 1993), p. 30.

3 Rodney O. Davis, 'Private Albert Cashier as Regarded by His/Her Comrades', *Illinois Historical Journal*, vol. 82 (1989), pp. 110–12.

4 Damian Shiels, *The Irish in the American Civil War* (2013), p. 168.

5 Ibid.

29. Eliza Lynch, First Lady of Paraguay

1 Richard Francis Burton, *Letters from the Battle-Fields of Paraguay* (London: 1870), p. 74.

2 'Irish "Grace O'Malley" in Paraguay', *The Irishman*, Saturday 18 July 1868.

30. John Philip Holland, Father of the Submarine

1 *Catholic Digest*, vol. 11 (St Paul's, MN: College of St. Thomas, 1947), p. 68.

2 'Holland Submarine Saved', *New York Sun*, 20 August 1916.

3 'Dinner to Major MacBride', *Western People*, Saturday 12 January 1901.
4 'The Holland Submarine Boat', *Irish Examiner*, Friday 17 June 1898.
5 'The Birth of a Submarine', *Edwardsville Intelligencer*, 22 October 1965.
6 La Salle Society dinner report from *Irish World*, quoted in Meath Chronicle, Saturday 5 January 1907.

31. Nellie Cashman, Angel of the Wild West

1 *Tombstone Weekly Epitaph*, Sunday 19 September 1897, p. 2.

33. Annie Moore, the First Emigrant Through Ellis Island

1 'A Cork Emigrant', *Cork Constitution*, 11 January 1892, p. 8.

34. Margaretta Eagar, the Last Tsar's Governess

1 Margaret Eagar, *Six Years at the Russian Court* (1906).
2 *Gentlewoman*, Saturday 21 January 1905, p. 21.

35. The Moore Brothers, Hollywood Stars

1 'Tom Moore is in Dublin', *Freeman's Journal*, Saturday 25 November 1922, p. 7.

36. Louis Brennan, the Wizard of Oz

1 *London Evening Standard*, 11 November 1909.
2 *Aberdeen Press and Journal*, Saturday 11 May 1907, p. 6.

40. Brendan Bracken, Churchill's Spin Doctor

1 Kay Halle, *The Irrepressible Churchill* (1966), pp. 52–53.

41. Patrick Gallagher, Vietnam Hero

1 James Durney, *Vietnam: The Irish Experience* (2008), p. viii. The Irish involvement in the war was a much neglected subject until 1998, when Declan Hughes (www.irishveterans.org) began the identification of the Irish who lost their lives in that war, at a time when few believed any Irish had been there.
2 Peter Berresford Ellis, *A History of the Irish Working Class*, new edn (London: Pluto Press, 1996), p. 254.
3 Gary D. Gullickson, *Vietnam: Our Story* (1992), p. 49.

BIBLIOGRAPHY

We live in an incredible age when the troves of newspapers past are now searchable online. As such, I salute the online Irish News Archive and British News Archive, which has made trawling through newspaper archives such a joyous and fruitful experience. Much of what appears in this book has been fished from the pages of archived newspapers such as the *Anglo-Celt, Limerick Reporter, Limerick Chronicle, Evening Freeman, Belfast News-Letter, Irish Times, Catholic Digest, Western People, New York Sun, Irish Examiner, Edwardsville Intelligencer, Irish Independent, Irish World, New York World, Meath Chronicle, Boston Post, Tombstone Weekly Epitaph, Kirkintilloch Herald, Daily Arizona Citizen, The Nation, Freeman's Journal, Northern Whig, Derby Daily Telegraph, London Evening Standard, Mayo Constitution, Chatham News, Aberdeen Press and Journal, The Times* and the *Daily Mirror.*

I also applaud the podcasts from Myles Dungan (The History Show), Patrick Geoghegan (Talking History), Fin Dwyer (irishhistorypodcast.ie), Zack Twamley (When Diplomacy Fails), Dan Snow (History Hit), Dan Carlin (Hardcore History), Melvyn Bragg (In Our Time) and BBC HistoryExtra.

The shelves of our home now groan with literally thousands of books, journals, pamphlets, magazines and other historical archives. While many of these were instrumental in helping me shape the stories in this book, I have also accessed manifold writings online through such wonders as Academia.edu and Google Books. The following titles will provide more information for those seeking further detail on the topics. For more please visit www.turtlebunbury.com and www.turtlehistory.com.

Introduction: Emerald Exodus

Chambers, Anne, *The Great Leviathan: The Life of Howe Peter Browne, 2nd Marquess of Sligo 1788–1845* (Dublin: New Island Books, 2017)

Crouch, Gregory, *The Bonanza King: John Mackay and the Battle over the Greatest Riches in the American West* (New York: Scribner, 2018)

Dietz, Maribel, *Wandering Monks, Virgins, and Pilgrims: Ascetic Travel in the Mediterranean World, A.D. 300–800* (Pennsylvania: Penn State University Press, 2010), pp. 194–95

Dunn, Richard S., *Sugar and Slaves: The Rise of the Planter Class in the English West Indies, 1624–1713* (Chapel Hill: University of North Carolina Press, 2012)

Emmons, David M., *The Butte Irish: Class and Ethnicity in an American Mining Town, 1875–1925* (Champaign: University of Illinois Press, 1989)

Gleeson, David T., *The Green and the Gray: The Irish in the Confederate States of America* (Chapel Hill: University of North Carolina Press, 2016)

Hamilton, P., 'Irish Women Immigrants in the Nineteenth Century', in James Jupp (ed.), *The Australian People: An Encyclopedia of the Nation, Its People and Their Origins* (Cambridge, UK: Cambridge University Press, 2001), pp. 456–59

Hogan, L., McAtackney, L., and Reilly, M., 'The Irish in the Anglo-Caribbean: servants or slaves?', *History Ireland*, 24 (2016), pp.18–22

McClaughlin, T., 'Irish-Protestant Settlement', in James Jupp (ed.), *The Australian People: An Encyclopedia of the Nation, Its People and Their Origins* (Cambridge, UK: Cambridge University Press, 2001), pp. 463–65

Reece, Bob, 'Irish Convicts', in James Jupp (ed.), *The Australian People: An Encyclopedia of the Nation, Its People and Their Origins* (Cambridge, UK: Cambridge University Press, 2001), pp. 447–51

Reid, Richard, *Not Just Ned: A True History of the Irish in Australia* (Canberra: National Museum of Australia Press, 2011)

Shiels, Damian, *The Irish in the American Civil War* (Dublin: The History Press, 2013)

Wray, Vamplew (ed.), *Australians, Historical Statistics* (Broadway, NSW, Australia: Fairfax, Syme & Weldon Associates, 1987), p. 8

1. Columbanus and the Merovingian Kings

Breen, Aidan, 'Columbanus (Colmán, Columba)', in James McGuire and James Quinn (eds), *Dictionary of Irish Biography* (Dublin and Cambridge, UK: Royal Irish Academy and Cambridge University Press, 2009)

Butler, Hubert, *Ten Thousand Saints: A Study in Irish & European Origins* (Dublin: Lilliput Press, 2012)

Cooper, J. C., *Dictionary of Christianity* (Abingdon: Routledge, 2013), p. 81

Couchman, John, *The Peregrinations of St Columbanus and the World He Lived In* (privately published, March 2020)

Dietz, Maribel, *Wandering Monks, Virgins, and Pilgrims: Ascetic Travel in the Mediterranean World, A.D. 300–800* (Pennsylvania: Penn State University Press, 2010)

Kenney, James Francis, *The Sources for the Early History of Ireland: Ecclesiastical: An Introduction and a Guide* (New York: Columbia University Press, 1929; rev. edn New York: Octagon Books, 1966)

Meeder, Sven, 'Irish Peregrinatio and Cultural Exchange', *Settimane di Studio del Centro Italiano di Studi sull'Alto Medioevo*, 66 (2019), pp. 427–51

O'Hara, Alexander (ed.), *Columbanus and the Peoples of Post-Roman Europe* (Oxford: Oxford University Press, 2018)

Ó Riain, Pádraig, *A Dictionary of Irish Saints* (Dublin: Four Courts Press, 2011)

2. Virgilius of Salzburg

Carey, John, 'Ireland and the Antipodes: The Heterodoxy of Virgil of Salzburg', *Speculum*, vol. 64, no. 1 (1989), pp. 1–10

Enright, Michael J., *Iona, Tara and Soissons: The Origin of the Royal Anointing Ritual*, Arbeiten zur Frühmittelalterforschung 17 (Berlin and New York: Walter de Gruyter, 1985)

Ó Riain-Raedel, Dagmar, 'Ireland and Austria in the Middle Ages: The Role of the Irish Monks in Austria', in P. Leifer and E. Sagarra (eds), *Austro-Irish Links Through the Centuries*, Favorita Papers (Vienna: Vienna School of International Studies, 2002)

Ó Riain-Raedel, Dagmar, "Wide-Reaching Connections": The List of Abbots from Iona in the Liber confraternitatum ecclesiae S. Petri in Salzburg', in Elizabeth Mullins and Diarmuid Scully (eds), *Listen, O Isles, unto Me: Studies in Medieval Word and Image in Honour of Jennifer O'Reilly* (Cork: Cork University Press, 2011)

3. The Carolingian Irish

Berardis, Vincenzo, *Ireland and Italy in the Middle Ages* (Dublin, 1950)

Byfield, Ted, *The Christians, Their First Two Thousand Years: Darkness Descends: A.D. 350 to 565, the Fall of the Western Roman Empire* (Christian History Project, 2003)

De Jubainville, Henry d'Arbois, *The Irish Mythological Cycle and Celtic Mythology* (Dublin: O'Donoghue, 1903)

Eastwood, Bruce, *Ordering the Heavens: Roman Astronomy and Cosmology in the Carolingian Renaissance* (Leiden: Brill, 2007)

Ó Riain-Raedel, Dagmar, 'St Kilian and the Irish Network in Early Carolingian Europe', in Wolfram R. Keller and Dagmar Schlüter (eds), *'A Fantastic and Abstruse Latinity?': Hiberno-Continental Cultural and Literary Interactions in the Middle Ages*, Studien und Texte zur Keltologie 12 (Münster, Germany: Nodus Publikationen, 2017), pp. 31–53

Stokes, Margaret, *Six Months in the Apennines or A Pilgrimage in Search of Vestiges of the Irish Saints in Italy* (London and New York, 1892)

Story, Joanna, *Carolingian Connections: Anglo-Saxon England and Carolingian Francia, c. 750–870* (Abingdon: Routledge, 2017)

4. Brendan the Navigator and the Monks of Iceland

Ahronson, Kristján, *Into the Ocean: Vikings, Irish, and Environmental Change in Iceland and the North* (Toronto: University of Toronto Press, 2015)

Boyce, John, 'The Arctic Irish: Fact or Fiction?', *History Ireland*, vol. 18, no. 3 (May/June 2010)

Fladmark, J. M., and Heyerdahl, Thor, *Heritage and Identity: Shaping the Nations of the North* (Abingdon: Routledge, 2015)

Flechner, Roy, and Meeder, Sven (eds), *The Irish in Early Medieval Europe: Identity, Culture and Religion* (London: Macmillan, 2016)

Lacy, Terry G., *Ring of Seasons: Iceland, Its Culture and History* (Ann Arbor: University of Michigan Press, 2000)

Phillips, J. R. S., *The Medieval Expansion of Europe* (Oxford: Clarendon Press, 1998)

5. Helias of Cologne

Hogan, J. F., 'Irish Monasteries in Germany', *Irish Ecclesiastical Record*, 4th series, vol. 3 (1898), pp. 526–35

Ó Riain-Raedel, Dagmar, 'New Light on the Beginnings of Christ Church Cathedral, Dublin', in Seán Duffy (ed.), *Medieval Dublin XVII* (Dublin: Four Courts Press, 2019)

Wattenbach, Dr, 'The Irish Monasteries in Germany', *Ulster Journal of Archaeology*, vol. 7 (1859), pp. 227–47

6. The Creation of the Irish Saints

Cooper, J. C., *Dictionary of Christianity* (Abingdon: Routledge, 2013)

Harbinson, Peter, 'Twelfth and Thirteenth Century Irish Stonemasons in Regensburg', *Studies: An Irish Quarterly Review*, vol. 64, no. 256 (Winter 1975), pp. 333–46

Healy, Rev. John, *Insula Sanctorum Et Doctorum, or Ireland's Ancient Schools and Scholars* (Library of Alexandria, 1897)

Levinge, Godfrey, *The Traveller in the East – A Guide* (1839)

Ó Riain-Raedel, Dagmar, 'Ireland and Austria in the Middle Ages: The Role of the Irish Monks in Austria', in P. Leifer and E. Sagarra (eds), *Austro-Irish Links Through the Centuries*, Favorita Papers (Vienna: Vienna School of International Studies, 2002)

Ó Riain-Raedel, Dagmar, 'Irish Benedictine Monasteries on the Continent', in Martin Browne and Colmán Ó Clabaigh (eds), *The Irish Benedictines: A History* (Dublin: Columba Press, 2005), pp. 25–63

Wycherley, Dr Niamh, *The Cult of Relics in Medieval Ireland: Power, Patronage and Devotion* (Turnhout, Belgium: Brepols, 2015)

7. Jacobo of Ireland and the Mongol Empire

Dwyer, Fin, 'The First Irishman in China (Outsiders Part II)' (12 Dec. 2017), *Irish History Podcast*, https://irishhistorypodcast.ie/the-first-irishman-in-china-outsiders-part-ii/

Jackson, Peter, *The Mongols and the West: 1221–1410* (Harlow: Pearson Longman, 2005)

MacMahon, Fr. Hugh, 'In the Footsteps of James of Ireland: Encounters with Irish Missionaries in China', in Jerusha McCormack (ed.), *The Irish and China* (Dublin: New Island Books, 2019)

Odoric, Friar, *The Travels of Friar Odoric: A 14th Century Journal of the Blessed Odoric of Pordenone*, intro. Paolo Chiesa (Grand Rapids, MI: William B. Eerdmans, 2001)

Chronica XXIV generalium ordinis Minorum (Ad Claras Aquas (Quaracchi): 1897), pp. 503–4

8. Luke Wadding and the Vatican Elite

Binasco, Matteo, 'Luke Wadding and Irish Diplomatic Activity in Seventeenth-Century Rome', *Studi Irlandesi: A Journal of Irish Studies*, vol. 6, no. 6 (2016), pp. 193–203

Binasco, Matteo, *Luke Wadding, the Irish Franciscans, and Global Catholicism* (Abingdon: Routledge, 2020)

Keogh, Dáire and McDonnell, Albert (eds), *The Irish College, Rome and Its World* (Dublin: Four Courts Press, 2008)

9. Don Guillén, the Original Zorro

Cline, Sarah, 'William Lamport/Guillén de Lombardo, 1611–1659: Mexico's Irish Would-Be King', in Karen Racine and Beatriz G. Mamigonian (eds), *The Human Tradition in the Atlantic World: 1500–1850* (Lanham, MD: Rowman & Littlefield, 2010), pp. 43–56

Crewe, Ryan Dominic, 'Brave New Spain: An Irishman's Independence Plot in Seventeenth-Century Mexico', *Past & Present*, vol. 207, no. 1 (May 2010), pp. 53–87

Lambert, Hubart Andrew, 'Lambert of Wexford', *The Past: The Organ of the Uí Cinsealaigh Historical Society*, no. 2 (1921), pp. 129–38

Prada, Natalia Silva, 'Irish News in the New Spanish Kingdoms: The Circulation of Political Information about William Lamport and Diego Nugent, 1642–1667', trans. Claire Healy, *Irish Migration Studies in Latin America*, vol. 7, no. 1 (Mar. 2009), www.irlandeses.org

Troncarelli, Fabio, 'The Man behind the Mask of Zorro', *History Ireland*, vol. 9, no. 3 (Autumn 2001)

Wilson, Peter H., *Europe's Tragedy: A New History of the Thirty Years War* (London: Penguin, 2009)

10. Lord Bellomont's Piratical Venture

Cabell, Craig, Thomas, Graham A. and Richards, Allan, *Captain Kidd: The Hunt for the Truth* (Barnsley: Pen & Sword Maritime, 2011)

The Tyburn Chronicle: Or, The Villainy Display'd In All Its Branches (London: Cooke, 1768)

11. George Berkeley, the 'Irish Plato' and Bermuda College

Atherton, Margaret, *Berkeley* (Oxford: John Wiley & Sons, 2019)

Berkeley, George, *The Works of George Berkeley, Bishop of Cloyne*, ed. A. A. Luce and T. E. Jessop, 9 vols (London: Thomas Nelson, 1948–57)

Berkeley, George, *Philosophical Works, Including the Works on Vision*, ed. Michael R. Ayers, Everyman edn (London: J. M. Dent, 1975)

Breuninger, Scott, *Recovering Bishop Berkeley: Virtue and Society in the Anglo-Irish Context* (New York: Palgrave Macmillan, 2010)

Downing, Lisa, 'George Berkeley', in Edward N. Zalta (ed.), *The Stanford Encyclopedia of Philosophy* (Spring 2013 edn), https://plato.stanford.edu/archives/spr2013/entries/berkeley/

Flage, Daniel E., *Classic Thinkers: Berkeley* (Cambridge, UK: Polity Press, 2014)

Jones, Dr Tom E., *George Berkeley: A Philosophical Life* (Princeton: Princeton University Press, 2021)

Kelly, Patrick, 'Anne Donnellan: Irish Proto-Bluestocking', *Hermathena*, no. 154 (1993), pp. 39–68

12. Richard Brew, Slave Trader

Anon., *A Treatise Upon the Trade from Great-Britain to Africa: Humbly Recommended to the Attention of Government by an African Merchant* (London: R. Baldwin, 1772)

Bean, Richard, 'A Note on the Relative Importance of Slaves and Gold in West African Exports', *The Journal of African History*, vol. 15, no. 3 (1974), pp. 351–56

Der, Benedict, 'Edmund Burke and Africa, 1772–1792', *Transactions of the Historical Society of Ghana*, vol. 11 (1970), pp. 9–26

Fynn, John Kofi, *Asante and its Neighbours, 1700–1807*, Legon history series (Harlow: Longman & Evanston, IL: Northwestern University Press, 1971)

Getz, Trevor R., 'Mechanisms of Slave Acquisition and Exchange in Late Eighteenth Century Anomabu: Reconsidering a Cross-Section of the Atlantic Slave Trade', *African Economic History*, no. 31 (2003), pp. 75–89

Micots, Courtnay, 'Status and Mimicry: African Colonial Period Architecture in Coastal Ghana', *Journal of the Society of Architectural Historians*, vol. 74, no. 1 (March 2015), pp. 41–62

Micots, Courtnay, 'A Palace to Rival British Rule: The Amonoo Residence in Ghana',

Critical Interventions: Journal of African Art History and Visual Culture, vol. 11, no. 2 (2017), pp. 132–54

Priestly, Margaret A., 'Richard Brew: An 18th Century Trader at Anomabu', *Transactions of the Historical Society of Ghana*, vol. 4, no. 1 (1959), pp. 29–46

Priestley, Margaret, *West African Trade & Coast Society: A Family Study* (Oxford: Oxford University Press, 1969)

Sanders, James, 'The Expansion of the Fante and the Emergence of Asante in the Eighteenth Century', *The Journal of African History*, vol. 20, no. 3 (1979), pp. 349–64

Shumway, Rebecca, *The Fante and the Transatlantic Slave Trade*, Rochester Studies in African History and the Diaspora Series (Rochester, NY: University of Rochester Press, 2011)

Sparks, Randy J., *Where the Negroes are Masters: An African Port in the Era of the Slave Trade* (Cambridge, MA: Harvard University Press, 2014)

Woolman, John, 'Considerations on the Keeping of Negroes: Extracts from a Collection of Voyages', in *The Works of John Woolman* (Philadelphia, 1774)

13. The Abbé de Firmont

Duchesse d'Angoulême, Marie-Thérèse Charlotte, *The Ruin of a Princess: As Told by the Duchesse d'Angoulême, Madame Elisabeth, Sister of Louis XVI, and Cléry, the King's Valet de Chambre*, trans. Katharine Prescott Wormeley (New York: The Lamb Publishing Co., 1912)

Edgeworth, C. Sneyd (ed.), *Memoirs of the Abbé Edgeworth Containing His Narrative of the Last Hours of Louis XVI* (London: Rowland Hunter, 1815)

England, Rev. Thomas (ed.), *Letters from Abbé Edgeworth to His Friends, Written Between the Years 1777 and 1807* (Longman, Hurst, Rees, Orme, and Brown, 1818)

Guinan, Joseph, 'Henry Essex Edgeworth', in Charles George Herbermann (ed.), *The Catholic Encyclopedia: An International Work of Reference*, vol. 5 (New York: Encyclopedia Press, 1913)

Woodgate, M. V., *The Abbé Edgeworth: 1745–1807* (New York, 1946)

Authentic Memoirs of the Revolution in France, and of the Sufferings of the Royal Family, Deduced Principally from Accounts by Eyewitnesses (London, 1817)

14. Hercules Mulligan, Washington's Spy

Frey, Holly and Wilson, Tracy, *Stuff You Missed in History Class* (podcast), 'Hercules Mulligan', Parts 1 and 2 (9 and 11 May 2016), iHeartRadio

Misencik, Paul R., *The Original American Spies: Seven Covert Agents of the Revolutionary War* (Jefferson, NC: McFarland, 2013)

Mulraney, Frances, 'Hercules Mulligan – The Irish-Born Tailor and Spy Who Saved Washington Twice', *IrishCentral*, 20 Jul. 2016, https://www.irishcentral.com/roots/history/hercules-mulligan-the-irish-born-tailor-and-spy-who-saved-washington-twice

O'Brien, M. J., 'Hercules Mulligan', *Journal of the American-Irish Historical Society*, no. 15 (1916), pp. 142–46

Troy, Gil, 'Hercules Mulligan: The Spy Who Saved George Washington – Twice', *The Daily Beast*, 24 Feb. 2019, https://www.thedailybeast.com/hercules-mulligan-the-spy-who-saved-george-washingtontwice

15. James Hoban, Architect of the White House

Bergin, Denis, 'In Search of James: Celebrating the 250th Anniversary of the Birth of James Hoban, Architect and Builder of the White House', *Old Kilkenny Review*, no. 60 (2008), pp. 70–77

Bushong, William, 'Honoring James Hoban: Architect of the White House', *CRM: The Journal of Heritage Stewardship*, vol. 5, no. 2 (Summer 2008)

Seale, William, *The President's House*, 2nd edn (Washington, DC: The White House Historical Association, 2008)

Seale, William, et al., *White House History: James Hoban: Architect of the White House*, no. 22 (2008). A Special Edition of the journal, dedicated to James Hoban.

Warner, William W., *At Peace with All Their Neighbors: Catholics and Catholicism in the National Capital* (Washington, DC: Georgetown University Press, 2004)

16. Hugh Gough, Conqueror of the Punjab

Brice, Dr Christopher, *Brave as a Lion: The Life and Times of Field Marshal Hugh Gough, 1st Viscount Gough* (UK: Helion & Company, 2015)

Donnelly, Jr, James S., *Captain Rock: The Irish Agrarian Rebellion of 1821–1824* (Madison: University of Wisconsin Press, 2009)

Farwell, Byron, *Eminent Victorian Soldiers: Seekers of Glory* (New York: W. W. Norton, 1985)

Rait, Robert, *The Life and Campaigns of Hugh, First Viscount Gough, Field-Marshal* (London: A. Constable & Co., 1903)

17. Pat Watkins, Crusoe of the Galápagos

Royal Gazette of Jamaica, 8 November 1817, p. 11

18. Chile's Irish Patriots

Fanning, Tim, *Paisanos: The Irish and the Liberation of Latin America* (Notre Dame, IN: University of Notre Dame Press, 2018)

Fanning, Tim, *Don Juan O'Brien: An Irish Adventurer in Nineteenth-Century South America* (Cork: Cork University Press, 2020)

Gay, Claudio, *Historia física y política de Chile (1749–1808)*, vol. IV (in Spanish) (Paris: En casa del autor, 1848)

Kerney Walsh, Micheline, *Spanish Knights of Irish Origin: Documents from Continental Archives*, vol. IV (Dublin: Stationery Office for the Irish Manuscripts Commission, 1978), pp. 16–19

Murray, Edmundo, 'Mackenna, John [Juan] (1771–1814)', *Irish Migration Studies in Latin America*, vol. 4, no. 4 (October 2006), www.irlandeses.org

19. John Field: A Muscovy Nocturne

Boland, Majella, 'John Field in Context: A Reappraisal of the Nocturne and Piano Concerti' (PhD Diss., University College Dublin, 2013)

Horton, Julian, 'John Field and the Alternative History of Concerto First-Movement Form', *Music and Letters*, vol. 92, no. 1 (2011)

Klein, Axel, *Irish Classical Recordings: A Discography of Irish Art Music* (Westport, CT: Greenwood Publishing Group, 2001)

O'Gorman, Marc-Ivan (writer and director), *Last Thoughts: The Life and Music of John Field*, RTÉ Lyric FM (4 Nov. 2018)

Piggott, Patrick, *The Life and Music of John Field, 1782–1837: Creator of the Nocturne* (London: Faber and Faber, 1973)

Dead in Moscow – John Field, RTÉ Television (1982). This seven-part series was made to mark the 200th anniversary of Field's birth.

20. Frederick Young, Father of the Gurkhas

Allen, Charles, *Soldier Sahibs: The Men Who Made the North-West Frontier* (London: Abacus, 2001)

Bonner, Brian, *Our Inis Eoghain Heritage: The Parishes of Culdaff and Cloncha* (Dublin, 1972)

Burke, Bernard, *A Genealogical and Heraldic Dictionary of the Landed Gentry of Great Britain & Ireland* (London: Harrison, 1863), p. 1724

Caplan, Lionel, *Warrior Gentlemen: 'Gurkhas' in the Western Imagination* (Providence, RI: Berghahn Books, 1995)

Coleman, A. P., *A Special Corps: The Beginnings of Gorkha Service with the British* (Bishop Auckland, UK: Pentland Press, 1999)

Gould, Tony, *Imperial Warriors: Britain and the Gurkhas* (London: Granta Books, 2000)

Harkin, Michael, *Inishowen: Its History, Traditions and Antiquities* (Carndonagh, Ireland, 1935)

Jenkins, Louisa Hadow Young, *General Frederick Young; first commandant of Sirmur battalion (Second Gurka rifles) the life-story of one of the old brigade in India: 1786–1874, including reminiscences of Ireland and India in the fifties* (London: G. Routledge & Sons, 1923)

Pemble, John, *The Invasion of Nepal: John Company at War* (Oxford: Clarendon Press, 1971)

Smith, E. D., *Britain's Brigade of Gurkhas*
(Barnsley: Pen & Sword, 1983)
Young, Amy, *Three Hundred Years in Inishowen*
(Belfast, 1924)

21. Dr James Barry, Caesarean Pioneer
Barry, Sebastian, *Whistling Psyche/Fred and
Jane* (London: Faber and Faber, 2004)
Dronfield, Jeremy, and du Preez, Dr Michael,
Dr James Barry: A Woman Ahead of Her Time
(London: Oneworld, 2016)
Gorelik, Boris, 'Dr James Barry, Hertzog's
Namesake', *Rapport* (Johannesburg),
4 October 2015
Holmes, Rachel, *Scanty Particulars: The
Scandalous Life and Astonishing Secret of
James Barry* (London: Viking, 2002)
The Gentleman's Magazine, vol. 76 (London:
F. Jefferies, 1806)

22. The Texas Revolution
Belfiglio, Valentine J., 'Italian and Irish
Contributions to the Texas War for
Independence', *East Texas Historical Journal*,
vol. 23, no. 2, article 7 (1985)
Tucker, Dr Phillip Thomas, *The Alamo's
Forgotten Defenders: The Remarkable Story
of the Irish during the Texas Revolution*
(California: Savas Beattie, 2016)

23. Sir George Gore, Buffalo Slayer
Pagnamenta, Peter, *Prairie Fever: British
Aristocrats in the American West 1830–1890*
(London: Gerald Duckworth, 2012)
'The Saguenay', *Harper's New Monthly
Magazine*, vol. 19 (July 1859)

24. Margaret of New Orleans
Kelley, Laura D., *The Irish in New Orleans*
(Lafayette: University of Louisiana at
Lafayette Press, 2014)
Luck, Katherine Adrienne, 'Finding Margaret
Haughery: The Forgotten and Remembered
Lives of New Orleans's "Bread Woman" in
the Nineteenth and Twentieth Centuries'
(2014), University of New Orleans
Theses and Dissertations, 1821, https://
scholarworks.uno.edu/td/1821

McGrath, Adrian, 'Margaret Haughery:
The Bread Woman of New Orleans', Old
NOLA Journal blog history (14 April 2009),
http://oldnolajournal.blogspot.
com/2009/04/margaret-haughery-bread-
woman-of-new.html
Neihaus, Earl F., *The Irish in New Orleans:
1800–1860* (Baton Rouge: Louisiana State
University Press, 1965)
O'Donnell, Rosie, 'The Caretaker – Margaret
Haughery (1813–1882)', in Mark Bailey
(ed.), *Nine Irish Lives: The Thinkers,
Fighters, & Artists Who Helped Build America*
(Chapel Hill, NC: Algonquin Books, 2018),
p. 29
Rogers, Rosemary, 'The Mother of
Orphans', *Irish America*, June/July 2016,
https://irishamerica.com/2016/06/
the-mother-of-orphans/

25. Children of the Great Hunger
Biography entries by: Murphy, David,
'Richard ('Dick') William Dowling';
Singer, Alan, 'Mary Harris – "Mother
Jones"'; Quinn, James, 'Thomas Francis
Bourke'; Evers, Liz, 'John Edward
McCullough'; Hourican, Bridget,
'James O'Neill'; and McCabe, Desmond,
'Timothy Deasy', in James McGuire and
James Quinn (eds), *Dictionary of Irish
Biography* (Dublin and Cambridge, UK:
Royal Irish Academy and Cambridge
University Press, 2009)
Bunbury, Turtle, *1847: A Chronicle of Genius,
Generosity and Savagery* (Dublin: Gill
Books, 2016)
Lonergan, Eamonn, *A Workhouse Story:
A History of St. Patrick's Hospital, Cashel
1842–1992* (Cashel: E. Lonergan, 1992)
McClaughlin, Trevor, *Barefoot and Pregnant?
Irish Famine Orphans in Australia:
Documents and Register* (Melbourne:
Genealogical Society of Victoria, 1991)
Reilly, Ciarán, *Strokestown and the Great
Famine* (Dublin: Four Courts, 2014)
Shiels, Damian, *The Irish in the American Civil
War* (Dublin: The History Press 2013)
https://earlgreysfamineorphans.wordpress.com

26. Little Al Cashier

Blanton, DeAnne, 'Women Soldiers of the Civil War', *Prologue Magazine*, vol. 2, no. 1 (Spring 1993)

Blanton, DeAnne, and Cook, Lauren M., *They Fought Like Demons: Women Soldiers in the Civil War* (Baton Rouge: Louisiana State University Press, 2002)

Clausius, Gerhard P., 'The Little Soldier of the 95th: Albert D. J. Cashier', *Journal of the Illinois State Historical Society*, vol. 51 (1958), pp. 380–87

Davis, Rodney O., 'Private Albert Cashier as Regarded by His/Her Comrades', *Illinois Historical Journal*, vol. 82 (1989)

Shiels, Damian, *The Irish in the American Civil War* (Dublin: The History Press, 2013)

Wood, Wales W., *A History of the Ninety-Fifth Regiment Illinois Infantry Volunteers* (Boone County Historical Society, 1993)

'Remarkable War Veteran: Woman Fought Three Years in Civil War', *Hartford Republican*, 6 June 1913

27. Thomas D'Arcy McGee, Father of the Canadian Confederation

Slattery, T. P., *The Assassination of D'Arcy McGee* (Toronto: Doubleday Canada, 1968)

Wilson, David A., *Thomas D'Arcy McGee: Passion, Reason, and Politics, 1825–1857, Volume 1* (Kingston and Montreal: McGill-Queen's University Press, 2014)

The Thomas D'Arcy McGee Foundation (thomasdarcymcgee.com) runs an annual summer school in Carlingford that tackles such thorny historical issues as the Great Hunger, Revolutionary Republicanism, Orangeism and Fenianism.

28. The Railroad Men

Ambrose, Stephen E., *Opening of the West: Undaunted Courage/Nothing Like It in the World* (Simon & Schuster, 2013)

Bain, David Haward, *Empire Express: Building the First Transcontinental Railroad* (London: Viking, 1999)

Heath, Erle, 'A Railroad Record That Defies Defeat – How Central Pacific Laid Ten Miles of Track in One Day Back in 1869', *Southern Pacific Bulletin*, vol. XVI, no. 5 (May 1928), pp. 3–5

Quigley, Hugh, *The Irish Race in California and on the Pacific Coast: With an Introductory Historical Dissertation on the Principal Races of Mankind, and a Vocabulary of Ancient and Modern Irish Family Names* (San Francisco: A. Roman, 1878)

Toponce, Alexander, *Reminiscences of Alexander Toponce, Pioneer* (1923), in B. A. Botkin and Alvin Harlow (eds), *A Treasury of Railroad Folklore* (1953)

Williams, John, *The Transcontinental Railroad*, ebook edn (New Word City, 2019)

'Completing the Transcontinental Railroad, 1869: Driving the Golden Spike', *EyeWitness to History* (2004), www.eyewitnesstohistory.com/goldenspike.htm

29. Eliza Lynch, First Lady of Paraguay

Esposito, Gabriele, *The Paraguayan War 1864–70: The Triple Alliance at Stake in La Plata* (New York: Bloomsbury USA, 2019)

Fanning, Tim, *Paisanos: The Irish and the Liberation of Latin America* (Notre Dame, IN: University of Notre Dame Press, 2018)

Lillis, Michael and Fanning, Ronan, *The Lives of Eliza Lynch: Scandal and Courage* (Dublin: Gill & Macmillan, 2009)

30. John Philip Holland, Father of the Submarine

Breen, Aidan and McGee, Owen, 'Holland, John Philip', in James McGuire and James Quinn (eds), *Dictionary of Irish Biography* (Royal Irish Academy and Cambridge University Press, 2009)

Goldstone, Lawrence, *Going Deep: John Philip Holland and the Invention of the Attack Submarine* (New York: Pegasus Books, 2018)

Whitman, Edward C., 'John Holland: The Father of the Modern Submarine', *Undersea Warfare*, no. 19 (Summer 2003)

'John P. Holland (1841–1914): The Liscannor Man Who Invented the Sub', *Clare Champion*, Fri. 9 August 1996

31. Nellie Cashman, Angel of the Wild West

Clum, John P., 'Nellie Cashman: A Modest Tribute to a Noble Woman Whose Energetic, Courageous, Self-Sacrificing Life Was an Inspiration on a Wide Frontier During Half a Century', *Arizona Historical Review*, vol. 3 (Jan. 1931), pp. 9–34; also published in Mary G. Boyer (ed.), *Arizona in Literature* (1935). John P. Clum knew Nellie Cashman and his article is based on interviews with the Cunningham family.

Dungan, Myles, *How the Irish Won the West* (Dublin: New Island Books, 2016)

Lydon, Dr Patrick P., and Chaytor, Donna, *Angel in Victoria: The Amazing Story of Nellie Cashman, "The Miners Angel"* (Victoria, British Columbia: Lydon Shore Publishing, 2017)

Monahan, Sherry A., *Taste of Tombstone: A Hearty Helping of History* (Albuquerque: University of New Mexico Press, 2008)

Zanjani, Sally, *A Mine of Her Own: Women Prospectors in the American West, 1850–1950* (Lincoln: University of Nebraska Press, 2000)

32. The Grace Brothers: Conquest of Peru

Clayton, Lawrence, *Grace: W. R. Grace – The Formative Years, 1850–1930* (Ottawa, IL: Jameson Books, 1985)

Hollett, Dave, *More Precious Than Gold: The Story of the Peruvian Guano Trade* (New Jersey: Associated University Presses, 2008)

James, Marquis, *Merchant Adventurer: The Story of W. R. Grace* (Wilmington, DE: Scholarly Resources Inc., 1993)

Quiroz, Alfonso W., *Corrupt Circles: A History of Unbound Graft in Peru* (Washington, DC: Woodrow Wilson Center Press, 2008)

Whittemore, Henry, *Long Island Historic Homes, Ancient and Modern: Including a History of Their Founders and Builders* (New York: Lewis Publishing Company, 1901)

33. Annie Moore, the First Emigrant Through Ellis Island

Smolenyak, Megan, '125th Anniversary of Annie Moore and Ellis Island' (10 January 2017), https://www.megansmolenyak. com/125th-anniversary-of-annie-moore-and-ellis-island/

'A Cork Emigrant', *Cork Constitution*, 11 January 1892, p. 8

34. Margaretta Eagar, the Last Tsar's Governess

Eagar, Margaret, *Six Years at the Russian Court* (London: Hurst & Blackett, 1906)

Slater, Sharon, 'Margaret Eager: The Tsar's Nanny', *The Old Limerick Journal* (Winter 2015), pp. 8–10

35. The Moore Brothers, Hollywood Stars

Brennan, Steve, and O'Neill, Bernadette, *Emeralds in Tinseltown: The Irish in Hollywood* (Belfast: Appletree Press, 2007)

Feeley, Kathleen A., *Mary Pickford: Hollywood and the New Woman* (Abingdon: Routledge, 2018)

36. Louis Brennan, the Wizard of Oz

Gray, Edwyn, *19th Century Torpedoes and Their Inventors* (Annapolis, MD: Naval Institute Press, 2004)

Hamer, Mick, 'Histories: The Spinning-Top Railway', *New Scientist* (18 November 2006)

O'Hara, Bernard, *Mayo: Aspects of Its Heritage* (Galway, Ireland: Archaeological, Historical and Folklore Society, 1982)

37. Violet Gibson: Killing Mussolini

Evers, Liz, 'Violet Albina Gibson', in Kate O'Malley (ed.), *Dictionary of Irish Biography Online* (Royal Irish Academy and Cambridge University Press, 2019)

Lynam, Siobhán, *Documentary on One: The Irishwoman Who Shot Mussolini*, RTÉ Radio 1 (21 June 2014)

Stonor Saunders, Frances, *The Woman Who Shot Mussolini* (London: Faber and Faber, 2010)

Violet Gibson (2020), directed by Barrie Dowdall; written by Barrie Dowdall and Siobhán Lynam

38. Don Patricio O'Connell, Barça's Saviour

Burns, Jimmy, 'Don Patricio O'Connell:

An Irishman and the Politics of Spanish
Football', *Irish Migration Studies in Latin
America*, vol. 6, no. 1 (March 2008),
www.irlandeses.org

Comer, Pat (director) and McElwain,
Gráinne (producer), *Paddy Don Patricio*,
Tobar Productions documentary for TG4
(3 October 2012)

Fitzpatrick, Richard (producer) with Kelly,
Ronan, *Documentary on One: The Man Who
Played Offside*, RTÉ Radio 1 (20 June 2015)

Lowe, Sid, *Fear and Loathing in La Liga:
Barcelona vs Real Madrid* (London:
Random House, 2013)

O'Connell, Sue, *The Man Who Saved FC
Barcelona: The Remarkable Life of Patrick
O'Connell* (Stroud: Amberley Publishing,
2016). Sue O'Connell is the wife of
Patrick's grandson Mike O'Connell.

39. Lord Haw-Haw, the Voice of Nazi Germany

Farndale, Nigel, *Haw-Haw: The Tragedy of
William and Margaret Joyce* (London:
Macmillan, 2005)

Kenny, Mary, 'Lord Haw-Haw and Ireland's
Dilemma over the War', *Irish Independent*,
7 May 2005

Walsh, Michael, *The Martyrdom of William
Joyce* (London: Steven Books, 2000)

West, Rebecca, *The Meaning of Treason*
(London: Penguin rev. edn, 1965)

40. Brendan Bracken, Churchill's Spin Doctor

Boyle, Andrew, *Poor, Dear Brendan: The Quest for
Brendan Bracken* (London: Hutchinson, 1974)

Halle, Kay, *The Irrepressible Churchill*
(Cleveland and New York: The World
Publishing Company, 1966)

Lysaght, Charles, *Brendan Bracken* (London:
Allen Lane, 1979)

Lysaght, Charles, 'Winston Churchill and
Brendan Bracken', in Robert McNamara
(ed.), *The Churchills in Ireland: Controversies
and Connections Since the Seventeenth
Century* (Newbridge, Ireland: Irish
Academic Press, 2011)

Lysaght, Charles, Brendan Bracken Memorial
Lecture, 9 May 2001, Churchill College,
Cambridge, UK

41. Patrick Gallagher, Vietnam Hero

Coogan, Tim Pat, *Wherever Green is Worn: The
Story of the Irish Diaspora* (London: Arrow
Books, 2002), p. 302

Durney, James, *Vietnam: The Irish Experience*
(County Kildare, Ireland: Gaul House
Press, 2008)

Gullickson, Gary D., *Vietnam: Our Story – One
on One* (Minnesota: VV Publishing, 1992)
www.irishveterans.org

42. The Irish and the White House

Boyd Roberts, Gary, *Ancestors of American
Presidents*, 2009 edn (Boston, MA: New
England Historic Genealogical Society,
2009)

Cheatham, Mark R., *Andrew Jackson,
Southerner* (Baton Rouge: Louisiana State
University Press, 2015)

Clinton, Bill, *My Life* (New York: Random
House, 2010)

Fitzsimons, Fiona, and Moss, Helen (Eneclann
researchers), 'Report on President Barack
Obama's Irish Ancestry' (2008),
www.irishfamilyhistorycentre.com

Graff, Henry F., *Grover Cleveland: The 22nd and
24th President, 1885–1889 and 1893–1897*,
The American Presidents series (New York:
Macmillan, 2002)

Hanna, Charles A., *The Scotch-Irish; or, The
Scot in North Britain, North Ireland, and
North America: Volume II* (Philadelphia:
Dalcassian Publishing Company, 1902)

Hood, Susan, *Royal Roots, Republican
Inheritance: The Survival of the Office of Arms*
(Dublin: Woodfield Press, 2002)

Jordan, John W. and Hadden, James (eds),
*Genealogical and Personal History of Fayette
County, Pennsylvania, Volume II* (facs. edn,
Westminster, MD: Heritage Books, 2007)

Kilroy, David P., 'From the White House to
the Thatched Cottage: American President
Visits to Ireland and the Immigrant
Narrative' (2017), CAHSS Faculty

Presentations, Proceedings, Lectures, and Symposia, 2445, https://nsuworks.nova.edu/cahss_facpres/2445

Meacham, Jon, *American Lion: Andrew Jackson in the White House* (New York: Random House, 2008)

Murphy, Celestine (Wexford County senior librarian, historian and genealogist), Kennedy family research, in Maria Pepper, 'Celestine Shines New Light on JKF Ancestor', *New Ross Standard*, 15 September 2018

Murphy, Sean, MA, 'American Presidents with Irish Ancestors', in Murphy (ed.), *Directory of Irish Genealogy* (2018 edn), Centre for Irish Genealogical and Historical Studies website

O'Donnell, Helen, with O'Donnell Sr, Kenneth, *The Irish Brotherhood: John F. Kennedy, His Inner Circle, and the Improbable Rise to the Presidency* (Berkeley, CA: Counterpoint Press, 2016)

O'Dowd, Niall, *Lincoln and the Irish: The Untold Story of How the Irish Helped Abraham Lincoln Save the Union* (New York: Skyhorse Publishing, 2018)

Schmuhl, Robert, *Ireland's Exiled Children: America and the Easter Rising* (Oxford: Oxford University Press, 2016)

Scott Berg, A., *Wilson* (New York: G. P. Putnam's Sons, 2013)

Swarns, Rachel L., *American Tapestry: The Story of the Black, White and Multiracial Ancestors of Michelle Obama* (New York: Amistad, 2012)

Whelan, Bernadette, *United States Foreign Policy and Ireland: From Empire to Independence, 1913–29* (Dublin: Four Courts Press, 2006)

Epilogue: Reflections on Irish Identity

Biagini, E. F. and Daly, Mary E. (eds), *The Cambridge Social History of Modern Ireland* (Cambridge: Cambridge University Press, 2017), especially Part III, 'Emigration, Immigration and the Wider Irish World'

Bunbury, Turtle, *Easter Dawn: The 1916 Rising* (Cork: Mercier Press, 2015)

Daly, Mary E., 'Migration since 1914', in T. Bartlett (ed.), *The Cambridge History of Ireland, Vol IV* (Cambridge: Cambridge University Press, 2018), pp. 527–52

Dowling, Michael J., and Kenney, Charles, *Leading Through a Pandemic: The Inside Story of Humanity, Innovation, and Lessons Learned During the Covid-19 Crisis* (New York: Skyhorse Publishing, 2020)

The Gathering Ireland 2013: Final Report, Dec. 2013, https://www.failteireland.ie/FailteIreland/media/WebsiteStructure/Documents/eZine/TheGathering_FinalReport_JimMiley_December2013.pdf

ACKNOWLEDGMENTS

A massive thanks to my agent Emma Parry for her positivity and focus, to Ben Hayes and Izzy Luta for their guidance and support, and to Jo Murray for her astonishing attention to detail. I am indebted to the genealogical brilliance of Maria O'Brien, the exceptional kindness of Dr Niav Gallagher and the legendary hospitality of the Tyrone Guthrie Centre at Annaghmakerrig. And to Ally, Jemima and Bay for the inspirational sounds of joy that echo across the garden to the timber studio wherein I write.

To Dagmar Ó Riain-Raedel, Kristján Ahronson and Matteo Binasco for their investigations into the holy men of a vanished world, to Professor Andrea Tilatti, Paolo Chiesa, Novella Scalzini and Huihan Lie for escorting me from Tolentino to the Mongol Empire, to Micheál Ó Siochrú and Liam Hogan for Caribbean insights, to Dr Tom Jones for realigning my thoughts on Berkeley, to Christopher Steed and Rebecca Shumway for their invaluable assistance on Richard Brew, to Denis Bergin for his excellent knowledge of The White House, to Jeremy Dronfield for helping me make sense of Dr Barry, to Laura D. Kelley who set me right on antebellum New Orleans, to Trevor McClaughlin for his work on the Earl Grey orphans, to Marc-Ivan O'Gorman for igniting my Fieldian interest, to Tim Fanning, Michael Lillis and Hiram Morgan for steering me across Latin America, to Karmendra Jaisi for guiding me into the Himalayas, to Jeff Kildea for Australian realities, to Brendan Matthews for his scholarship into the Hodgers family, to Megan Smolenyak for her work on Annie Moore and the Obamas, to Seán Murray for going beyond the call to trace the Grace mausoleum in Arles, to Darina Molloy and Jim O'Connor of Castlebar Library for checking the facts on Louis Brennan's family, to Brian Hobson for his work on the torpedo man, to Barrie Dowdall and Siobhán Lynam for their outstanding work on Violet Gibson, to Sue and Mike O'Connell for managing my tale of Don Patricio, to Charles Lysaght for his forbearance with my account of Brendan Bracken, to Teresa Keegan, Pauline Gallagher, James Durney, Martin Durkan, Declan Hughes and Brigadier General Michael Neil for keeping me on track with the Vietnam War.

I also thank the good people of the Irish Georgian Society, iBAM! Chicago, the Centre Culturel Irlandais, the Irish Cultural Centre (Hammersmith), the Ancient Order of Hibernians (Savannah), the Center for Irish Research and Teaching (Georgia Southern University), Web Summit, the Chalke Valley History Festival, Fáilte Ireland and EPIC – The Irish Emigration Museum for inviting me to speak of the diaspora in recent years.

And for disparate assistance on the diaspora, for helping me dig a little deeper, for setting me on the right path, for going beyond the call to guide me, for so many details, great and small, I thank the late Charles Allen, Mike Allen, Chris Aubin, Sebastian Barry, Marti Bellingrath, Alex and Daria Blackwell, Meike Blackwell, Karen Wardamasky Bobrow, Alice Boyle, Mette Boye, Herbie Brennan, Dr Christopher Brice, Jacquie Burgess, David John Butler, Dr David Butler. Liam Campbell (Fáilte Ireland), Cliff Carlson, Val Carry, Ann Loughrey Casey, Maurice Casey, Mark Clinton, Johnny Couchman, Michael Counahan, Alastair Hubert Bao Butler Crampton, Jane Cregan (Irish Rail), Catriona Crowe, Alison Deegan, Gerard M. Delaney, Matthew Dennison, Matthew C. Donahue, Darragh Doyle, Fin Dwyer, Myles Dungan, Rory Everard, Ronan Fanning, Tommy Fegan, Will Fennell, Mark Fitzell, Richard Fitzpatrick, Fiona Fitzsimons, Commandant Dave Foley, Patrick Geoghegan, Dr John Gibney (Royal Irish Academy), Paul Gorry, Shane Gough, Miriam Nyhan Grey, Mervyn Greene, Patrick Greene, Winnie Healy, Catherine Ann Heaney, Mart Hintz, John Horne, Vicky House, Neville Isdell, Rebecca Jeffares, Arthur Johnson, Christopher Johnson, Howard Keeley, Martin Kelly, Ronan Kelly, Kaz Langley,

Tom LaPorte, Susan Leggett, Kirstin Lemon, the late Melosina Lenox-Conyngham, Maria Levinge, Wanda Lloyd, Katherine Adrienne Luck, Seán Mac an Ultaigh, John McCartin, Tim McCoy, Catherine McDonnell, Stewart D. McLaurin (White House Historical Association), Katherine McSharry, Patrick MacCionnaith, Nathan Mannion, Martin Mansergh, Dr Guillermo MacLoughlin, John Mee (Castlebar Parish Magazine), Marie Milner, Grace Moloney (Clogher Historical Society), Nicola Morris, Helen Moss, Sean Murphy, Ceallaigh Ni Bheirnigh, Pádraigín Ní Ghallchóir, Una Ni Ghabhláin, Isabella Rose Nolan, Christopher Normand, James O'Fee, John Onions, Gregg Patrick (Central Statistics Office), Kenny Pearce, John Pemble, Jen Pike, Michael Purcell, Gillian Quinn, Charlie Raben, Ciarán Reilly, Terry Reilly, Stan Ridgeway, Fiona Ross, Martin Russell, Bruce Seymour, Damian Shiels, Bobby Singh, Jessica Slingsby, Dan Snow, Frances Stonor Saunders, Rory Sweetman, Tom Sykes, Kenny Timmons, Jessica Traynor, Zack Twamley, Louise Walsh, Meghan Walsh, Prof. David Wilson and Tom Wood.

ILLUSTRATION CREDITS

Map of Ireland by Drazen Tomic
© 2021 Thames & Hudson Ltd, London

1   Museum Plantin-Moretus, Antwerp
2, 3 De Agostini Picture Library/Getty Images
4   Bibliothèque Nationale de France, Paris
5   Photo National Gallery of Ireland, Dublin
6   Timken Museum of Art, San Diego
7   National Portrait Gallery, London
8   Photo Christophel Fine Art/Universal Images Group via Getty Images
9   Library of Congress Prints and Photographs, Washington, DC
10 Maryland Historical Society, Baltimore
11 National Army Museum, London/ Bridgeman Images
12 Photo The Gurkha Museum, Winchester
13 Science Source/akg-images
14 Museo Histórico Nacional, Santiago. Album/Alamy
15 Library of Congress Prints and Photographs, Washington, DC
16 Samuel Kessler/Alamy
17 Yale University Library, New Haven
18 Private Collection
19 Granger/Shutterstock
20 Science History Images/Alamy
21 Private Collection
22 New York Public Library. The Miriam and Ira D. Wallach Division of Art, Prints and Photographs
23 Matteo Omied/Alamy
24 Everett Collection, Inc./Alamy
25 Library of Congress Prints and Photographs, Washington, DC
26 Shutterstock
27 Daily Mail/Shutterstock
28 Keystone/Hulton Archive/Getty Images

INDEX